A Tenner and a Box of Kippers

THE STORY OF
KEITH HOUCHEN

A Tenner and a Box of Kippers

THE STORY OF
KEITH HOUCHEN

JONATHAN STRANGE

For my Mother

First published 2006

Stadia is an imprint of
Tempus Publishing Limited
The Mill, Brimscombe Port,
Stroud, Gloucestershire, GL5 2QG
www.tempus-publishing.com

British Library Cataloguing in Publication Data.
A catalogue record for this book is available from the British Library.

ISBN 0 7524 3796 8

Typesetting and origination by Tempus Publishing Limited
Printed in Great Britain

Contents

The Author

Jonathan Strange was born in Dorset in 1952. He is a freelance musician and writer. He has travelled the world as a violinist in Britain's major orchestras, while pursuing a wide interest in sport. In the studios, he works with the stars of rock and pop and on the scores of Hollywood movies.

For Tempus, he has also written *Coventry City FC: A History in 50 Matches.* He is chairman of Coventry City London Supporters' Club, is a member of MCC, reads Wallace Stevens, and lives in Wembley.

Acknowledgements

My overwhelming thanks go to Eric A. Thorn who has enabled me to overcome the more taxing demands of my computer as well as assisting me with the proofs. I am deeply indebted to Eric for his wisdom and good counsel as well as his professional skill and insight over so many aspects of this project.

I am profoundly grateful to Sue Cook who has faithfully and devotedly transcribed my interviews with Keith, and to Philip de Bary for his careful reading and advice over the text.

I wish to thank Dave Batters, Bob Bradshaw, Jim Brown, Tony Brown, Terry Frost, Billy Horner, Barry J. Hugman, Michael Joyce, John Malcolm, Kevin Monks, Barry Nicholls, David Phillips, John Sillett, John Wallace, Michael Williams and all those others whose contributions and help have played such a crucial part.

I would like to pay especial acknowledgement to the *Coventry Telegraph,* the *Hartlepool Mail* and *The Northern Echo.*

I would like to thank the *Coventry Evening Telegraph*, *Newcastle Chronicle and Journal*, *The Northern Echo* and *The Yorkshire Evening Press* for the use of their photographs. I am grateful to Frank Reid and Graeme Rowatt for the use of individual photographs, and to the *Daily Mirror* for the *Griffin's Eye* cartoon. I would like to acknowledge the *Hartlepool Mail*, *Ilford Recorder* and *Mirrorpix* for their assistance in trying to identify certain photographs, and to thank Keith and the Houchen family for making prints and family photographs available to me. I am grateful to Richard Simmons and Bonasta Photographic for the photograph of the author.

Whilst every effort has been made to trace the copyright permission for all material used in this work, we apologise if any parties have not received due acknowledgement.

Preface

'Have you fallen out yet?' my friend enquired, pointing to notorious bust-ups between biographers and their subjects.

He was only half joking, but such ructions are less common over sportsmen's tales. Cups and caps and runs and goals, in themselves, are about as contentious as a string of traffic cones. And cliché and hyperbole soon supervene once you seek to evoke the essence of the performance itself. Words miss the point.

I have aspired, therefore, to do more than just turn the pages of a scrapbook in writing about Keith. Above all, this is the story of a human being, of the towns and cities where he worked, of the football clubs themselves, and of the ether and ethos of the game as he experienced it. It is a travelogue, a documentary, a life, written for the general reader as much as the 'anorak'.

Keith Houchen spent twenty years in the football profession. His career started and finished at the same unfashionable club and, in between, arched itself in an unexpected rainbow. His is a story of ambition, hard work, disagreement, and regret, lit up by several notable triumphs, and characterised increasingly by problems with officials. However, whilst he might still dispute a penalty, Keith Houchen has found and fulfilled a life beyond.

My answer to my friend's question was: 'Certainly not! Indeed, quite the reverse.' And, in intruding on their lives, I would like to thank Keith and Yvonne for all their help, and for their continuing warmth and friendliness.

Jonathan Strange, Wembley, 2006

Middlesbrough to Chesterfield

A lanky teenager stood at the barrier at King's Cross Station. It was one of those hot summer's days when even the pointing in the brickwork seems to expand to swallow you in the swelter of the metropolitan afternoon. This was the path of the *Flying Scotsman,* the youngster's first glimpse of London. Approaching the terminus, he'd caught sight of Highbury, home of Arsenal. The train eased its way into the platform; doors creaked; the sedate atmosphere gave way to the urgency of arrival, of destinations beyond, of relief and expectancy, of life being gathered up again in the click of heels and shouts from adjoining platforms. Intimacy gave way to the raucousness of a ticking clock, but one young man remained bemused. He had been told that someone would be there to meet him. His dad had put him on the train at Darlington with instructions to 'phone home if there was a problem. It would be all right because he would catch up with two other boys on the train who were going to the same place, but he hadn't bumped into them yet.

I was a romantic type of kid, I read books and stuff. It was like me setting off to London to make good type of thing. I remember that. But then I got scared stiff. I got off at King's Cross. It's this big scary place isn't it? People and trains and noise…

He didn't know what the other boys looked like. What should he do? With bag in hand, he was about to make his way to a 'phone box. He was not to know that in London in the 1970s you were lucky if you could find a payphone that actually worked. Fortunately, as he stirred himself for the first challenge of this wider world, he could see a figure running towards him across the concourse. The dishevelled and breathless appearance of an adult amidst a giant world of bricks and the disorder of impersonal faces was an enormous relief.

'Is your name Houchen?'

'Yes'

'I'm from Crystal Palace. I'm sorry I'm late; I got stuck in the traffic. Where are the other two lads?'

'I don't know. I didn't see them on the train.'

The man's slightly exasperated expression gave way to relief as the other two boys, shirts untucked and bags swung over their shoulders, sidled into view.

'You must be Terry and John.'

Terry and John Fenwick had been trawled from the North-East along with Keith Houchen.

The North-East has always been one of the richest shoals, small fish kicking footballs around by the thousand in a pageant of school and junior clubs, eager teams with eager kids seeking to make names for themselves, to be paid for their recreation. Mums and dads parade along the touchline. There are little pals and others to show off to, tracksuited Sirs barking instructions and then the occasional faceless figure, stocky and bandy like an ex-pro, fingers indifferently twitching, a cigarette jostling with a pencil as he scribbles a note. Are these the unseen eyes of Darlington or Hartlepool, or even Newcastle, Sunderland or Middlesbrough? Is this uninvited guest the person to open a career and life ahead? What does he see beyond the youthful instinct and enthusiasm? What is it that takes flesh in his mind, transfers itself to Ayresome or Roker, or has the child heaving, coaxing or belting the ball across the green sward at St James'?

Crystal Palace were one of the most talked about clubs of the time, the team of the future with a scouting network scouring the country for the talent to confirm it. The competition was stiff with other top quality youngsters such as Vince Hilaire and Billy Gilbert. Gilbert, Hilaire and Terry Fenwick were almost a year older than Houchen. They had big careers ahead of them. Terry's brother John, however, didn't make the big time.

The boys were whisked across London to one of those relentless terraces in the shadow of the mast at the old Crystal Palace. Beyond lay Brighton, the sea and the other end of the country.

These were happy days for the teenager, doing what he loved and dreaming that one day the terraces at Selhurst Park would reverberate to his name.

It was not to be. He was too thin, too lightweight, they said. 'You've got something but you should go away and drink some Guinness.'

It was Malcolm Allison, probably, who made the decision not to offer Keith a contract, before handing over his cockney cigar and fedora to Terry Venables. Crystal Palace 'phoned Keith's father, thinking that he might like to tell his son before the club did. Mr Houchen was more surprised at the news than anyone, but he didn't know much about football. It broke Keith's heart but he returned home not with his tail between his legs, but rather with a lesson in life. The family met him off the train at Glasgow Central – his sister and three brothers, Mum and Dad, Gran and Gran Pop, a sardine tin on wheels setting off on a precious holiday.

Keith later had an unsuccessful trial at Aston Villa but there was to be another professional club that did show an interest. The cobbles of Chesterfield and the sleepy football ground at the top of the town were a long way from Roy-of-the-Rovers, but it was a start.

The crooked spire of the fourteenth-century parish church of St Mary and All Saints is as peculiar to Chesterfield as the leaning tower to Pisa. Beneath a lead covering, the 69m (228ft) spire is constructed of timber, which has warped and twisted to bring the top nearly three metres off centre.

Simon Jenkins, in *England's Thousand Best Churches*, wrote:

> One theory is that the devil rested on his way from Sheffield to Nottingham, another that a virtuous maiden sent the spire wild with admiration… On the east wall is an astounding memorial of three allegorical figures, representing Youth, Old Age and Death, with beneath them a shrouded corpse. Below are a skull and gravedigger's tools, a most ghoulish portrayal of death.

George Stephenson, born in Newcastle and engineer of the Stockton and Darlington Railway, is buried in the churchyard of Chesterfield's Trinity Church.

It was the year of the 'Silver Jubilee'. Keith spent the summer training with Chesterfield and scrambled up one of the floodlight pylons to get a view of the Queen on her visit to the town.

I was a non-contract apprentice, which in effect really meant being a general dogsbody with a bit of football thrown in. The chores were never ending. A typical day meant walking five miles from my digs, getting there early enough to clean all the pros' boots, mashing up massive pots of tea and cleaning up after the players had gone.

Being the pre-season, we had to paint the corridors, the dressing rooms and of course the ground itself. After all that was done, it was time to start helping the groundsman to prepare the pitch. This was all very labour intensive, digging every inch of the pitch with pitch forks and barrowing tens of tons of sand to be spread on it.

The groundsman, Jim, imparted a vocabulary lesson to any apprentices presuming on his beloved turf for an impromptu game. The morning's work done, he reclined in the shadow of the stand with his lunch box. Every now and again, Jim would rest the wife's sandwich and gather up an old air rifle perched beside him like a faithful pet. On letting loose a volley at the pigeons stalking his seeds, the crack would clatter their wings over the town below.

Sweeping out changing rooms, washing floors, cleaning shelves encrusted with painted-over plooks of dust, were the privileges endowed on aspiring young professionals at any club. At Saltergate, the wooden floors were the originals and you could have swept for a year without making an impression. Perhaps that was the point, and you just hoped that the coaching staff were in a good mood when they checked. Privy to the ether of heroes, you were lucky to be cleaning the sod from their boots. For many youngsters, a lifetime of labour exchanges beckoned at the other end of the players' tunnel.

It was the first time Keith had played for a professional club in a proper fixture. The manager was the intimidating figure of Arthur Cox. Cox, with an accent straight out of *Crossroads,* compensated for a promising career shattered by a broken leg when playing for Coventry Reserves by hanging his years on the peg of many a club as a coach and manager. He was dour and tough, his CV chiselled out of the very fabric of the game. He had been assistant to Bob Stokoe at Sunderland on one of those days of fantasy which Keith Houchen would come to know. Having left Sunderland, he was grateful for a spell coaching in Turkey, at a time when Turkish football was as low as Luxembourg's. Grateful for the opportunity at Chesterfield, Cox's career was soon in the ascendancy and eventually at the service of Kevin Keegan in the England set-up.

First impressions are indelible wallpaper to the young. The youth team coach seemed a bit of a tough nut too, but with the deftness of a conjurer he could sometimes disarm the kids in his charge with an unexpected sensitivity.

One day at Chesterfield, a young copper got on the team coach. The uniformed 6ft 4ins belonged to Steve Ogrizovic who was soon to follow in the footsteps of a previous Chesterfield player Gordon Banks and become a great goalkeeper.

Chesterfield won through to the finals of the DFS six-a-side competition at Bakewell by beating Nottingham Forest and Northern Premier League side Buxton. The squad was made up of Steve Ogrizovic, Len Badger, Steve Cammack, Les Hunter, Gary Pollard, Gary Simpson, Andy Higgins and Keith Houchen. Aside from Ogrizovic, Cammack would one day be a team-mate during Houchen's brief spell at Scunthorpe. Len Badger was one of two very experienced right-backs on Chesterfield's books at the time, the other being Wilf Smith.

Somehow, Keith never expected that he would be offered a professional contract at Saltergate, and thus it turned out.

The north-east England of Tyneside and Middlesbrough was one of the foremost regions of the great iron-masters, carried forward into the age of steel. On 25 July 1867, in Ohio, USA, barbed wire was first patented. In a prefab in Middlesbrough on the same day in 1960, Keith Houchen came into the world. All of the Houchen children were born at home.

What would we want to go to hospital for?

The Houchen family lived in the Newport Bridge area of Middlesbrough, which used to be one of the rougher parts of town. Home was about five minutes from Ayresome Park. Newport Bridge, a vertical lift construction built in 1934, continues to span the River Tees, but in 1995 the home of Middlesbrough FC moved to the Riverside.

Middlesbrough Football Club was founded as the result of a discussion during a tripe supper at the Corporation Hotel. The club turned professional, but reverted to amateur status, beating Old Carthusians in the FA Amateur Cup Final of 1895. In 1898, Middlesbrough's semi-final against Thornaby was postponed because of a smallpox epidemic in the two towns. Given the risk of deadly disease, Darlington demurred at the FA's proposal that they should host the fixture and it was eventually played at the remote village of Brotton. Spectators were banned. By the time Middlesbrough came to defeat Uxbridge in the final at the Crystal Palace, the threat had presumably receded. *The Daily Telegraph* observed that the crowd was made up largely of a 'few hundreds who had been beguiling away their time by watching a game of lacrosse on the neighbouring enclosure'.

In 1893, Middlesbrough Ironopolis, who played at a venue called the Paradise Ground, had preceded their amateur rivals briefly into the Football League. Middlesbrough returned to the professional ranks and Archibald Leitch was commissioned to design Ayresome Park.

Leitch's burgeoning reputation as the doyen of football ground designers had nearly been scuppered as a result of the disaster at Ibrox Park. Leitch's Glasgow palace was the largest purpose-built football stadium in the world when it opened in 1900. Leitch himself bore witness to the horror at the Scotland *v.* England international in 1902 when part of the terracing opened like a chute under the spectators' feet. Of the hundreds of people piled like rubble beneath, twenty-six eventually died. Leitch wrote: 'I need hardly say what unutterable anguish the accident caused me, surely the most unhappy eyewitness of all.' At the end of the game, Doig, the Scotland goalkeeper, was chaired off the field by a section of the crowd oblivious of the disaster.

In 1903, his reputation tainted as it was in some quarters, Leitch set to work at Middlesbrough. The theatre he built provided the stage for Common, Camsell, Mannion and Clough, and bore many characteristics of his distinctive style. It provided a galvanising backdrop for generations of local youngsters, Keith Houchen among them.

There were times when a desiccated sense of propriety such as occasionally prevailed at other professional clubs was amply reflected at Ayresome Park. In 1905 eleven of the twelve directors were suspended by the FA for making irregular payments. The succeeding chairman – a churchman, freemason, watchmaker and wealthy jeweller by the name of Lieutenant-Colonel Thomas Gibson Poole – also came unstuck. He was eventually suspended from the game for life for his part in

attempting to bribe the Sunderland team. Poole perceiv
over Middlesbrough's local rivals on 3 December 1910
his prospects in the following week's General Elec
Sunderland's players, contemptuous of inducement, ·
Tories. Middlesbrough still won, but so did Poole's Liberal oppo..._
who retained his seat with an increased majority. Poole, whose rank was
derived from the First North Riding Volunteer Artillery, became a phil-
anthropic pillar of local society. He enjoyed three terms as mayor of
Middlesbrough, and was knighted by George V. When he died a year
after the King, the fulsome obituaries managed to avoid any mention of
his ever being involved with football.

Ken and Vernie Houchen had five children at two-year intervals:
Jimmy, Dennis, Jackie, Keith and Patrick. The five are now dispersed
throughout the country. Keith's three brothers all joined the Coldstream
Guards and were stationed at Chelsea Barracks in London. Jimmy had
gone into the Paras when he left school and joined the Guards after five
years out of the army working at British Steel's Clay Lane works. He
has served in Kenya, Canada, Germany, Northern Ireland and Cyprus.
He was an outstanding 1,500 metres runner. Dennis left after eight years
and became a member of Cleveland Constabulary. He later received a
commendation from the Chief Constable for apprehending an armed
robber. Rick lives in Somerset working with horses – both riding and
transporting them – and Jackie still lives in Middlesbrough where she
had her sixth child twenty years after the first one. At a time when he
was being knocked back in his efforts to become a professional footballer, Keith also considered following his brothers into the Guards.

It is not clear why Keith should have been given the names Keith
Morton. His father had the same ones and Keith has passed Morton on
to his son Ross.

When Keith was a toddler the Houchens lived in a council house in
Gleneagles Road. It was close to St Mary's College where Keith later
went to school. It was a tight fit and Keith remembers walking up the
road and noticing how the posh end of it had gardens at the front.

*It was a struggle as kids and very hard work for Mum and Dad, but they made
sure we had what we needed and we always went on holiday. Two weeks every
year we went away. My dad used to have a big old Bedford van which he used to
keep on the road himself – he was a good mechanic. He got us there somehow. We*

ould either go up to Scotland, to the Highlands, and camp – Fort William and all round that way – or go down to Devon and Cornwall and stay on campsites. In those days you could go on a campsite for next to nothing. It could take a few days to get to Devon. Everybody went, my gran, me granddad, all of us.

Gran Pop had been in the Merchant Navy during the War. My gran was told at least twice that he was missing presumed dead. He was sunk four times, once when he'd just been picked out of the water.

We used to sleep on the side of the motorway at night time. I suppose they weren't motorways then, but a lot of A roads. I can remember sleeping in the van, and that noise. There were very few cars around when I was a kid. We had the only one in the street for a long time – a big old Zephyr we had. It's all cars now, isn't it? As a car went by it would go mmmmm, mmmmm, and the van would rock. Then you would go back to sleep, and then mmmmm as another car went by.

One time we set off for Scotland and we only got as far as Barnard Castle. It seemed like miles at the time as a kid, and the van broke down so we pulled into a little campsite. There was just us and one brick toilet block thing. There were maybe two other tents in the next field and it was right by a river under the castle. My dad fixed the van, but we stayed there for two weeks – it was one of the best holidays we have ever had. We were fishing every day. I've got pictures of us all – there was Jackie, then me, then Dennis and Jimmy. They always stood us in a row with the fishes we had caught. One time, my dad shouted, 'Come on, get back over the wall.' Suddenly there was this bloke shouting, "'Ere, you!" We were obviously poaching weren't we, thinking back now. We all asked Dad what the matter was, but he just said, 'Come on.'

We would explore. Dad would take us, get us to where we wanted to be. Then he'd go to the pub. He used to love the pub and stuff. I had a great childhood, a really, really happy childhood. I can honestly say that.

My dad did a bit of everything. When we were really small, he worked at Smith's Dock on the shipbuilding and what have you. He ran the parts department for a garage for a while. He turned his hand to most things, especially when we were kids, because there were five kids and he had to get the money in. Then, he went on to work in pubs. He trained to be a steward in a working men's club and did that for twenty-three or twenty-five years. Mum and Dad both trained up to do it. My mum was a school dinner lady when I was very little. So they both spent twenty-five years running social clubs before they retired from that and ended up living in Cyprus.

My dad was a very dominant figure, very disciplined. If you did wrong, he would slap you – it's against the law now. In my dad's era, if you did something wrong you got punished for it. Looking back, we were all a bit wild really – the only way to keep us in place was to give us a smack. And my mum wasn't scared to give us a whack. She was a lovely mum but she put us in our place as well. I think her loudest refrain was, 'Wait till your father gets in here.' I think that was the noisiest thing in the house.

It was a working-class household. As you came in from school, it was freezing in the house and you would have to light the fire and get the paper on it, blaze it up.

We had moved from Gleneagles Road when my dad bought a three bedroom terraced house in Orwell Street – for £350. My sister had a tiny box room and us four lads shared a small room with two bunk beds either side. So we all slept together as kids. We were very close growing up, and spent a lot of time together.

Keith was brought up as a Catholic and went to Sacred Heart Primary School next to Ayresome Park. It was at Sacred Heart that his footballing instinct first manifested itself.

I remember being really good at football; I was the best player in the playground and had a real interest in the game. A new teacher came over from New Zealand, a Mr Turnbull. He was very enthusiastic, properly organising football in the playground and getting a school team together.

The playground was the pitch. There was no grass to play on. Keith used to go next door to Ayresome Park and see the players and run errands for them. It was not many years since Ayresome Park had played host to North Korea's three qualifying matches in the 1966 World Cup. Pak Doo Ik's goal knocked out Italy and subtly modulated the axis of world football for ever.

I used to go to the little shop on the corner on little errands for George Smith, who finished up as my coach at Hartlepool, getting him orange juice and bottles of milk. It was something to brag about.

Normally, you could not play in the school's senior team until the final year but Keith was so much better than anyone else that he was being picked when he was only nine. It was when he got to secondary school that he realised that he was very, very good at football. The Houchens were a sporty family and all the children were made to do sport, in particular karate. His two older brothers were both black belts and Keith and his younger brother were just off that as browns. His father thought that karate was a useful defence and discipline in such a tough area. He would take the boys in their karate suits to Albert Park in the middle of the town and get them to run round the park barefooted to harden up their feet as he rode alongside them on his bicycle.

The eldest brother, Jimmy, became a runner and ran for the town and the county. He set a record at the local stadium for the mile which still stands.

We used to go and watch Jimmy. We'd sit having picnics watching him on the track, the old cinder tracks. I can remember the excitement of all that, seeing him way back, coming and coming and getting there right on the line. It's things like that which stick in my mind: 'Oh God, I would love to be able to do that, be the one winning the races.' I was a good runner at school but not at that kind of level. But I found out very early on that I could be top dog at football. My dad used to take me to watch Jimmy playing football. I loved the crowd watching him, someone being better than everybody else. I realised that football was going to be my 'out'.

Dennis was an outstanding swimmer and had a trial for England Schoolboys. He became a keen water polo player.

Mr Houchen was more passionate about athletics and swimming than he was about football, although he always came along to watch. He felt most engaged when he could take the children out on a cross country run.

As a young man, he had had a bad motorbike accident:

It absolutely demolished his right leg. It was a horrible shaped right leg. He had it for the rest of his life and really struggled with it.

He had been in the Merchant Navy and the Army and it was probable that other than for a little karate he was living his sporting aspirations through his boys.

It was all about getting this idea into your mind about being a winner, being better than the next man, always standing up to the next man, never backing down to anybody. Be true to yourself; don't look for trouble or start any, but never back down. He was always preaching that to us as kids. If you were running the 800 metres, for instance, you got that horrible pain but you ran through it. It was like this mind theory: if you can run through the pain, you can beat everybody else. I hated running, at that age anyway, so football was my natural outlet, something I was particularly good at.

Both Keith's parents were Middlesbrough born and bred. His mum's side had come from Ireland. At school, Keith was neither shy nor extrovert. He had plenty of friends, but also plenty of trouble with teachers.

I followed my brothers through school and I think your brothers carry a bit of a reputation before you. There might have been a little bit of that. They were frustrating years, if anything. I just had it in my mind I was going to play football. I was always first in the school side from my first year at secondary school and then I went straight into the town team.

The headlines followed: HOUCHEN HITS SIX IN BORO DOUBLE and HOUCHEN HITS THE WINNER FOR BORO. The six were in a 7-5 win for the Under-14s against North Yorkshire Boys at Thirsk.

I was the first person in Middlesbrough to be picked for Cleveland when it changed from Yorkshire. I had trials for England Schoolboys, but never got picked. There were very few from the North-East – you Southerners had the monopoly in my day.

I didn't have many other hobbies. From the background that I came from, you took catapults. These tatty old towns are getting done up now but you could go to Newport Bridge and it was awful. The River Tees was a disgusting river in those days; dumping everything in it, weren't they, but you could go over there for hours shooting catapults at the rats, big rats coming out of the river. It was a typical Sixties childhood really.

We would be in a gang and we would all build a bonfire on 5 November and whoever had the biggest bonfire had the biggest credo. We counted it on the number of doors we managed to bring along. We were surrounded by derelict houses and you would go and get doors and floorboards from them. I suppose it's different in the gangs now.

Very occasionally on a Saturday afternoon Keith and other boys got up to a particular prank. They would break into cars near the football ground and reposition them around the car park like chess pieces. But it was more joy-parking than joy-riding.

We would go shoplifting and all the daft things that people do without being really bad at it. You would get in the wrong area and end up fighting. When I was at St Michael's, the first secondary school I was at, I got caught up in a fight with a lad from another school. I had had a few fights and would stand up and fight if I had to fight. We had been at this school for a swimming gala. I had a bit of a reputation as a fighter. A mate of mine got into an argument with somebody at this school and the top man at the school wanted to fight the top man at our school. It had nothing to do with me; I was on my way home from school. They were walking out behind and I got told I had to fight so-and-so. It was on a playing field on the way to the bus.

I was taught through karate not to get in too close. If you get too close, fighting gets messy – they can grab you and drain your strength. He got in very close, very early. I was quite slow on the day. He was a bit of a tough nut and had me in this headlock. It seemed like an eternity; I couldn't get out. I tried every move I had ever been taught by my dad. I tried grabbing his knackers – he wouldn't let go; poking his eyes – he wouldn't let go. It was uncomfortable. I couldn't breathe for a long time. He was joking and laughing with the crowd, and the crowd were laughing.

This was not Tom Brown and Harry Flashman. The violence was public rather than institutional, the crowd partisan but at the same time indifferent to the protagonists.

Scores of kids came out to gawp, the whoops and chatter, laughs and cries, detached in the afternoon air. Keith sweated as he felt the grip of the other boy's arm, the intimacy of his grubby hand, dirty nails and ink stained uniform. Keith's head was touching the ground. Grass was for playing football on – only on holiday had he ever breathed it in. Now, his senses were being confronted by the silence of ants. It was like watching television with the sound turned off.

It went on for a long time, and eventually he must have started to weaken. I got out of the headlock, and went loose on him. I absolutely pummelled him. That was the end of the fight. He lost, I won; who's laughing now? Then I went home.

Keith was about thirteen. He had been in trouble with the police for little things when he was growing up. He had to go to the local magistrates' court a couple of times. He was told that he was a good lad and shouldn't get dragged down, and was made to do a few hours community service, 'cleaning people's cars and that sort of thing'.

We had the police come round to our house. The kid had gone home and was in a right mess. I didn't realise how much I had hurt him – his nose was broken. He said I jumped on him and beat him up, so the police came and arrested me for assault. He wasn't such a tough nut in court, with his mum and dad. I felt hard done by because I hadn't started it, I hadn't instigated it. I had to put up with him holding me in a headlock for it must have been about fifteen minutes. I remember when we went to court, having to demonstrate karate to the magistrate. I said that once I got out of the headlock I was able to hurt him, but only in self defence. But apparently I took two of his teeth clean out. He deserved it.

Did this tough background help him to cope with the rough and tumble of the football world? The assumption is too glib for Houchen and his reaction is characteristically more subtle: 'Maybe I coped despite it.'

There had been no interest in Keith from the football profession until one evening there came a knock at the door. It was six o'clock and Keith's dad was eating his tea. The man introduced himself as Owen Willoughby, a scout who had seen Keith playing for the County. He was there on behalf of Crystal Palace Football Club.

2

First Hartlepool

Many are called but few are chosen, even at Chesterfield and Keith Houchen found himself spat out like so many others. Arthur Cox opted instead to sign another young striker called Phil Walker. Walker was three years older than Houchen, and stronger; Chesterfield got five years and 48 goals out of him. Keith went on the dole and worked for a month in the markets in Newcastle and Chester-le-Street. Would he now decide to join the Army like his three brothers or keep trying to be a professional footballer? The decision was soon made for him.

As Lady Godiva rides naked through Coventry, so the monkey hangs over Hartlepool. During the Napoleonic Wars, a French ship was wrecked off the Hartlepool coast. The townsfolk, primed for invasion, remained vigilant as the vessel lost its struggle in the storm. Amongst the flotsam was a sole survivor: a monkey clad in a military costume. The locals, unable to distinguish an ape from a Frenchman, sought to cross-examine the creature. A kangaroo court was convened on the spot. The accused – impervious it seemed to the charges of espionage – was sentenced to death, the mast of a coble serving as a ready gallows.

On 16 December 1914, the ghost of the monkey could afford a wry smile. Shortly after 8.00a.m., three battle cruisers emerged from the mist. For about forty minutes, from as close as 4,000 yards, the *Seydlitz, Moltke* and *Blücher* rained 1,150 shells onto gun emplacements and the docks. There were 119 deaths and over 200 people wounded. It was the first time that mainland Britain had been hit by German fire.

Nearly thirty years later Hartlepool lost one of its favourite sons to the next war. Henderson Rowntree, better known as the crooner Chick Henderson, was a vocalist with the Joe Loss Band. His recording of Cole Porter's *Begin the Beguine* was the only British record of the 1930s to sell a million copies. Henderson had just been promoted to naval sub-lieutenant when he was accidentally killed by a piece of shrapnel from a British ack-ack gun firing over Southsea.

After the war many a British theatre audience was kept amused by *Whisky Galore,* a fictional account of the sinking of a ship laden with whisky on the island of Eriskay. Its author, Compton Mackenzie, was born in theatrical digs in Hartlepool in 1883 when his father was playing at the Gaiety Theatre. West Hartlepool's contribution to culture was most singularly represented by being the birthplace of Lionel Tertis, who became the world's leading exponent of the viola.

Hartlepool is only a few miles away from Middlesbrough, close to home for Keith Houchen. Keith had scored the winning goal at the Victoria Ground in an FA Youth Cup-tie for Nunthorpe Athletic. Nunthorpe was a successful Junior club in Middlesbrough for which Houchen guested. After the game, the Hartlepool manager Billy Horner took the youngster into the office and invited him to train with the club the following week.

Mrs Houchen drove her son into Hartlepool. It was a grey, wet, windy day. With a quick 'Good luck', she pulled back into the heavy flow of traffic, leaving Keith standing outside a tall wooden fence. The Victoria Ground was a shambles of a place but nonetheless a League football ground.

It wasn't Selhurst Park, nor even Saltergate, but this was the start. It was one of those moments, like the first day at school, like the chill sense of isolation when manoeuvred into that fight, of responsibility for himself, of moving on, of fresh excitement and challenge.

Young Houchen found his way along a passage and ran into Roy Hogan, another recent beginner. Houchen helped Hogan sort out the players' kits; it eased his first day nerves. Hogan was the only apprentice – at Chesterfield there had been five or six to bow and scrape to the seniors' needs.

The players sauntered in, some laden with bags, actors without their make-up on. There were jagged ends to conversations, a titter or expletive, and just an occasional glance or wink at the stranger in the corner. The flip of an eyelid does not necessarily invite a handshake or the return of a smile;

it's more of a matey put-down to keep the distance. Gradually, however, the faces began to break into a welcome, and there was immediate recognition from Trevor Smith, a first-year pro whom Keith had played against in local football. It certainly made it easier having a pal on the inside, and Trevor was one of the very best. Eventually he became Keith's best man.

They were the liveliest, most down-to-earth bunch of characters I had ever met in my life and I learnt very early that one of the most important things I was going to need was a sense of humour… I was a little awestruck to be sitting next to and changing with some of my heroes from the Middlesbrough team I had supported as a boy – people like Derrick Downing, Eric McMordie and George Smith – the players I had run messages for at Ayresome Park.

The weather was Napoleonic. With the town covered in snow, the club found a big gymnasium in which to train. The youngster enjoyed himself. He loved to dribble, and no one had much success at prising the ball away from him.

The week became several weeks and Keith played well enough in training to be offered non-contract forms at the club. This meant that he could play for the reserves and also in any emergency for the first team. He continued to turn out for Nunthorpe but the FA Youth Cup run was brought to an end by Middlesbrough with a 6-1 defeat in the second round at Ayresome Park.

One morning, on 9 February 1978, Billy Horner called Keith into the office. The reserves had registered a good win that week and four of the goals were scored by Houchen. 'Sit down,' Billy gently instructed.

A Hartlepool manager had reputedly once signed a player for a tenner and a box of kippers. Billy Horner was offering something a little more straight-forward.

I desperately, desperately wanted to be a professional football player so it was just amazing for me when they offered me a professional contract, a year's contract, thirty pounds a week. I wanted to play high up. I wanted to be a top footballer. I can remember having to stop myself from jumping out of the chair opposite the manager.

Here I was outside this run-down little fourth division ground in the pouring rain. I was walking on air all the way out to the car where Derrick Downing was waiting to run me home.

I said to Derrick that I couldn't believe that at last I was a pro footballer. He replied: 'Great, but all the hard work is yet to come.' He was right of course but I will never forget that moment or being able to walk into the local dole office in Middlesbrough where I had been signing on for the last two months to say: 'I won't be back, I'm a professional footballer.'

Hartlepool United used to be called Hartlepools United. Through a curiosity of local government, Hartlepool and West Hartlepool were united into one municipality only in 1967, with the football club reinventing itself the following year as Hartlepool AFC. The new title derived partly from a misconception of continental chic resulting from the muddle we still get into over the names of foreign clubs. For instance, Italians no more talk of 'AC Milan' than we do of 'Liverpool FC'. For that matter, we still tend to describe Internazionale or Inter as 'Inter Milan', but when did you ever hear Highbury resounding to cries of 'Arsenal London'? Perhaps it is no more than the quirk of condescension by which we define Thierry Henry, say, as a 'French' international – with a mere adjective – but David Beckham always – and more correctly – as an 'England' one. Even Richie Benaud colludes at this, describing his fellow countrymen's Test side as the 'Australian' team.

Nationhood is not a distinction we readily endow in reference to those beyond the Channel. Alan Hansen wrote in *The Daily Telegraph* about the 'great difference' with a 'foreign player': 'Usually, when his back is to the wall, you will get a positive response from a home-grown footballer, but there is no guarantee of that when you are dealing with a foreigner.' And therein lies the dichotomy. In the grander stands of the game, the names of players from foreign tribes trip gleefully off the tongue and there is talk of 'getting into Europe', but some people – not especially Hansen, and not especially in football – scrutinise any such familiarity with suspicion.

Some Bournemouth fans still refer to their club as 'Boscombe', in deference to Bournemouth and Boscombe Athletic. On one occasion, a visitor to Dean Court, intrigued by the regular exhortations of 'Come on Boscombe', enquired what number he played. In 1971, the club sought to leap to the top of the alphabetical league with the ghastly 'AFC Bournemouth', which is nonetheless preferable to 'Bradford Bulls' or 'Sussex Sharks', the acne of Stars and Stripes that has sprouted over Rugby League and Cricket. 'Hartlepool AFC' jettisoned its suffix in 1977 and reunited without sigmoidal end.

The 'Pools or the 'Pool hold the record for the most applications – fourteen – required for re-election to the League. However, on 5 January 1957, they came within a whisker of knocking the Busby Babes out of the FA Cup. There was a record crowd at the Victoria Ground of 17,426 for a game that Matt Busby later described in his autobiography as 'the most exciting match I've ever watched'. Three down within half-an-hour, Hartlepools fought back to 3-3 before Whelan scored a winner for Manchester United in the dying minutes. The team might well have gone on to clinch promotion had it not been for the death four weeks later of manager Fred Westgarth, one of the great figures of Hartlepools football. With one team only promoted from each section of the Third Division, the 'Pools finished second to Derby.

In the 1960s, Brian Clough, making fewer mistakes than are expected of a first-time manager, steered Hartlepools away from the crumbling cliff. A year after his departure, the team ascended for the first time to the Third Division. One season proved enough.

Clough wrote in his autobiography, 'Hardly any of them could play in the first place, and money was in such short supply that if we'd needed a new shit-house door, I'd have been expected to provide it and fit it.' As an economy measure, he even took lessons to drive the team coach.

Clough's short reign at the club was eventful in other unexpected ways. Shortly after his appointment, Clough was surprised when the police interrupted a training session in order to arrest one of his top players for non-payment of maintenance.

When Keith Houchen arrived, Hartlepool were ninety-first – last but one – in the Football League. A fortnight after he signed pro, and with Bob Newton suspended, Houchen was running out in front of the home fans for his League debut, against Crewe Alexandra. An early shot went just wide and, shortly before half-time, the offside flag robbed him of a dream debut when he cleverly latched on to a through pass and neatly flicked the ball past Geoff Crudgington. Hartlepool scored with an own-goal and the veteran Wales centre forward Wyn Davies equalised twelve seconds from time. It was at the Racecourse Ground on 3 March 1962 that Davies, not much further on in his career than Houchen, scored a hat-trick within the first half-hour as Wrexham beat Hartlepools 10-1.

Three days after the Crewe game, young Houchen was on the winning side at the Vic against Southport.

It was very hard at first. I was always up and down but I knew I could make it and gradually I found my feet.

Billy Horner, too, had plenty of confidence in his raw recruit:

> In terms of skill, I rate him just as highly as Malcolm Poskett, whom we sold to Brighton for £60,000 a few weeks back. If Keith lacks something at present it is a little aggression. He doesn't put himself about considering his size. But that isn't uncommon in a youngster. It comes with experience and confidence.

The talent that Horner had recognised was expressed in determined dribbling but Horner, George Smith and Willie Maddren got to work on Houchen's physical strength in order to turn him into an adult centre forward. The youngster was taught the trade: to battle for the ball, keep it up, flick it on, play it off an opponent's legs, to jump at the right moment. He was shown how to protect himself from being hit, to bring other players into the game.

I had always been the best player locally because I could get the ball, run past people and score goals. It's all instinct in kids' football, what comes naturally to you. But when you go into professional football all of a sudden there are things which you hadn't even thought about.

I think I learnt to be a professional footballer once I got in at Hartlepool and it was a tough, tough, very tough league and big, monstrous teams and players you were playing against. They would break your leg and smile at you and lads on our side would do it too. When I first got into the team, those big centre halfs would just go straight through me and knock me over.

We used to have training sessions when they would put a big centre half on me. I would have to hold the ball and hold him off for a certain number of seconds.

I remember having to learn when to stand, when to run into the channel, changing over so the centre half doesn't know whether you are going to the channel or going to stand. We would develop it with a couple of players running from midfield, learning the right time to release the ball to them. All of a sudden you've started to become a player then.

I worked for hours at getting above my man in the air but, instead of heading the ball, just glancing it to put people in. It was all about teaching you how to be strong, how to get your arms up, how to jump with your elbows.

I was forever getting whacked on the head – I used to get a migraine quite easily.

You are protecting yourself, not actually trying to elbow anybody. It was hard for me by the time I got to thirty-four because I was being penalised for things I used to work at on the training pitch when I was seventeen. The game changed: I was starting to get booked and sent off for things that I had been coached to do.

Houchen was fortunate to have such mentors. They had done the rounds at the blunter ends of football pitches. Maddren, the legendary former Middlesbrough defender who should have played for England, succumbed later to motor-neurone disease. He raised thousands of pounds for research into it before his death in 2000. He was a devoted coach and would tell Houchen which forwards to watch and how to learn from them, like Mike Tyson sifting the archives for a composite of heavyweights' strengths:

'So-and-so is not particularly good at this, but good at that…Watch this forward – he is not particularly good in the air but suddenly he will peel into space when there's time…Watch that forward because he's really good at holding it up and knows exactly when to lay it off – left, right or back.' I think when I was at Hartlepool we had a lot of old pros that had been fantastic players: Eric McMordie, Paul Bielby – these type of people, who had just had enough of football, were disillusioned, picking up their wages and, to be honest, not really bothering. I think there was a lot of that going on. I don't know, maybe I was different, I was the enthusiastic one. I can remember training for hours on my own, so obviously none of the others were that enthusiastic or they would have been out there with me wouldn't they? But I think there was a lot of disillusionment and there were some real bad pros. Some of the older ones obviously hadn't been bad pros because of the good careers they'd had, but they were at the stage where they weren't bothered anymore.

We used to have a mad rush to get to the bank to pay in our cheques. Only about six of them would go through and the rest would bounce – oh yes, it was that sort of club, so you can imagine the old pros not being that inspired to do anything. It was run down; it was falling apart; it was tough.

But George and Will would quite happily spend three hours with you at the nuclear power station. It was just me and them, whatever I was weak on. George, everyone at the club, knew I could play high up and wanted me to play higher up, so if I was prepared to listen they were prepared to put the time in, and I will always be grateful for that.

George took me to one side and said, 'You are going to play higher up and I am going to make sure that you do…You can do this more; you can do that more. You are a big strong lad; you need to be a big, strong centre forward.'

They always said that I was too weak physically. So the big, strong centre forward I ended up at the end of my career I wasn't when I started.

I had wonderful ability with my feet. It was the other stuff I had to work on: all that heading and holding people off. They would spend hours doing that. They'd bring in an apprentice and I would just play balls with him like Shearer does. I was all floppy and I had to work at that a lot. I worked for hours at volleying. Someone had to go really, really tight on me. I would have to be on the half-turn so he couldn't get round me. George crossed the ball and I had one touch and a shot.

There were lots and lots of things. That's why I think by the time I was twenty-six I was ready to play at the top level. My really productive years as a footballer were from twenty-six to thirty-three when I changed my game which meant I did more but scored less.

There were other things I remember from my first year. Allan Clarke nearly did me when he was playing for Barnsley. How he didn't break my leg I don't know. I sat down on the floor and looked up at him. 'What's the matter, what are you looking at?' he said. Norman Hunter was altogether different. 'I'm sorry, I'm a yard short these days,' he'd say.

Some players really set out to hurt you. I had broken ribs, broken backbone, all sorts of things in my early days at Hartlepool. I got hit playing at Portsmouth and I finished right underneath the boards. They nearly killed me, because I wasn't strong. You look at the Shearers of this world – they run in a balanced way so when they get hit they don't go flying, even if it puts them on one knee. I had to learn to be a professional footballer which is different from being a really good football player.

Alan Foggon taught me in training how to intertwine my arms with an opponent's when jumping for a header. It stopped them getting off the floor. The ref doesn't see it, nobody sees it. I really was very good at it. There weren't many people, if I was marking them at corners, who scored against me. I learnt some really clever stuff like that but not easily. It took me a while because I was a big, soft, nice boy.

Bob Newton, one of 'Pool's tougher eggs, returned to the team for the long haul to Bournemouth.

He was the local favourite, a beast of a man with a bull neck, massive barrel chest, and thighs as big as my torso, with a temper to match, but a very funny man and a great bloke to have in the dressing room and in the side.

The first time I met Bob was at the gym that first day I came to the club. He walked towards me whilst our teams were resting between five-a-sides. I wasn't sure if he was coming over to beat me up for tackling him or to introduce himself. I found that I got on with him quite well and in the next four years we struck up a great partnership on the field.

On 24 March 1978 Houchen led the attack at home to Barnsley. 'Pool lost, but for Houchen one memory will never fade – that of his first goal. Taking possession, he ran to the edge of the box at the Town End before slotting the ball past Peter Springett. The ball struck the upright before tantalisingly rolling back across the line. It was Good Friday. For the first time, Houchen's name would be in every newspaper, if only as a statistic.

On Easter Saturday, Hartlepool went to Darlington. This was Everton *v.* Liverpool and Arsenal *v.* Tottenham rolled into one. And a scrawny teenager became the talk of Cleveland with his second-half winner. On April Fools' Day, 'Pool played a strong Swansea side at the Vetch. Three goals in twelve minutes in the first half and five goals in eighteen minutes in the second were no joke for Hartlepool but, on the following Tuesday, Houchen gave 'Pool victory at Rochdale with the only goal of the game. In eleven days the youngster had played 4 games and scored 3 goals. It ensured his place for the rest of the season, and – against Newport – he scored again. Hartlepool rose to twenty-first in the division by the end of the season but it was not enough to avoid re-election, passing Barrow's record of eleven applications in the process.

Re-election was the annual beauty contest for the four ugly sisters who finished at the bottom of the League. The rules required the four to retire and re-apply. The full members – the clubs outside the First and Second Divisions were only associates – cast votes for the four failures and any new applicants. There was anxious lobbying lest any aspiring debutante seduce the bejewelled jurymen.

In 1972 Barrow had become one of the occasional discards when Hereford squeezed them out after a second vote. It was against Barrow on 4 April 1959 that Hartlepools, seven up at half-time, had recorded their biggest Football League victory, by an improbable 10-1. 'Please may we come back and play again in August,' an application might plead, and sometimes almost as succinctly. In 1983 the Hartlepool chairman addressed eight short paragraphs to the 'Dear Sirs' of Lytham St Annes, of which the most pertinent was the following:

> The unemployment situation in the north-east of England is still a massive problem, and this town has suffered very badly with closures. It would be a hard blow to this area if there were no League Football in the Town as information given to us indicates that many prospective new businesses are attracted to towns which support a Football League Club.

Gateshead had been snuffed from the consciousness of many beyond the Tyne Bridge with its enforced retirement from the football coupons, although the name remains embossed on the cistern of many a football ground lavatory manufactured in the town. The ghosts of clubs like New Brighton continue to echo gauntly as if from a memorial plaque. To this day, on account of Bradford (Park Avenue) who were ejected in 1970, football fans of an older generation rarely refer to Bradford City as simply Bradford.

It was not often that the black cap was donned and, in 1932, it didn't need to be as Thames Association, deciding not to reapply, disappeared like a disused Underground station. Accrington Stanley ostentatiously died in the middle of a season.

Gateshead's ejection in 1960 remained the subject of grumblings in the North-East. Hartlepools had lost 29 of their 46 fixtures and conceded 109 goals. They finished the season six points behind Gateshead but polled sixteen more votes. It was not a case of Hartlepools being more experienced letter writers than Gateshead, as neither club had been forced into re-election since 1939, rather the impressive insistence of Peterborough's pleas for election. When Workington gave way to Wimbledon in 1977, they had teased tolerance too far with a fourth consecutive application, although Hartlepools's in 1960 was the first of five on the trot. In 1978, Southport were thrown out after a second ballot in favour of Wigan Athletic.

Southport had enrolled in the new Third Division (North) in 1921 – the same year as Hartlepools. Travelling from Hartlepool to London in those days demanded a trawl through *Bradshaw's* almost as long as the journey itself. So, with the potentially sympathetic Newcastle chairman John Oliver – a prominent member of the League Management Committee – suffering a serious stroke at breakfast just before the Special General Meeting, Hartlepools could have felt rather lonely, but there was no need to fret that their journey was wasted as they were duly elected.

In 1984, another letter from the Hartlepool chairman arrived for consideration at the League's AGM at the Café Royal. Towards the end of the season, the attendance at the Victoria Ground for the Stockport game had been only 790, one of the lowest for a Football League match anywhere since before the Second World War. It turned out to be Hartlepool's last application. In 1986, automatic promotion and relegation was introduced between the top club in the Alliance Premier League (Gola League as it had become) and the bottom club in the Football League. You could say that Hartlepool have repaid the faith in them by finishing in the bottom four only once since that last application. You might add that they have finished in the bottom five or six on six further occasions.

As well as the thirty-three votes of confidence and one in three additional customers, the money from the sale of Malcolm Poskett provided a solid base for Hartlepool's marked improvement in the 1978/79 season. On the opening day, after leading 3-1 at half-time, the team surrendered at home to Doncaster, but only one game was lost in the next eight. Hartlepool were seventh. Houchen lost his place after the Wimbledon match on 9 December when Bob Newton returned from suspension. He was now doing a lot of weight training to build up his strength so that he could enforce his height and physique. His ability on the ball was not in question but he needed to add some of the rough and tumble of the burly Newton who was over a stone heavier. Houchen and Trevor Smith would spend afternoons at the Clairville Stadium in Middlesbrough doing extra work on this. Gradually, the stringy boy gave way to the predatory adult, less prone to being bullied from the ball, more insistent in his initiative.

Houchen was only out of the starting line-up for four League matches but, in the days before climate change, this meant that it was 10 February before he returned to the side for the game against Torquay. There had been only one home match since before Christmas – a pantomime season with just a single performance. It would have strained the coffers of any club, let alone Hartlepool, had there not been the gala benefit of drawing Leeds in the third round of the Cup. Never mind the 6-2 defeat. There were 16,000 at the Victoria Ground to see it.

Houchen scored in his first four games back in the team. In the last of these, against Crewe, Trevor Smith became the fifth Hartlepool player to be sent off that season – a record for the club.

Billy Horner talked to Arthur Pickering in the *Hartlepool Mail* on 24 March 1979 about 'Pool's poor disciplinary record. His comments were prescient and perceptive:

> Disciplinary problems have caused us several headaches at the Victoria Ground this season, and we don't need to be reminded that one more sending-off this season will create a new Football League record.
>
> We are not at all proud of this situation, and we know that we must accept that we could do with tightening-up in this respect.
>
> But though we have had five players sent off this season, only two of them in my view deserved to be shown the red card – the others went off in regrettable circumstances.
>
> Billy Ayre deserved his marching orders at York, and so did Trevor Smith in our recent home match with Crewe. Both players should know better than to do what they did, and both will have to learn their lessons the hard way.
>
> But the other three players to be sent off this season deserve some sympathy at least.
>
> Martin Gorry reacted to severe provocation at Bournemouth when one of their players stood on his ankle for ten seconds after the referee's whistle had blown.
>
> Derek Loadwick didn't touch the man he was alleged to have kicked when he was sent off at Aldershot. He had been the victim of about 15 fouls from one player, when he lunged at the man as he was on the floor – but didn't intend to make any contact.
>
> Bob Newton was sent off at Torquay for retaliation, yet I have never seen him retaliate in my life. He went past two of their players and had only the goalkeeper to beat.
>
> Two tackles from behind failed to bring him down, but a third desperate attempt succeeded at the expense of a free-kick to us. Bob got up and pushed the centre half away… and was sent off.
>
> We see reactions from players on television ten times worse than this, yet they often aren't booked. I want to know why.
>
> …

We also have referees like the one we had this season who throughout the game spoke to players saying he would love to get the chance to book them or send them off.

He apparently said to Bob Newton: 'I have had you before, and I would love to have you again.'

After a quiet game from Bob I gave him a roasting because I thought he wasn't trying but then I discovered from him and the others that the referee had frightened him with his threats.

…

I can't tell players to stop tackling. If every manager was forced to do that by bookings and so-on the game would turn into a Sunday school outing. We can't allow it to lose its physical edge because of fear of referees and a committee in London.

I can only remember two players going off this season with injuries received in games against us, and the two Hartlepool players who caused the injuries were not booked. So we can hardly be described as a dirty team, otherwise we would be leaving a trail of destruction behind us after every match.

A lack of experience has a lot do with some of the trouble we have had. Trevor Smith, for instance, was sent off because his lack of experience allowed him to lose his head and lash out when a more experienced player provoked him.

He and our other young players are learning this season that this sort of thing goes on all the time in League football. The game is about skill and scoring goals, but it is also full of people who goad, provoke and tempt players to get into trouble with the referee.

Trevor was fined £45 by the club for his offence, but sometimes I feel awful fining players because, although they have been booked, their offences have been too trivial for words.

…

Players who are booked for dissent or retaliation deserve their punishment and the referee is more often than not right in sending them off when he does. He has a very difficult job to do, and all dissent and retaliation does is make it harder for him.

But a lot of bookings in Division Four, from what I have seen this season, have been earned by offences which would only warrant a lecture in Divisions One or Two. In our home game against Wimbledon this season, four players from each side were booked – yet the game wasn't at all dirty.

We have tried to do something about it by fining the players who get themselves into trouble. We have had referee Pat Partridge at the ground to talk to us, and I have invited referees to join us in training and control some of our practice matches.

I believe they should be more involved than they are, and even if their jobs prevent them from taking part during the day they can come on a night when part-timers and young players train.

I have played in matches against referees, and they have kicked me as much as I have kicked them. They have done things which would earn bookings if they were refereeing.

They have surely got to make allowances for the human element in the game.

The general theme in refereeing seems to be to play everything by the book, but the game is all about players and they need to be understood and treated with some measure of consistency. The ref has to make split-second decisions which are often difficult, but they often make it hard for players.

Most important of all, the gap between players and referees must be closed before it becomes too wide.

After their victory against Torquay on 10 February 1979, Hartlepool United went sixteen matches without a win. Houchen scored an equaliser against Wigan and another in the last minute to save the game against Bradford City. There were further goals from Houchen at Scunthorpe and Wimbledon, but the team had tumbled down the table. Astonishingly, Hartlepool then finished the season off with five wins in their last six games. Victory at Darlington helped push Darlo into re-election, and Mark Lawrence scored all four goals against Halifax. Hartlepool finished thirteenth and Houchen ended his first full season as top scorer with 13 goals.

Smith and Lawrence were Houchen's best mates during his early years as a pro. One summer, Lawrence and Houchen got a rap over the knuckles from the FA for accepting an invitation to appear in an informal five-a-side tournament in Middlesbrough. The jaunt cost Lawrence his career. He broke his leg so badly that at the age of twenty-four, Houchen's friend , 'a really, really good footballer', was left contemplating an alternative future. He had a brief spell at Port Vale and played non-League but the dream had snapped. He and Houchen had been pals at school. They are now business partners.

There was a little group of us. I'd played with Trevor at school. He was a good defender but prone to mistakes which is why his career fizzled out.

There was another good friend, Billy Ayre. Billy was eight years older than Keith which seemed quite a lot to a gawky teenager.

He was the toughest bloke I had ever seen, even when he was training. Some nasty stuff used to go on in the corridors when we played southern sides, such as Wimbledon who'd just come into the League. Billy used to out-tough them just by looking at them. But he was a lovely man and he gave me loads of compliments, 'You are such a good footballer,' 'You're going to play at the highest level.' I used to talk to him all the time. He was a fantastic person to base yourself on.

Billy Ayre later applied his humanity to coaching and management, most notably at Halifax and Blackpool.

Footballers keep in touch through the grapevine, one that evokes names and connections beyond the back page and the patter of club programmes. Years later Keith got a call from Billy. They hadn't spoken for months. 'What about lunch at The Quayside?'

Mark, Keith and Billy met at the Newcastle restaurant. Mark and Keith were taken by surprise – the indestructible pillar of Billy looked emaciated and gaunt. 'I've got to have an operation. It'll be OK but I shall be off for a few months,' he confided as they chatted over old times and talked of families and real lives.

It was time to go, one last laugh – a player or a place stalled by the memory as they continued to chat through the car window. Only later did Keith and Mark realise that Billy had come to say good-bye. Within weeks he was dead, from lymph node cancer. He wasn't yet fifty.

Houchen started his second full season as a League footballer. Pompey, at the Vic, was the first engagement in the diary, on 18 August 1979. The Fourth Division has been akin to the show on the end of the pier for quite a few famous clubs, with Huddersfield and Portsmouth faded comics eking out a laugh beside more predictable Punch and Judys. However, both clubs were on the way to convalescence with promotion at the end of the new season, Pompey kicking off with a 3-0 win. Hartlepool, with a history that had gone but never quite come, followed up with a win at Scunthorpe and defeat at Rochdale.

Houchen went close to scoring in the first three games and got off the mark with the only goal of the match against Aldershot. It was one of those sticky afternoons when summer refuses to yield to autumn. Player-coach George Smith was injured. He was replaced in midfield by Paul Staff, still two days short of his seventeenth birthday. Staff swung over an unexpected cross and Houchen rose to head home. The strong presence of Bob Newton was welcome support. Newton was returning to the side after serving six months out of a nine-month prison sentence imposed as a result of a motor accident in which a young Hartlepool player had been killed.

It was a briefly prosperous Christmas and New Year: a run of four wins and two draws put 'Pool into eighth place by the end of January. Houchen scored 5 times in a run of 4 consecutive matches. By the beginning of April the team were still in the top half of the table, but a run of only 2 points from their last 9 matches consigned 'Pool to finishing the 1979/80 season sixth from bottom. Houchen, who had been ever-present, missed 5 of the last 6 matches but was top scorer again with 14 goals.

The players returned to training in July with Houchen top of the shopping list for several clubs on the lookout for a tall striker. Third Division Reading were told by Vince Barker that even if he was available, they would not be able to afford him. Houchen was presented with a trophy as top goalscorer, and the chairman crowed:

> He could have gone this week but he's happy to stay at Hartlepool United, and one of these days he's going to be a great star.

It had become a Hartlepool tradition to take a tour to Scotland prior to the grouse shooting. The location of many a Scottish club is camouflaged by its title, thus Methil is home to East Fife and Perth to St Johnstone. The players could indulge a smokie in more familiar Arbroath, confident that the Red Lichties were not up to emulating their world record score against Bon Accord in 1885, in a match so one-sided that the Arbroath goalkeeper reputedly spent most of the game smoking a pipe whilst his comrades guzzled their 36 goals at the other end. Although the beaters were not yet out, Billy Horner was happy with the prospects and with his new signings: Bobby Kerr, John Bird and Geoff Forster. A few days away, with a round or two of golf, cushions the impending stress of a winter of wasted dressing rooms and journeys through the night. It helps imprint the names you'll need to shout, coerces a spent cartilage or two, and charges you up with banter and bull. It provides insulation from the lesions of life and a League table that never lies.

Wigan were first up in the League. Television viewers were used to the sound of Eddie Waring commentating from Central Park, where the heritage of Eric Ashton, Billy Boston and so many others was pivotal to the story of Rugby League. Any significance in events at Springfield Park sank with the first reading of the football results. Wigan Athletic, however, had enjoyed a good first year in the Football League, but Hartlepool's 3-0 win put the teams at almost opposite ends of the new table.

Expectations of Keith Houchen, who had left his teens behind in the close season, had become more rigorous. He scored against Wigan but in neither leg of the League Cup tie against York. Failure to score in the second League game, a home defeat by Bury, cost him his place. Back in the team for the League trip to York, he chipped the goalkeeper from just inside the area with a finely taken first-half winner. Defeat followed at Bournemouth, but Billy Horner was not unhappy:

> It gave me and everybody else who was there a lot of satisfaction to see a Hartlepool team perform so well down in the South, where the club has been one of the Northern laughing stock teams for a long time. We won't be a laughing stock at Bournemouth now, and while that is no compensation for not getting a result, it's better than nothing.

Aside from two bad defeats at Southend and Wimbledon, 'Pool were shaping their season with some good football. Houchen was continuing to raise eyes with several outstanding goals – what a pity the cameras were not there. At Stockport, Houchen set off on a forty-yard run and rounded the 'keeper before angling the ball into the net. In the home game against Wigan, he showed tremendous pace in moving onto a through ball from Roy Hogan before accurately placing his shot. The victory against Wigan was the twelfth of the season and put 'Pool into third place. There were over 5,000 at the Vic, and the feeling was that with such pace and skill throughout the team promotion was a strong possibility.

A week later, with optimism in the air, a thousand Hartlepool fans made the journey to Scunthorpe for an FA Cup tie. When the home team clinched victory with a dubious second-half penalty, morons amongst the visiting support were quickly to the fore. With less brains than most of the creatures you would expect to come across at a venue called the Old Show Ground, they hurled missiles which struck both the Scunthorpe goalkeeper and a policeman.

Hooliganism is not the exclusive preserve of the modern world. At Shildon, once the catalyst for Timothy Hackworth and other railway pioneers, Shildon Athletic entertained Hartlepools in a North Eastern League fixture on 13 March 1909. The local team conceded a last minute equaliser, which did not meet with universal acceptance. Colin Foster, in *Hartlepool United: in the Beginning 1908-1921*, describes events:

> Mr Brown, the referee, who hailed from Middlesbrough, had experienced difficulty throughout in keeping the game under control. Most of the 750 or so spectators did not see eye to eye with his decisions. Immediately after the whistle was blown for full time, a section of the crowd allowed their anger to outweigh discretion. The referee was being treated badly and as he crossed the ropes to go to the dressing room area he was surrounded by about fifty people. Stones and mud were thrown at him. One stone hit him on the right side of the face causing a large abrasion, whilst a half brick narrowly missed his head. Some officials of the club attempted to stop the trouble to no avail. Fortunately for the referee, two officers of the law arrived to quell the disturbance resulting in one of them being hit by a stone too.
>
> Finally the police escorted the referee to a nearby hotel and then the railway station for a hasty departure... Due to the assault the referee had to miss four days work. He submitted a claim to the Durham FA for lost earnings. The Shildon club later admitted the assault took place but claimed that it was only of a trivial nature. They had put the matter in the hands of the local constabulary but still no arrests had been made. At a hearing 18 days after the game took place, Shildon were found guilty and had to pay the referee's lost earnings and the Doctor's bill. They were reprimanded further, for evidence had proved that two members of the club's committee had sworn at the referee after the game in his dressing room, resulting in them being suspended until the end of the season. The use of their ground was suspended for two weeks and they couldn't play within six miles of Shildon. They were also fined the princely sum of £3.

Returning to their League fixtures after the Cup-tie at Scunthorpe, Hartlepool's form sagged but the chairman was uncowed, 'I think we're certainties for promotion, and I believe we've got the young players coming along that could make us a force in the Third Division next season.' Vince Barker was a Yorkshire farmer and a genial and benevolent character.

He was really strange. He loved me. He didn't want me to go and that probably held me back a couple of years.

Driving along the A66 for the local derby at Darlo, Houchy was astonished to hear the chairman announce to the local radio audience: 'We're going to beat 'em 10-0 today.' Barker endorsed it in the dressing room with, 'I've told 'em on radio, so don't let me down.'
His favoured phrase to the troops before matches was always, 'All the best lads, and don't forget.'
    'And don't forget what, Mr Barker?' Bob Newton once enquired.
    'Joost don't forget!'

When you went in to ask for a rise, he would say, 'Ungrateful little booger'. You went out feeling over the moon if you got an extra tenner.

When Plymouth and Cardiff each offered the best part of a £100,000 for Hartlepool's young star, Barker was quoted in the local press as saying, 'They're not having him for nutmegs.'
    At the end of January, Houchen was first to the ball when 'Pool were awarded a penalty against Rochdale. He sent the 'keeper the wrong way but later admitted that he had never taken a penalty kick in his life. Bob Newton, the normal penalty-taker, was out of the side. Houchen's bravado was further evident with the other goal. Roy Hogan and Derek Hampton combined in a crowded penalty-area to work the ball to him and he went round a defender and the goalkeeper before letting rip with a right-foot shot – 'a piece of brilliance,' commented Billy Horner.
    Hartlepool were still in the promotion hunt until the end of February but a run of five defeats killed things off. Tyne Tees TV cameras were at the last of these and although the highlights were kind to Hartlepool, Horner was more discerning:

I couldn't bear to look for much of the time. I've never been so embarrassed in my life. To say we were awful would be understating it – I can't think of the words to describe it.

The team had responded to the midfield guile of Brian Kerr, the former Sunderland Cup Final hero, and scored enough goals, but if only the money had been available to strengthen the defence. Hartlepool finished ninth, with Houchen top scorer with 17 goals.

These were difficult times for football. The state of the economy and the hooliganism that had been evident at Scunthorpe was fuelling a growing disaffection. The vast improvement in Hartlepool's form had only brought an extra two hundred customers through the turnstiles. The Football League decided to pep things up and address the negative nature of much of the football. Three points for a win were introduced.

Alan Durban, the Sunderland manager, was at Hartlepool's friendly against Bolton before the start of the 1981/82 season, with Arthur Pickering observing in *The Northern Echo*:

> He must have noticed the form of Pool's annual top scorer Keith Houchen who scored once last night and might have added one or two others. He occasionally tended to overdo things but he showed again that he has the skill and strength required to make a success of the game at a higher level.

'Pool made a mess of their part in the inception of the new Football League Group Cup, losing all three games, and then lost their opening two League matches. After the Colchester game, Pickering didn't mince his words:

> shocking... it would have been impossible for them to be any worse... 'Pool need new players. I have said it before, Horner says it, chairman Vince Barker has agreed. So when are they going to get them?

Rochdale, whose victory was inspired by Essex boy Eugene Martinez, were given a better run for their money and Pickering reported that 'Houchen could have won the game virtually single-handed.' The player's diving header for the opening goal would one day spawn a famous successor.

Fans put the poor form down to what they referred to as the 'Victoria Ground Saga'. This had begun in January 1977, when the club offered to buy back the ground from the local Council for £24,000, a bid which the Council rejected. Ed Law, in *Hartlepool United: A History of one of the North-East's Oldest Cubs*, describes what happened:

In October the same year [1977], the Council proposed that the club buy back the ground for the sum of £60,000 on a 99-year lease. The club accepted the offer and negotiations began.

In February 1978, United stated their intention to pay cash for the purchase of the ground and the Council passed outline planning permission for ground improvements. Two months later, the club cleared their rent arrears, this before the Council passed planning permission for a new gymnasium, social club and changing rooms in May 1978.

Little or nothing was heard of matters from then until February 1979, when United chairman Vince Barker broke silence to accuse the Council of 'delaying tactics'. Five months later the chairman threatened 'drastic action' if the deal was delayed any longer. Despite his protestations, it was February 1980 before the two factions got together at the Victoria Ground. The result of this meeting was that the club agreed to forego rights to compensation, apart from such for the new boundary wall to be erected when the new road on the Clarence Road side of the ground was built.

Come July 1980, Vince Barker accused the Council of going back on their agreement of the sale price for the ground. Although no figures were revealed, the difference between the club's and the Council's price was believed to be in the region of £30,000. Barker went further and threatened that if the delay continued he would move the club out of the town. At the end of the month the Council stated that the contract for the sale of the ground was ready.

The wrangling continued and in March 1981 the club queried four clauses in the contract. This brought an immediate response from the Council, who threatened a time limit on the deal after which they stated they would end negotiations. The club's supporters were up in arms in May of that year, when it was alleged that Barker was planning to move their club lock, stock and barrel down the coast to Scarborough, having declined an offer of financial help from local businessmen Harold Hornsey and Frank Owbridge.

Significantly, neither Vince Barker nor the Scarborough Football Club chairman, Don Robinson, denied the rumour and the secretary of the Football League, Graham Kelly, elected to make 'no comment'. Earlier that season Scarborough failed in a bid to take control of Halifax Town.

Gloomy as the portents were, Hartlepool found the elastic in their socks with 5 wins in the next 6 games, including a second-leg victory against Northampton in the League Cup. This, however, was not enough to prevent 'Pool going out in the first round of the competition for the seventh year running. Bob Newton was back after a summer playing in the United States and John Linacre from squabbling over his salary, but Mark Lawrence's recovery from a broken leg was less negotiable. Cardiff manager Richie Morgan came sniffing again for Keith Houchen but was not prepared to meet the price. How Hartlepool would come to regret it. Back on par from the end of the previous season, 'Pool were in ninth spot.

Sendings-off in consecutive matches did not endear the officials to Arthur Pickering, who wrote in *The Northern Echo*:

> Referee Don Shaw likes to come to Hartlepool to take charge of matches at the Victoria Ground so he can take some fish back home to Sandbach – but on Saturday he took home more than just fish.
>
> There was criticism from every quarter for Mr Shaw's performance... and he appeared to deserve it all... nobody had a good word for him.
>
> Mr Shaw is not likely to be made too welcome next time he comes to Hartlepool.
>
> I am no great lover of Football League referees, but Mr Shaw's performance – even allowing for bias and the fact that I saw it from the stand instead of from the pitch – was one of the worst I can remember from an official.
>
> It would be easy to say that the sending-off of Alan Sweeney was the incident which showed up his form, but there was far more to it than that. In fact, his refusal to give Pool a penalty five minutes before half-time was possibly the most amazing single decision I have seen from a referee for years.

A draw at Bramall Lane rather than home defeat by Peterborough is always going to reflect better in your assessment of the ref, and Pickering believed that 'Coventry's Keiran Barratt, refereeing only his fourth Football League game, handled it well enough to suggest that all is not lost with officials.'

'Pool were rewarded for their 500-mile round trip to Colchester with a draw that should have been a win. The Oystermen were amongst the pacemakers in the division, but at 3-1 down 'Pool's Mike Fagan launched himself across the turf to contribute a spectacular headed own-goal. Houchen scored twice for the visitors, once from the spot, but was emphatic that Martin Bodenham erred in giving the penalty from which Colchester made it 3-3:

I had made a clearance and the lad came in and caught my foot. I hadn't even seen him, then he dived and got himself a penalty.

Billy Horner was impressed, 'It was the best acting dive I have ever seen – even better than some of Bob Newton's.'

Two days after the Colchester trip, the players found themselves kicking their heels on the side of the A1 for forty-five minutes after a tyre blow-out. When they finally got off the coach, they beat Stockport 2-0. As James Bond observed in his match report, the players 'could not be blamed for looking a little jaded'. Stockport manager Jimmy McGuigan, back for his first match in four months after a series of stomach operations, said, 'Hartlepool aren't a bad side at all. They play with keenness and method and have some skilful players.'

The hunt was on for Houchen, who was scoring regularly and attracting increasing attention. Middlesbrough were short of goals and the local boy could have been the answer but manager Bobby Murdoch didn't see it that way. Bids from other clubs had been declined whilst some whirled in the ether of murky corridors, agents' pockets and newspaper speculation.

Vince Barker confided to reporter Mike Spence with the air of a salesman:

Arsenal seem very keen on Houchen and their chief scout has watched him very closely in our last few matches. I know Bolton's manager rated Houchen very highly in the days when he was manager of Bradford City. Now, Oldham have joined in, while Newcastle's Joe Harvey hardly ever misses one of our home games and I'm sure he would love to take Houchen to St James's. Unfortunately, they have financial problems and I would only be interested in a cash deal. I am not interested at all in player-exchange deals, unless of course there is also a large cash element... If Boro came onto me and started to talk in terms of £100,000 plus for Houchen, I would listen with interest. Sunderland spent £350,000 on Ally McCoist and I don't rate the player in the same class as Houchen – I told Sunderland's directors so.

Only Vince Barker could have had the nerve for 'the pot calling the kettle black' bit about Newcastle's finances or, in the same interview, to chide his most valuable asset for saying on the local radio that he wouldn't want to sign a new contract with Hartlepool. Footballers were still mere hunks of meat to be traded from the hook. Only a few months later, with the abattoir in danger of collapse, Barker would be grateful to unlock the door of the fridge to any bidder.

Houchen felt that a lot of people misunderstood his comments:

I don't have anything against Hartlepool… They gave me a chance when I was thrown out by Chesterfield, and I am grateful for that. I would want to be away no matter which club I was playing for. But if Hartlepool were in the Second Division I would probably be happy. The point is that I am ambitious and I feel I have proved what I can do in the Fourth Division. I would now like the chance to show that I can also do it in the First or Second.

The continued absence through injury of Andy Linighan was making serious demands on 'Pool's rearguard. Although only nineteen, Linighan's strength in the air, and his spidery stretch in the tackle, were sorely missed. At Boothferry Park, Houchen scored both the visitors' goals – the first a neat angled chip, the second a penalty – but Hull ran in five. Pickering of the *Echo* was critical of referee Brian Martin, 'who ignored so many fouls that one spectator thought he was a Rugby League official who had gone to the wrong ground in Hull'. The Hartlepool players were asked to autograph the match ball after Les Mutrie's hat-trick, but Pickering conceded that 'it wouldn't be surprising if they wrote "with compliments from the Hartlepool defence" on it'.

A week later it was Houchen who was taking home the match ball after scoring his first Hartlepool hat-trick, the quickest to be completed in a Football League match since 14 November 1931. On that occasion, Dixie Dean scored his third goal after fifteen minutes of Everton's home match against Chelsea, a good ten minutes faster than Houchen. Geed up by his usual pre-match diet of sherry and eggs, Dean added two more by half-time and could have had another if his boot had not stuck in the mud when he had only the goalkeeper to beat. Poor visibility dictated that the teams turn round immediately at half-time, and Everton won 7-2.

Only a week before, Billy Richardson scored four times within nine minutes of the start of West Bromwich's First Division match at West Ham, having already missed twice in the first five minutes. Richardson had been signed from Hartlepools United and was known at the Hawthorns as 'Ginger' so as to distinguish him from the other William Richardson in the side. He scored 202 goals in 320 League appearances for Albion and won one England cap. A product of the United Bus Company FC in Hartlepool, Richardson was born in Framwellgate Moor near Durham, from where George Camsell had also come. Camsell's League scoring record of 59 goals in a season had stood for just twelve months when it was passed by Dixie Dean.

Manchester City's Fred Howard completed a hat-trick within thirteen minutes of his League debut against Liverpool on 18 January 1913 and went on to score a fourth in the second half.

Despite Keith Houchen's threesome, Hartlepool were held 4-4 at Peterborough. The scorer had an unusual explanation for his prolific burst against Hull and Peterborough: a niggling knee injury.

Because I am never quite sure how long the knee will last in a game before it starts to give me problems, I might be trying that little bit harder in the back of my mind. I suppose I want to make my mark on a game before I start to limp… They would have had to carry me off in that game. I was only passed fit less than an hour before the kick-off, but hitting a hat-trick so quickly meant that I was in no mood to be substituted.

In the following game, Houchen was not on the mark. Sheffield United brought hooligans with them and, on the field, 'Pool's profligacy contributed to the visitors' 3-2 win.

Arthur Pickering didn't pull any punches about Tranmere's visit the following Tuesday:

> The match started badly and gradually got worse, finishing up as a blow-football farce nobody deserved to watch. It wouldn't have been so bad if the wind had been warm, but it was so bitingly cold that most spectators must have spent the rest of the night struggling to get warm… the most boring match I have seen for a long time.

Pickering was probably right, but as Stephen Kelly observed in his introduction to *The Kingswood Book of Football*:

Football… is a ninety minute rush, little time to think or deliberate. It's all over in a flash with maybe half an hour to file that report as you sit in a dreary stand in the back streets of Hartlepool, the wind ripping in from the North Sea, all the lights, bar one, switched off to save the electricity bill.

The transfer deadline was approaching and local talk was on the likelihood of Keith Houchen joining his home-town club, Middlesbrough.

I read about clubs being interested in the papers or hear it on the grapevine and then nothing happens. It's been a bit of a saga for a while now and it's got to the stage where people are asking me when I am going to Middlesbrough. I can't answer them because I am the one who knows the least.

As things are I am in a state of limbo because I don't know where my future lies. I want to get married, but it's difficult to make arrangements when you don't know where you might be going… Every time I think I have done well in a game I sit at home waiting for the 'phone to ring with the manager telling me that someone has come in with a bid. But you get lots of downs to go with the ups, and the 'phone hasn't rung yet.

It was actually a problem for Houchen that he was more than just a goal poacher:

I feel one of my strengths is running at defenders, which can often create chances for team-mates.

However, the likes of Middlesbrough were more concerned with the deadliness of the ammunition than the overall quality of the weapon. Cyril Knowles, who was then 'Boro's first-team coach, did not endear himself by saying that Houchen had been playing in the Fourth Division too long for clubs to be interested in him.

Middlesbrough would have been a fantastic move even if they hadn't put me in the side – just to take me down there and feed me in. But, you know, you can't change anything. I wouldn't change anything after looking back, because it all culminated in 1987. It all came together, all of the things that happened in the Cup run, everything that went before, especially for me. This was my time.

Meanwhile, Houchen had one more goal to score for Hartlepool – at Crewe, and only 1,116 people turned up to watch. Four days later, at home to Aldershot, he was playing his last match for the club.

The youngster possessed boundless ambition and the self confidence to believe that he should be performing at a higher level.

I was handing in transfer requests from the age of nineteen. I can remember walking into Billy's office and Billy just ripping them up and putting them in the bin and I would turn round and walk out until the next day. My worst nightmare would have been to play at Hartlepool for my whole career, but they just didn't want me to go.

I didn't want to be playing at that level, in small grounds with small crowds. I wanted to be playing where the proper football was played in the big stadiums.

They didn't discuss any formal bids with me. I had a yearly contract. It didn't make any difference to them whether you signed for ten years or one year because you were their player and they could stop you going anywhere else. They used to do it in the lower leagues – they used to stop players from playing by keeping their registration, and that was it – which was why it all had to change.

He had listened and learnt in his time at the club, prompting Billy Horner to recall:

> I remember when we put Keith in the first team, he was only seventeen but he did very well. At first he was quite weak and easy for defenders to knock over but we worked on toughening him up and it seemed to work. The thing that struck me about Keith was he was very ambitious; he was always knocking on my door asking if anyone had made an offer for him which was quite rare for a young lad.

A scoring record of 65 goals in 170 League appearances, and at Hartlepool of all clubs, was a good 'Get out of jail' card. Keith Houchen's appeal was about to be granted.

3

Great Dunmow

It was a morning like any other morning – the usual breakfast, a glance at the paper, the drive to the training ground. Preparation for Saturday's game would be stepped up, there'd be a laugh with the lads, a drink perhaps after training, and Yvonne – his girlfriend – in the evening. But it all turned out rather differently. The door of the other hut, the one that served as an office, was flung open. Billy Horner leaned out and shouted:

> Over here, Houchy. We've had Orient on the 'phone. They want to sign you. The chairmen are haggling over the fee on the 'phone at this moment. It's a pittance but we need it if we're going to stay in business.

Orient had been in touch the previous day and Hartlepool were hanging on in the hope that one of the other clubs to have shown an interest in the player would come in with a bigger offer before Thursday's deadline. Orient's tender was an insult. Hartlepool had turned down various bids for their star goalscorer including £80,000 ones from Cardiff and Portsmouth and one of £60,000 from Plymouth, but things had become desperate for the club, even more desperate than normal. The Inland Revenue had demanded payment of £60,000 in respect of outstanding PAYE contributions. In the event, the £25,000 from the sale of Houchen, plus £4,000 raised by the supporters, gained the club a stay of execution.

It was the last straw for a lot of Hartlepool supporters. Within months, an action group was formed which criticised the club for its lack of ambition, the failure to support Billy Horner in signing new players, the inadequate ground facilities, lack of communication and not coming to agreement with the Council over the purchase of the Victoria Ground. For all this, Bob Newton demonstrated that there was still some heart in the club when, on hearing of an attack on a York pensioner, he organised a whip-round amongst his colleagues and sent the lady a bouquet of flowers and a get well card.

Hartlepool were not the only club in the North-East in trouble. Earlier in the year, Darlington had had to raise £50,000 all of a sudden in order to stay in business. Supporters and townsfolk stumped up. Several other clubs confronted oblivion – an oblivion nonetheless that in modern times had suffocated (and in the process uniquely immortalised) only Accrington Stanley. Hull City had been in receivership and Bristol City were within twenty-four hours of resigning from the League. There were plenty of others who did not welcome a knock at the door. The recession was biting, and people were less ready to spend money supporting their struggling local team.

'How much time have I got to decide?' Houchy asked.

'You haven't, they want you down there tonight.'

Houchy went out and sat on the hoardings with Bobby Kerr. Bobby, a midget of a man born in Alexandria, had been the captain of Sunderland's Cup-winning side. He knew the form.

Was this the moment Houchy had been waiting for all these years, the chance at last to prove himself on a bigger stage, to fulfil the dream that had briefly been rescued by Chesterfield, and on which Hartlepool had finally given him a toe-hold?

Years before, Bob Paisley had been at Edgeley Park one night when Hartlepool were playing Stockport. The in-talk was that Paisley had his eyes on two young strikers at the time, and that he had come to make a final decision about one of them called Houchen. Houchy played a blinder. As he left the field, the two big Stockport centre-backs offered their praise, 'Don't forget us, will you. We'll be looking out for you on the telly. You'll definitely be on your way to Liverpool after that.' 'Good luck, Houchy', his team-mates said as they shook his hand in the dressing room, sensing that their pal had just played himself out of wooden huts for ever. Houchy had the skill perhaps but not the electrifying pace of the other young striker. He played for Chester – his name was Ian Rush.

I used to say that it was as good as it was going to get for me. 'They've signed Ian Rush, Liverpool, they could have had me.' I would like to know what happened there. Billy Horner went missing for two days as well, and I have always wondered what went on, people congratulating me and saying: 'You've done enough, you're off,' and Bob Paisley sitting there. Can't ask him; he's gone now Bob.

'Where is Orient?' Houchy asked.

'Somewhere in east London,' volunteered one of the reporters.

'It's nice down there, you'll like it.'

'How much should I ask for?' Houchy asked Kerr.

'Just take what you can get,' Kerr shrugged.

There were no agents, no advisers, and little help for youngsters fighting for their aspirations. Players were cuts and joints and a club's property, in or out of the fridge. But the time had come when Hartlepool's survival depended on selling their son.

Houchy 'phoned Yvonne at the boutique where she worked, and then his mum. He had never lived away from home. This was the biggest decision of his young life. It was all such a rush that he can no longer recall going home to pick up a bag. It was probably a moment of greater significance for his mother, personal needs packed for one last time at the launch of her son's journey. He left his old banger at the front of the house. Mark Lawrence drove him over to Darlington to catch the train. He thought of his dad taking him to Darlington station the very first time he went to London. Then, it was in hope of being offered a contract with Crystal Palace. Now, he was actually going to sign for Orient. Then, he was a carefree and occasionally wanton teenager. Now, he was a young man of twenty-one.

The atmosphere in the railway carriage had changed. The world within was of routine thoughtlessness – of unharnessed kids, the gormless spillage of personal stereos. Journeys no longer seemed so significant, merely a hinge between somewhere and somewhere else. For Keith Houchen though, this was more like a voyage. He was taking his destiny into his own hands. Hartlepool hadn't given him much of a choice, and Orient wasn't exactly a terminus, but the journey he was making was a precious one.

Orient had amended their name and, like Hartlepool, come to regret it. They were misguidedly embarrassed at the parochial prefix of Leyton, and the change had not required a deed poll. Orient were bursting to

break free from under the shadow of West Ham United, a club still reso-
nating with cosmopolitan assurance from the days of Hurst, Moore and
Peters.

Orient were struggling in the Second Division but it was an opportunity for a young player to prove himself under the metropolitan spotlight.
Hit a good run, stave off relegation, score some goals, and London – this
self-contained country above and beyond his experience – could place
him on the platform of his ambitions. Besides, Orient had some players
who had climbed out well beyond the small print.

This time, the welcoming party was prompter than it had been when
he first alighted at King's Cross as an adolescent. The chill of the spring
evening and the abandoned swathe of platforms lent urgency to the
station at this late hour. Isolated figures plunged into cabs, weary twos
or threes disappeared into the Underground. At that time of evening,
motorists drew up in York Way, wound down their windows and bartered
for bodies, whilst kebab houses opposite glared vacantly into another day.

The young shank of a Yorkshireman was gobbled up by an awaiting
car, the glamour of lights soon receding as the driver headed east. On
arrival, the chauffeur needed to convert his brusqueness at the wheel
into secretarial deftness with a fax machine in order to wire the forms to
Lytham St Annes. Houchen had never played at Brisbane Road and did
not even glimpse the workplace to which he was entrusting his future
before signing his contract in the Orient boardroom.

The fire was alight. A man was sitting in front of it, brandy in hand.
The Orient director was surprised by Houchen's comment:

*I'm really looking forward to some proper training facilities and being able to work
on my technique.*

Professionals are supposed to be finished articles. You don't expect your
new acquisition, who is costing tens of thousands of pounds, to volunteer an apparent lack of confidence at the very moment he is putting
pen to paper. It may have characterised the player's dedication but, being
football, it was taken like a pantomime performer announcing that he is
looking forward to working on his timing.

*It was only later that I found out that their training facilities were no better than
Hartlepool's. In fact, they didn't have a training ground.*

After the signing, the director drove his new charge to South Woodford to one of the club houses. Woodford is a bit further along the Central Line than Leyton and full of terraces of trim semis. This would be home for the time being, although Keith had to spend Thursday night in a hotel. It was the 'settling in' moment which fans don't see when the new jigsaw piece is laid out for their delectation. The director gave Keith a brief tour of the property, less like a host revealing his house than an estate agent joining in a look around. Each flick of the switch revealed a neat, clean potential – cupboards to open, beds to make, a kettle to boil. In the kitchen, a half-used bottle of washing up liquid was bathed in the purr of strip lighting, fresh soap adjoined the bathroom taps. There was post on the door mat. Keith wondered whether it would show a familiar name, or just another player passing in the night. Ken Knighton was actually living there at the time. And at the end of a long day as Keith heard the director drive away, there was the 'phone, a chance to be himself and to call home, to tell Yvonne the exciting news with all the implications about their future to be considered. And then sleep.

From backyards beyond, the chink of milk bottles, casual chuckles and chatter, and the urgent patter of schoolchildren began to etch themselves into the dawn. The light had already been fading on Wednesday when the paternal figure of Billy Horner leant out of his hut. During the intervening darkness, Keith's life had changed for ever.

That's it, it moved on in only a day from just being a kid in my mum's house.

Now, there was a shower to operate, a toaster to understand, a new view from the window, and a different light to the day ahead.

He tried to remember what colours Orient played in as he ran the soap over himself. He'd never played against them and they were hardly regulars on *Match of the Day*. He tried to bring to mind the names of his new team-mates. Who plays in that position, he wondered. And what did this mean for his future with Yvonne?

It's like being welcomed to the school gang when you join a new club. Some of them you know, some you don't, some you recognise from the telly or the back page, some you simply think, 'Who the fuck's he?'

The bell rang. Keith had made himself spick and span, or as spick and span as you do to take your clothes off as soon as you get to work. He zipped up the toilet bag his mum had packed and shoved it into the hold-all. The boots were still encrusted with locks of northern turf.

Keith was showered with asides from his driver about the surroundings framed in the windscreen before him. The floodlights of Brisbane Road came into view. Soon, he would be mucking in to a new family and needing to hang out an image for himself, like a puppet on its own string. As with any new player at a club, he would need to care about the image he conveyed – neither too brash nor too coy.

I was very quiet, quite shy.

Some of the greetings were laced with banter and familiarity, others with disinterest. Ken Knighton stood up to introduce the newcomer. There was a clattering of feet and ironic cheers, all naughty boys together. Welcome aboard, it said, you're one of us.

Training lasted most of the morning. Morning gathered up the afternoon and swept Keith into a familiarity of person and place. Someone returning along the passage registered a smile, a new team-mate asked about a friend at Hartlepool, words were shared over an unexpected discovery of something in common. Each hour became a day and by the time he got on the team coach the next morning it seemed as if he had been in London for a lifetime.

He felt like a yo-yo, returning immediately to the North. However, he would not be going to the Victoria Ground to pull on a blue shirt with no.10 on it for the visit of Bradford City but to Hillsborough to play Sheffield Wednesday.

Everyone seemed to know the driver and a club official made an announcement concerning the journey ahead. Off they went, and out came the cards and the papers. Some chatted over quiet concerns whilst others occasionally turned to harangue a pal or take the piss. Staying in a hotel was not an unfamiliar luxury. At Hartlepool, surprisingly, they had stayed in quite reasonable ones from time to time. Orient were about to turn all their journeys into day trips in order to cut costs.

Sheffield Wednesday was one of the biggest clubs Keith had ever played against; the Hillsborough stadium which dominated the valley around it the biggest he had played in. Not only was the 16,460 crowd one of the largest he had played to, but there would be a huge invisible audience later that evening to view and analyse his performance – on

Match of the Day. The players had already been told. O's fans who had not made the journey would get a preview of whether the twenty-five grand's worth they would be cheering out at the next home game was worth the money.

Orient had been hanging on in the Second Division for years. There was one exceptional season in 1973/74 when they finished fourth and were pipped for promotion by Carlisle. Otherwise, they had not finished higher than eleventh since being promoted in 1970, although they had reached the FA Cup semi-finals in 1977/78. There had been one hapless season in Division One back in 1962/63.

The story of Orient had been a similar one of survival to Hartlepool but with an occasional extra nought tagged on the end. Between 1966 and 1981, the O's sold eight home-produced players for a total of nearly £1.5 million, including Glenn Roeder to QPR for £250,000, and Tony Grealish for £150,000 to Luton.

Under Jimmy Bloomfield's management, Orient had been determined to build a team capable of challenging for promotion. In July 1980, Bloomfield signed Stan Bowles from Nottingham Forest for £90,000, and in November the same year paid a club record fee of £150,000 for Tottenham's Peter Taylor. But, during the following August, he was forced to sell John Chiedozie. Chiedozie had arrived in east London from his native Nigeria at the age of thirteen. Rejected by West Ham, he signed as an apprentice for Orient and made his League debut when he was sixteen. Chiedozie established himself in the right-wing berth vacated by Laurie Cunningham on his sale to WBA, and soon emulated the skills of his predecessor.

The sale of Chiedozie prompted the resignation of Bloomfield. Bloomfield's successor, Paul Went, lasted only a month. The O's were at the foot of the table, and in October the club appointed Ken Knighton as manager. Frank Clark, Knighton's former assistant at Sunderland, joined him a month later. Knighton was the Houchen connection and had tried to sign the player for Sunderland. Houchen respected him and it was one of the main reasons for him accepting terms with Orient.

'I was Orient's best player by half-a-mile,' is Houchen's wry recollection of his new team-mates that afternoon. Kevin Taylor and Gary Megson scored in the second half to give Sheffield Wednesday a 2-0 win. Afterwards, Ken Knighton gave Houchy a lift home across the Pennines. He was still living in Sunderland and commuting weekly to London.

Houchen and Knighton made arrangements for the drive back to London after the weekend. For now Houchy was home in Middlesbrough. His mum was there to welcome him and there was plenty to tell Yvonne.

The 'Pool had lost 2-0 at home to Bradford City. Houchy's no. 10 shirt had been given to a seventeen-year-old local boy David Linighan – at 6ft 2ins Hartlepool could save on the need to buy a new shirt. David later made his mark in the centre of the Ipswich defence and was from a footballing family which included brothers Andy and Brian.

The weekend was spent packing a bigger case and planning for a new life in the capital. The Saturday evening with Yvonne presented more than the usual respite from the knocks and bruises of the afternoon, more even than the opportunity to watch himself on *Match of the Day*. The tracing of a future life together had been drawn into sharp relief by the decisions of the last forty-eight hours.

Going to London by car was a new experience. All signs pointed to the giant city, miles of suburbs drew you in, and even the limits of Brisbane Road bore the hint of a portentous world. The voices were different from the Victoria Ground where the dressing room was inflected with short 'a's and the curl of Geordie. Here, the sounds were more widely collected but, even with the Kensington born Nigerian Tunji Banjo, predominantly cockney. Barry Silkman, a useful inside-forward on his eighth club and as cockney as they come, christened Keith and Yvonne Mr and Mrs Hovis. Yorkshire was as far away as London was to Houchen.

It was all real broad cockney, 'Leave it owt. Fuckin' 'ell, what are you talkin' about, 'Ovis?'

When we came out of the ground, we had an old bus to take us to training. I had a car all rusting and full of holes. 'Whose car is that, somethin' fuckin' eaten it?'

When we went to the end of season do, they were fascinated by the way we talked, as if we had come from Mars.

As at Hartlepool, there were several who had been around the block but at Orient there were players whose signatures had adorned much bigger autograph books. Ralph Coates had played for the club until recently and both he and Peter Taylor for England. In defence, there was another former Spurs player Keith Osgood. David Peach, one time Southampton left-back, arrived at about the same time as Houchen. West Ham lads such as goalkeeper Mervyn Day and centre half Tommy Taylor were more than the left overs from Newcastle and Middlesbrough but characterised the Hartlepool squad.

Houchen felt that he was joining a club on the up, with some quality players. Life was very different from the Victoria Ground – there was a canteen and free lunches, and kit was neatly laid out in the dressing room.

Goalscoring had been the main problem for the O's for months. Early in the season they went seven consecutive games without scoring. Chiedozie had left, Stan Bowles too. The mercurial Bowles was no longer as sharp as in his QPR and England heyday, but was still capable of springing from midfield with punishing effect. Against Preston earlier the previous season he had bewitched his way past three players before turning and scoring with a searing left-foot shot. In every sense, Bowles wore his hair long. However, his penchant for gambling probably didn't commend itself to the new manager. Peter Taylor had broken his ankle in December and Billy Jennings, another ex Hammer, left for Luton soon after Houchen had been bought to play alongside him. Orient had scored twenty-five goals in twenty-eight games. Their top scorer, with five goals, was right-winger Kevin Godfrey.

Houchen's introduction to Orient was in a fortnight of four away games. After Hillsborough, there were further defeats at Luton, QPR and Cardiff. The newcomer eventually made his home debut in a 0-0 draw on a Monday evening against Cambridge United. Only 3,162 people came out to look. Even fewer turned out on the Saturday to see struggling Bolton. It was only the third time that season that the O's had scored as many as three goals. Things were looking pretty desperate.

Had he made the right move? He thought of previous moves that had not materialised, of Cardiff bidding £90,000. He had yet to score in his ten games and relegation looked a certainty.

Chelsea were in the doldrums of the Second Division, caught between a past of Ted Drake and Charlie Cooke and the brazen oil billions of today. They had become like a face you recognise in the street, only to realise that it's from Tesco not the telly. There were only 6,009 people at the Orient game which remains the lowest League crowd at Stamford Bridge since the War. Chelsea were two up at half-time but, after fifty-eight minutes, Houchen scored his first Orient goal. Two minutes later,

Gary Locke put through his own net to give the O's a point. It was not enough.

Levity does not usually commend itself in a situation where hara-kiri might appear more honourable, and Ken Knighton – giving up the ghost on any idea of avoiding the drop – felt sufficiently riled to tell the press boys:

> I am disgusted at being relegated but some of the players were laughing in the bath only ten minutes after the game. What I saw in the first forty-five minutes really concerned me and changes will be made next season. It is an affront to me because I have three years of a contract left and I still want success for Orient. The supporters have been badly let down tonight.

The O's must have taken their manager's words to heart as they put three past Leicester at Brisbane Road on the last day of the season, but the hinges had already dropped off the stable door.

The first months in London presented other hazards for Woodford's new residents:

We went for a big Indian. I was saying that nobody ate Indian in Middlesbrough, but South Woodford was all Indian restaurants. I used to get doner kebabs – I had never seen anything like that in the North-East.

I picked a vindaloo. It was burning the skin on my lips but I couldn't leave it because we were being taken out. I went to get up for training. We had this huge, long bathroom. I was thinking, 'Shit, I'm going to be late,' but every time I tried to get up, 'Ooh,' I had to sit down. I was late and got fined £25 which was a fortune, and that was my first Indian. Now you go there and know exactly what's what, all blasé. We were just naïve – the first time we went shopping we spent loads of money but it was all nonsense, pineapples and things, nothing actually for dinner.

Relegation and professional disappointment were countered by personal joy. In July, Keith and Yvonne got married. They were living in the club house where Keith had been deposited that first night, a big two bed-room flat overlooking South Woodford Green. Now it was time to have a home of their own and to invest in the future.

I met her at Roy Hogan's twenty-first birthday party at the Staincliffe Hotel in Seaton where we later had our wedding reception. We went after a match, and there were also local people there. I immediately noticed Yvonne.

As you grew up you started to meet girls at the local youth club and I went out with the girl from the next street for a while. I stayed on to the Sixth Form in the College, and I got girlfriends there but nobody I was amazingly in love with.

Yvonne lived in Seaton. It's got a nice beach but the problem is you can see all of ICI on the corner. Yvonne was born at Wheatley Hill which is mining country over in Geordie-land. It's not somewhere I particularly like, to be honest. I like the stretch after Newcastle but not the bit down to Hartlepool. It doesn't do anything for me, all those pit villages type of area. I don't like it, never have done. And when you get over to Tow Law it's like being on the moon.

But that doesn't matter. Yvonne was gorgeous; she was a really sexy, attractive girl. I took her home that night, and that was it. I didn't think I would marry her but that was 1978 and I was eighteen and Yvonne was seventeen.

The couple were soon engaged and even if the move to Orient was not a fulfilling one it confirmed their future together. Yvonne was different, an independent spirit, shy but self-assured, vivacious but not pushy. She was pretty, very pretty, her look dark and direct but watchful even when not watching. The two pairs of eyes had met, and met again, like butterflies nervously fluttering, delicate but sure. The intensity was immediate.

We organised the marriage straight away, got married – on 17 July 1982 – and both moved down together. Her parents are wonderful, so supportive; they've always been dream in-laws.

We had gone from being kids to suddenly buying houses and becoming parents. Cara was born while we were there. She was born in Chelmsford.

I rang up to ask about houses for sale over the road. They were £55,000. I nearly fainted, £55,000 my God, so we started looking further and further out.

Epping was very expensive, Harlow a soulless new town which they hated. Their researches took them to Great Dunmow, forty miles from London on the A120 between Bishop's Stortford and Braintree, 'all thatched cottages, village greens and ducks in the pond – it was gorgeous'. The terraced cottage with three bedrooms, and garden front and back, cost £24,000.

Dunmow gave rise to one of Britain's oldest popular ceremonies – that of the Dunmow Flitch – dating back to at least the fourteenth century. The flitch, a cured and salted side of pork, is given to a couple who can prove that not once in a year and a day have they regretted marrying. One of the earliest references is in *The Canterbury Tales*, where the Wife of Bath boasts that none of her five husbands would have dreamt of claiming the flitch. At various times the custom died out, but it has been continuous (held now in each leap year) since it was revived in 1885 with the addition of a mock court involving judge, jury and witnesses.

The trip to Chesterfield on the opening day of the 1982/83 season was more than just a return to humbler fields, it was a reminder of where his career had tentatively dipped its feet. Orient's ambitions had been sapped by relegation, average attendances were down to 4,419 and there was no money to spend on new players. After the second game, injury kept Houch out for the next 14 matches. For Orient, goals were almost as scarce as they had been before relegation and, despite a 4-0 thrashing of Cardiff, form was wretched. Having conceded six goals at Huddersfield at the end of September, the O's were beaten 5-1 at home three times in the space of six weeks. Houch was back for the last of these fiascos and scored Orient's goal. Confidence amongst the customers was at a low ebb and the gate for the next home game was down to 1,668. But Preston were beaten and Christmas was kinder. Houch scored the only goal of the game against Millwall and the last of five against Bournemouth.

The tide looked as if it was turning. Houchy had new support in Peter Kitchen. Kitchen had been playing for a club called Happy Valley in Hong Kong. Orient had once paid Doncaster £30,000 for him and received five times that amount when they sold him to Fulham. Despite defeat at Bramall Lane on New Year's Day, the O's won another three games on the trot.

Come 1 March, Houch stepped up to bury the winner against Gillingham with David Peach, the normal penalty taker, out of the side. With better support, and goals from Kevin Godfrey and young midfielder Mark McNeil, Houch was beginning to find the net more regularly. He scored two and McNeil three in a 5-1 defeat of Exeter. A draw at Portsmouth was followed by defeat at Cardiff in the penultimate game. Survival all depended on the last match against Sheffield United at Brisbane Road.

Doncaster and Chesterfield were already six feet under. Reading were third from bottom on fifty points, with the trap door the difference between Orient (-27) and Wrexham (-19) who were both a point ahead. The drive from Denbighshire should have been quite pleasant on this early summer's day. Reading, however, could still save themselves by defeating the travellers – should Orient not win. The Royals were ahead at half-time with a goal by Kerry Dixon, but Orient had also set about The Blades. The O's were 2-1 up with goals from Houchen and Kitchen. Kevin Godfrey and Bill Roffey added two more in the second half. Orient were safe; it didn't matter that Reading had beaten Wrexham. Houchen was spared playing in the Fourth Division the following season – against Hartlepool. Orient, he had hoped, was the stepping stone to the big time. He had worked hard, heeded his coaches, kept his head down, and believed in his own ability. His life changed completely that evening he boarded the train at Darlington. Was it a mistake? Should he really have let Hartlepool sell him at that moment? What had he gained? He and Yvonne were married and loved their new home. But a battered car and the constant cost of petrol to get to work were a sobering reminder of a contract negotiated in the middle of the night, without experience and counsel to ensure that basic needs could be met and paid for, in a deal that suited a couple of employers. How much had the welfare of the player mattered in all this?

I was dead naïve. I was earning £120 a week at Hartlepool and Orient gave me £225, which sounded a lot at the time, but I didn't think to ask for a fee for removals, solicitors and all the rest. I had never had commitments before. I had been living in my mum's house, driving up and down to training in my old Ford Capri and having enough money to take Yvonne out. The club should have said 'We will pay this, we will pay that.' I think they did actually give me a £1,000 signing-on fee or something daft. If I had stayed for the full length of my four-year contract at Orient, I would also have received £2,000 in loyalty bonuses. But it was a massive struggle. We got married and had a baby. We didn't have enough money coming in. We literally couldn't pay the bills while I was at Orient. I don't think the club realised how bad it was, how skint we were. Yvonne started to do some work in a chemist in Great Dunmow but the money I was paying in petrol to get into London every day was equivalent to the mortgage we had.

After five matches of the 1983/84 season Houchen was beginning to feel a little more confident about the move after a fine goal from Kevin Godfrey at Rotherham had put the O's top of the table. But he and the Brisbane Road faithful were rewarded the following week with a 1-0 defeat by Bristol Rovers, and the team did no more than nibble at promotion before starting to slip after Christmas. As the worst of winter approached, the defence began to leak goals like a burst pipe. Richard Key, a former Coventry junior, recovered the ball from his own net four times at both Millwall and Bradford City, and five times at Oxford.

A 6-2 home defeat by Wimbledon at the beginning of February turned out to be Keith Houchen's last full appearance for the club. Houchen, top scorer with nine League goals (four of them from the spot), was dropped. Deprived of Colin Foster for much of the season, it was lagging at the other end that had been needed. So universally was Foster addressed as 'Munster', after the comic-horror hero of the American TV series, that Houchen momentarily struggles to recall his real name. A hat-trick by centre half Tommy Cunningham provided one of the few highlights of Orient's season, at bedraggled Exeter. The Exeter interlude was followed at Bramall Lane by another six-goal thrashing. Houchen came on as sub the next week, but had now slid off the manager's team-sheet.

Ken Knighton had made a reputation as a tough disciplinarian, an old fashioned carrot-and-stick manager, who finally talked himself out of the dressing room with such press pronouncements as, 'If there was a way I could stop their wages, I would.' Houchen, however, was privy to his more benevolent side.

When Knighton was sacked as Orient manager in May 1983, his assistant Frank Clark stepped up. Clark, a laboratory technician, had won an FA Amateur Cup winners medal for Crook Town when you could still play good football just for fun, but turned his test tubes in for a career at St James' Park. He went on to Nottingham Forest where he became a vital cog in Clough's all-conquering team. Unusually in a walk of life where the first whiff of relegation tickles the chairman's pistol, Clark spent eight years as manager at Brisbane Road before ascending into the board room. He was only tempted back onto the treadmill by the opportunity to replace the retiring Brian Clough at the City Ground.

Houchen never hit it off with Clark, who was himself from County Durham:

For whatever reason, he didn't take to me. I was the only bloke from the North-East; everyone else was a southerner. Looking back, I would have thought he would have gone out of his way to help me integrate, and give me more of a chance. But I always felt he went the other way.

I was young, very young, going from Hartlepool to Orient – first house, kid, struggling, struggling for form. If he had a modicum of common sense, he wouldn't knock you all the time. He would try and give you some confidence and build you up.

I scored in the League Cup at Aldershot, and was playing really well, I thought, when I came in at half-time. But he had a go at me, 'You, YOU!' He was one of those sort of managers, 'YOU keep out the way, YOU ever fucking do that again!' He once ran ten yards to kick Mervyn Day's backside. Merv would admit that he's got a fair backside, and Frank came off worse.

What had apparently set the bawling off on this occasion was something trivial in the pre-match warm-up when Houchen failed to take turns at shooting, inadvertently striking a ball at the 'keeper at the same moment as a team-mate was taking aim.

Then, after the match, dead calm and condescending, he said to me, 'I knew I could get you going.'

Years later, when Brian Clough was saying that Frank Clark was the best manager in football, I remember thinking, 'How does he know Frank Clark is the best manager, how could he say that?', because he patently wasn't. He was a poor man manager, poor manager. He was one of the old type. He would shout, and rave and rant, and tactically he wasn't particularly brilliant.

I remember when we started to travel to every game by train on the morning of the match. They got rid of overnighters, so we had to get to King's Cross or wherever for six o'clock in the morning. I had to leave my house at 4.30a.m. to get in. Frank and the physio would get all the stuff into their car and I'd follow them to the station because I could never find my bearings in London. It all looked the same to me. I remember on two or three occasions they left it late and were jumping red lights, and I was having to follow. I got pulled up by a copper one morning. I got done for thirty or forty quid and I was borassic. I went to see Frank and said, 'I got this off the police; it was your fault; you were jumping all the red lights, I was trying to stay with you. Will the club pay this fine for me?' 'No, you pay.' I just didn't have a good rapport with him. He didn't like animals, didn't like dogs. The groundsman had a little beagle – dead cute and that. He hated it and I thought if he doesn't like dogs and animals he's got something wrong with him anyway.

Years later when I was player-manager at Hartlepool and he was manager at Nottingham Forest, he was the guest speaker at the North-East awards. I was there with my players as the Hartlepool nominee for North-East Player of the Year. His speech was actually quite good, and he said, 'I see Houchy's in the room, another player I got rid of! Shows you what I know.' I thought, 'Let bygones be bygones.'

I didn't really want to, but I said I better go and say hello to Frank. He was talking with Viv Anderson, because they were old team-mates. So I went over to say hello, but he didn't make much of an effort so I walked away. So whatever it was with Frankie, it wasn't for me, that's for sure. Years later, in a newspaper article before the Cup Final, all of my ex-managers and coaches, Ken Knighton included, said they never had any doubt that I could play at the top level. Frank Clark was the only exception. He said he was very surprised.

I was never bolshy with coaches or managers. It was only later, when I left Coventry, that I thought, 'That's it, nobody's going to treat me like crap again without me really letting them know about it.'

Some weeks after the Aldershot incident, Houchen submitted a transfer request, stating that the manager 'didn't like him', and left it on Clark's desk. The player was shaking when Clark called him into the office. He was twenty-three and this kind of working confrontation was new to him.

'Why do you say I don't like you? I'll put it in to the chairman, but don't you want me to take that bit out? It sounds stupid putting that down.'

'I don't think you do like me. That's what I want put in.'

The transfer request was granted and the player was phased out. It felt like being in quarantine, except he had deliberately gone out of the way to court the infection. It was a new and lonely gamble. It wasn't like being thrown out of the classroom at school, when you knew that eventually you'd be called back in. This was his decision, final and absolute. He had put himself out on a wing, there but not there, no longer belonging, and an outsider amongst his mates. He was certain he was right, but would others share the belief? And where to now?

Houchen never received the same degree of coaching and encouragement as George Smith and Willie Maddren had granted him at

Hartlepool, except perhaps from Ralph Coates. However, the depressing train of unrequited effort that had characterised Houchen's career up to now was about to be rewarded by an unexpected change of colours – and mood. One morning, Houchen was told that York City were coming to watch him in a reserve fixture at Bishop's Stortford.

You don't travel all the way from York to watch Orient Reserves play just on spec. Houchen himself was to discover that a manager spends a lot of time thumbing through *Rothmans* as if it was the Yellow Pages. But as manager Denis Smith later told him, 'Anybody who could score sixty-five goals playing for Hartlepool must have something,' and Smith had a good idea of what he was getting.

Two years before, Houchen had set off for London in conscientious pursuit of a move dictated by circumstance but invested with hope.

I got down there, signed at midnight, had a little training session on the pitch, travelled to Sheffield and stayed in a hotel in Sheffield, played against Sheffield Wednesday – it was the game for Match of the Day *– and so it was like everything happened in two days.*

Nobody knows you, nobody is bothered and then, all of a sudden, they wanted to know me. It's like anything in a career, I suppose: you move slowly – unless you're Michael Owen and the first thing you do the world knows, and it's all captured. Some of the goals I scored at Hartlepool when I was seventeen to twenty-one were just out of this world – phenomenal – but no one ever said. A fifty-year-old bloke might come up and tell you now, but it was never captured for posterity.

The young footballer's ideals were built up and then, bit by bit, filed down by his experiences at Orient. For the first time, the world at his feet was a disappointment.

It was all very strange. They were odd times, and it was very difficult for me. It was very hit-and-miss. It was like they had spent twenty-five grand, brought me in and wanted me to be like Maradona. I did help them, I got to double figures both seasons and I scored some pretty good goals at times, but it was hard, it was a struggle.

Orient were in the doldrums forever, and I think they have got worse and worse since. When Dave Speedie was working his balls off at Darlington to get a move, I was working mine off at Hartlepool. He went to Chelsea shortly after I went to Orient, when they were playing to a few thousand in the Second Division.

Chelsea had a big tradition and all of a sudden they could get 20,000 or 30,000. I went to Orient who were getting 4,000, and if they played for a thousand years they would still get 4,000, so maybe I shouldn't have gone, maybe I should have turned the move down. But I'd had that many near misses and I just wanted to prove myself somewhere else.

York City may not suggest a promising convalescence for a career but York had been top of Division Three all season. For the first time, there was the prospect of playing in a side that really regarded victory as their right, not just a bonus. Keith Houchen certainly hadn't kicked the ball around the playground at Sacred Heart fantasising about re-election or relegation battles.

4

York

Daniel Defoe made York the birthplace of Robinson Crusoe, and Dick Turpin was hanged on the Knavesmire in 1739 having dispensed a lengthy and amiable conversation with his executioner.

The city meets at several crossroads in our heritage. St Peter's School, to this day, foregoes any fireworks and fun on 5 November out of respect for an ex-alumnus, Guy Fawkes.

York fell to the Romans, and later to the Danes. In 948, Eric became York's last Viking King. Eric was one of the many sons of King Harald Finehair of Norway, and secured his father's inheritance by murdering most of his own brothers – hence his sobriquet as Bloodaxe. He enjoyed a shortish sojourn, and was murdered at a bleak moor land spot at Stainsmore on the A66.

In 1066, King Harald Hardrada of Norway beat the English at Fulford Ings, only to be defeated by King Harold of England in a rematch at Stamford Bridge. This was three weeks before the latter's disappointing display at Hastings.

York City Football Club, known as the Minstermen, have played at Bootham Crescent since 1932. The venue, close to the old lunatic asylum, was formerly a cricket ground. Yorkshire even played a County Championship match there in 1890. *Wisden's Cricketers' Almanack* reported:

Owing to the non-arrival of three of the Kent team in sufficient time to take their innings, the chances of the Southern eleven were severely prejudiced, and in a terribly bad light the seven wickets were got down by Peel and Ulyett in an hour for 46.

York Minster has towered over the faith of the nation since the Middle Ages, but the message it enshrines has a chocolate rival. The alliterative urge to re-brand the football ground as KitKat Crescent stemmed from the interest of the local firm of Nestlé Rowntree.

Healthy teeth, it could be inferred, are not a feature crucial to an athlete's anatomy. Certainly, they are no more guaranteed than spiritual salvation, and their illusion can always be conjured with the snap of a telephoto lens.

At 54 Bootham, in 1907, W.H. Auden was born, but the Auden family moved to Solihull before young Wystan was old enough to be able to enjoy a Fruit Pastille.

In recent years, the Ghost Research Foundation officially declared York to be the Most Haunted City in Europe. Among the local spectres are Mad Alice, executed in 1825 for the then capital offence of dangerous insanity, and the Grey Lady, the wraith of a woman bricked up after an illicit love affair.

In February 2004, though, the Asda store at Monk's Cross became the first British supermarket to hold a wedding ceremony. The couple had met at the checkout.

After London, York was the biggest city in the country when the Normans came, with an estimated population of 8,000. In the Middle Ages it continued to develop as a trading centre, exporting wool to members of the Hanseatic League until the ships grew too large for the River Ouse.

Richard Plantagenet, Duke of York – but probably not 'The Grand old' one, established the House of York. Centuries of trans-Pennine rivalry are characterised to this day at Headingley and Old Trafford and in the more parochial jousts of Rugby League, although the Yorkists had originally attracted a more Southern-based support. Richard succumbed to the Red Rose at the Battle of Wakefield in 1460, and his head was displayed on York's city walls adorned with a paper crown.

During the Civil War, York was held by the Royalists until it fell in 1644 after the nearby Battle of Marston Moor.

In 1828, George Hudson – a local draper – invested a legacy of £30,000 in the North Midland Railway, enabling York and the noble sweep of its station platforms to be at the centre of the railway age. Cocoa from Liverpool and fruit from Scotland facilitated the sweet trade, and Hudson became the 'Railway King'. Some dubious financial dealings later proved to be Hudson's undoing, prompting Charles Dickens to describe him as 'The Giant Humbug of this time, and not a pleasant illustration of our English virtues.'

A few years later, Dickens – his mistress beside him – was a passenger on the railway train involved in the disaster at Staplehurst in Kent. He wrote to his GP:

> I was in the terrible accident yesterday, and worked some hours among the dying and the dead.
>
> I was in the carriage that did not go down, but hung in the air over the side of the broken bridge. I was not touched – scarcely shaken. But the terrific nature of the scene makes me think that I should be the better for a gentle composing draught or two.

On 22 March 1984, York City agreed a deal with Orient for their footballer. Keith Houchen moved north, faster even than Black Bess, and Orient received a purse of £15,000.

At the time, fresh battle lines were being drawn up over Yorkshire. On 5 March, plans had been announced to close the Cortonwood Colliery near Barnsley. Miners at Cortonwood, and all over Yorkshire, went on strike. Arthur Scargill, the president of the NUM, became the most ubiquitous figure on the airwaves, and brought to a fine art the evading of questions he did not care to answer. On a wall of Doncaster Railway Station, to the legend, ARTHUR SCARGILL IS A WANKER, someone had appended the observation, PITY HIS FATHER WASNT.

Keith signed his contract and stood outside the club offices, looking back towards the city centre and the Minster above. There was space, and green coloured space at that. Where the streets were narrow, they honoured the mediaeval history of which many of them had been a part. Gone were the stifling, monotonous, arterial terraces of east London. Bootham Crescent was more than a blob on an A–Z in a web of streets granted identity only by an index. The atmosphere around the ground was relaxed. A few workmen in overalls were applying their hammers and chisels to some specific but minor repairs; the receptionist was easy, the coffee drinkable. A couple of OAPs queued at the ticket office as their dogs, tails nervously quivering, summed each other up. When the sun came out, it spread itself evenly, not in clammy angles and shadows. Yvonne smiled. Cara was a tot, just a few months old. They all went for a bit of lunch, and on to Houchen's mum's in Middlesbrough.

It was perfect before we could sell the house down South. It was a completely fresh start, and a breath of fresh air, with a really happy club on the up, lots of good players, and winning games.

The contract was for two years at £225 a week, the same as he got at Orient. There were certain provisions: the player (together with his family) should become resident within twelve miles of Bootham Crescent by 31 March 1985; the club would reimburse him with reasonable expenses incurred in moving to York, including estate agents' fees, removal costs and legal fees up to a maximum of £1,000; the club would pay £30 a week in accommodation and travelling expenses for the first seven weeks, and contribute £41.66 per month direct into the player's pension scheme for a period of twenty-four months. A year later, Houchen signed an improved contract for £250 a week.

It may have been Fourth Division but this time it was clear which way his new club was going. Two happy seasons followed in a contented dressing room.

Houchen's first appearance was at Aldershot. He came off the bench to replace Steve Senior who broke his right leg during the second half. It was a short but eventful debut. He missed a penalty, scored York's second goal and got himself cautioned.

There were other eventful features to Keith's early experiences at York, not least the training facilities, which in their own way were as characterful as at Hartlepool. Keith was struck by the proprietorial attitude adopted by a lady gathering up footballs from the bushes. He observed that the balls would sometimes need to be gently wrested from her grasp. He was also intrigued by the sudden presence of someone matching him step by step in a sprint. He was surprised not so much by the unfamiliarity of his new partner – after all, he was still getting to know some of the faces – as by his rather unusual training kit, consisting of bedroom slippers and pyjamas. Keith's colleagues seemed to take this all in their stride, even when the anonymous gentleman could be seen crumpling to the ground in the far distance. Keith, it transpired, had swapped a power station near Hartlepool as a training ground with the loony bin at Clifton Moor.

Four more substitute appearances followed in a continuing torrent of victories before Houchen made his official bow in the penultimate game at home to Bury. With John Byrne and Keith Walwyn in such prolific form, Houchen wore the no.6 shirt. Manager Denis Smith had suggested that he play a similar role to John Wark at Ipswich. It was endorsement, perhaps, of the creative aspect to his game which had attracted Hartlepool when they took him on. Nowadays, we would describe his role as being 'in the hole'.

I had a defensive midfield which covered for me and I was given licence to get in the box every time we attacked. The next season, I finished as top club scorer with 18 or 19 goals – all from centre midfield. I couldn't play at centre forward because they had two great players up front. John Byrne was a top-level player and moved on to better things; Keith Walwyn was not the greatest touch player but a really big, strong lad and great in the air.

It was a happy camaraderie type of club, and Denis got good players, the likes of John MacPhail from Sheffield United, Ricky Sbragia – a centre half, and Gary Ford on the wing.

Denis Smith and Viv Busby were very astute coaches. They got you to play in a certain way. If you were switched on, in a good solid side, were positive and knew what you were doing, you were more likely to get good results than bad results. They got the formula right, and when you start winning it becomes a habit. At all my other clubs, if you went a goal down, it was 'Oh God, no.' At York, it wasn't a problem.

York finished the season with defeat at ecclesiastical rivals Hereford. Long since crowned Champions, they finished with 101 points. Three points for a win had been introduced in 1981/82, and it was the first time that a League club had reached three figures – 'Team of the Century', as *The Yorkshire Evening Press* headlined it. York, who won 31 of their games, finished sixteen points clear of runners-up Doncaster. Byrne scored 27 of the 96 goals and Walwyn 25. Houchen had not made enough appearances for them to strike him a medal, but at last he was on the up. There could be no doubt about the wisdom of this move.

It was fantastic, after four years at Hartlepool where it had been a massive struggle year after year, and then two years at Orient where it didn't work out and we got relegated one year and almost relegated the next. All of a sudden, I was playing with these lads who had this self-belief that they were going to win every time they went out. They just used to pass the ball, create chances and score goals and there was always a smile on everybody's face and drinks on the bus coming back, everyone really happy. I couldn't believe the difference.

The crowd used to love it. It brought some colour – it was a flamboyant team. I scored all those goals from centre midfield, and the training was fantastic. It was like someone took a jacket off me, and away I went. But even playing at that level, I wanted to be doing it at the very top.

Playing at a higher level prompted no compromise in form as York City set about the Third Division at the start of the 1984/85 season. Six wins and two draws in the first eight games propelled the Minstermen to the top of the table. But a home win against Bristol Rovers was followed four days later by a home defeat by Bristol City. A Tuesday night stuffing at Bournemouth later in the month saw the team start to pitch. However, at the beginning of November, Gillingham – who went on to finish fourth – were thrashed 7-1 at Bootham Crescent. Houchen scored a hat-trick, only his second in senior football.

On 17 November, a crowd of 3,836 gathered for a first round FA Cup tie at Bootham Crescent. If you had wanted to locate York's opponents Blue Star, as they were still called, you would have needed to take the metro to Kenton Bankfoot and then a bus to the Wheatsheaf Sports Ground in Woolsington, four miles north of Newcastle. In 1978, the Wearside League club had won the FA Vase at Wembley.

A goal in each half from the brace of Keiths, Walwyn and Houchen, put paid to any giant-killing. The significance, as with Coventry's third round win against Bolton in 1987, lay more in the veil of fate it had lifted.

In the next round, York travelled to Hartlepool. Old friends welcomed Houchen home, and a large crowd of 8,554 was there to see him add to John MacPhail's goal, and put York into the draw for the Third Round. It was truly a purple patch for Houchen. Starting with the hat-trick against Gillingham, he netted 10 goals in a run of 10 consecutive League and Cup games.

In August, the Fourth Division Champions had kicked off in the Third Division with a home game against Walsall. As football seasons started to take shape, it was the FA Cup that used to be most eagerly anticipated.

After Saturdays of surprise, the draw for each round would be awaited with fervour for two whole nights, like the climax of Test Matches when Sunday was always a rest day. At last, on Monday morning, listeners to the wireless and *Music While You Work* were transported to FA headquarters at Lancaster Gate. The door opened onto, 'The next voice you will hear…', and you were ushered into an atmosphere heavy with pipe smoke and watch chains to eavesdrop on this arcane procedure. Clearly, the draw had not been the only item on the agenda. That aura of AOB about it, the sense that it is not actually quite the most important thing in the world, is blown away under the eye of television.

If you had slain a giant or were likely to, if you were poised for Olympus or had already adorned it, the BBC's interlocutor would enlighten the audience with some of the juicier numbers on the balls. Otherwise, as the sheet drew back, witnesses paused before each identification, and prayed that Ernie might yet come to life.

What egalitarian balls they were! Having charted the progress of Bishop Auckland, the same number might later secure the destiny of Liverpool. It could be made up as the *Mayor of Casterbridge,* but happily recast as Hotspur. What life do they have away from the spotlight, these balls, as they plod the beat for the FA Vase or the FA Sunday Cup? Where do they reside? Do they sit perkily on trays like eggs, or jostle in bags aside the brooms and the Brasso?

The balls rattled in their mysterious pouch, squirming like sperms, immediately identifiable from their emerging heads. The Coventry City's of this world hoped they would avoid the York City's (in 1938 they didn't, and duly lost), and the York City's that luck might favour their fantasies with a more glamorous victim than Coventry City. Half-stifled guffaws gave shape to the room – like *The Archers* behind their microphone – as a committee member's own club found itself assigned a slippery Somerset challenge. The bag got snappier the emptier it became. Survivors were glad to know they had avoided so-and-so, only to discover that they were drawn against…Walsall.

After gung-ho wins against Preston and Burnley, York lost to both Hull and Derby by the odd goal in New Year League matches before taking on Walsall in the Cup.

In the third round on 14 January 1933, Walsall had created one of the most celebrated of FA Cup legends when they knocked out Arsenal.

In *Cliff Bastin Remembers,* the Arsenal player recalled:

Never have I seen Herbert Chapman look so miserably unhappy. He made a brave, desperate, but unavailing effort to cheer us all up. 'Never mind, boys,' he said, 'these things do happen.' But we were all inconsolable, and so, for that matter, was he. I think he felt the blow more than any of us. Here was the team which he had come to when it was struggling pathetically at the bottom of the first division; the team which he had made one of the greatest in the history of football, beaten by a fifth-rate side. Napoleon must have felt like that in Russia, a hundred and twenty-one years before.

Of all the players, I think I felt the effects of the defeat most deeply. At twenty years old, I was the youngest in the side, so perhaps this was only natural. On my way home to my lodgings that night in the underground railway, I felt positively suicidal. Visions of the Arsenal goals that might have been rose up before my eyes; hopes that the events of the afternoon had been nothing but an evil nightmare would delude me for a brief moment, only to be banished away by the cold, grim reality.

Goals from Butler, Walwyn and Hay were enough to enable York to see off the Saddlers. Many times was the name of Walsall invoked after Arsenal's ball followed York's out of the bag in the draw for the fourth round.

Except for a short spell in the Second Division in the 1970s, York City have been permanently amongst the lower orders since joining the League in 1929, and had to apply for re-election on seven occasions. This has made their quite extraordinary record in the FA Cup even more noteworthy.

In their first season in the League, York took Newcastle United, fielding the immortal Hughie Gallacher and six other internationals, to a third round replay after holding on for a draw in a severe snowstorm at St James'. Having seen their heroes depart on the seven o'clock train, 'these happy undaunted enthusiasts then went back into the Tyneside city and revelled in the gayest of spirits'.

In 1938, less than sixteen years after the club's formation, York City took Huddersfield to a quarter-final replay having disposed of two other First Division clubs, Middlesbrough and West Bromwich. York had played sixteen FA Cup-ties in two seasons.

In 1955, York became only the third Third Division club, after Millwall (1937) and Port Vale (1954), to reach the semi-finals. Victories against non-League Scarborough and Dorchester Town were followed by a 2-0 win at Bloomfield Road in the third round. This was the great Blackpool side of Matthews and Mortensen, victorious in the celebrated Final of Coronation Year.

After victory at Amateur kings Bishop Auckland, came Tottenham and another famous triumph, York winning 3-1 at Bootham Crescent in front of a 21,000 crowd. The quarter-final then presented an awkward trip to Meadow Lane, but Second Division Notts County were beaten 1-0.

Dave Batters, in *York City: A Complete Record 1922-1990,* describes events after the Notts County match:

> There was great excitement in York as news came through of the result. Progress of the match had been relayed to Clarence Street, where York RL were in action, and the biggest cheer of the afternoon followed the announcement of City's win. There was cheering in local cinemas as the result was flashed on the screens. Telegrams of congratulations poured into Meadow Lane and the Victoria Hotel in Nottingham where City had based themselves. Amongst these were messages from York MP Sir Harry Hylton-Foster, York Rugby League Club and Brighton and Hove Albion, who congratulated City on upholding the prestige of the Third Division...
>
> The scenes in the city of York that Saturday night were quite incredible. The first of 14 special trains arrived back at 8.10p.m. and many people assembled at the station to greet those who 'had been there'. To the roar of rattles, bells and wild cheering, the supporters arrived back in triumph. Red and white favours, top hats, umbrellas, even suits in red and white were everywhere and the station remained a cauldron of noise and excitement until midnight, when the last train arrived. By 9.30p.m. a crowd of several hundred had congregated in Blossom Street, waiting for the arrival of the City team by coach as they arrived along Tadcaster Road. They had a celebration dinner at the Victoria Hotel. A police car escorted the coach into York and the team were given a heroes' welcome.

The City team made their headquarters at Matlock before the semi-final at Hillsborough. The manager of the Lilybank Hydro Hotel organised a special dinner on the night before the game and set the table out as a football pitch with cardboard caricatures of the players. Twenty-one thousand people – a fifth of the population of York – journeyed forth on 26 March 1955 to see York take on Newcastle. The West Yorkshire

Road Car Co., alone, organised forty-three motor-coaches, and Pullman Coaches sent twenty-six. There were twenty special trains.

York fell behind to a fourteenth minute goal from Vic Keeble but, after half-an-hour, Bottom robbed Bob Stokoe and ran thirty yards before placing the ball past Ronnie Simpson in the Newcastle goal.

On the following Wednesday afternoon, the two teams replayed at Roker Park. The city of York came almost to a standstill with factories and schools glued to the wireless commentary, and a large crowd congregated in the market-place where a loudspeaker had been installed. Newcastle went straight into the lead, and completed their 2-0 victory before half-time, but for a Third Division team to be amongst the last three surviving sides in the FA Cup was unique. Milburn, Mitchell and the rest went on to beat Manchester City and lift the Cup five weeks later. It was a wonderful season for York City, and an exceptional one for Arthur Bottom who scored 39 goals in 46 League and Cup games.

The Minstermen were still at it in more recent times when, in the second round of the Coca-Cola Cup in 1995, they knocked out Manchester United after winning the first leg 3-0 at Old Trafford.

Meantime, the aura of 1955 had begun to cloy for the class of 1985. Nobody really expected that York could beat Arsenal, but few fans had been optimistic all those years before.

I was twenty-four, and had had nothing but struggle. Football is not all about the grander people. I had struggled and struggled and struggled, and then I suddenly came into this club, where we won our league, and everyone was happy and dancing. Then we had this Cup run and drawn one of the massive clubs at home, and I was going to be playing.

Unlike in 1955, the cameras were there. Deeds of derring-do would defy the illusions of sepia and legend. York tore into their distinguished visitors from the start. Unable to play a cultured passing game on the bone-hard, rutted pitch, Arsenal were rattled throughout and struggled to impose themselves. Both sides had their opportunities and York could have had the game sewn up with Houchen and Gary Ford – twice – having first-half chances. Keith Walwyn, who had to replace a split right boot, had a lob headed away from near the line after beating Lukic, and Houchen was only inches away from connecting with a Walwyn cross.

They just didn't want to play. They seemed to spend half their time moaning at each other. They certainly didn't have the enthusiasm for the game we had.

Steve Williams never wanted to get on with the game. He was always shouting and cursing at his team-mates. You can't do that and still give your best.

With the game in its final moments, Arsenal must have been anticipating the comfort of replaying on their own carpet with the York directors licking their lips at the prospect of the extra income from a trip to Highbury. Suddenly, Steve Williams pushed Keith Houchen over in the box. The ref pointed to the spot. Ten thousand York supporters exploded as if it was a goal. Houchen got up and dusted himself down.

I knew it was close to time but didn't know exactly how long there was to go. It seemed to be ages between being fouled and when I was able to take the kick.

I had made a run and got on the goal-side of Williams when I felt him tugging at my shirt and his arms then went round my neck. The referee was only ten yards away when I looked up after going down under the challenge.

The goalkeeper made up my mind for me. I saw him leaning to his left, and so I thought I would have a go at the other corner.

Houchen despatched the ball a yard inside John Lukic's right hand post. One of the photographs captured the very moment the ball crossed the line, a split second before the surge of the crowd's reaction. It was the moment when a child claws open a present, a loved one waits on a smile, excitement delivers unrestrained joy. York had won.

Suddenly, all the curiosity of the camera and the printing press swivelled towards Keith Houchen. That one strike of the ball had lifted the player out of the coterie of the back page, the club programme, the nestling interest of aficionados, and into a face with a tag, a name stamped with a story. (Sadly, he no longer has his tape of the *Match of the Day* coverage. Some time later, when a tummy bug hit the Houchen household, someone was sick into the video machine with the tape in it.)

It was only the second penalty I had taken for York. I'd always liked taking free kicks and penalties, but I wouldn't have known until the moment I took the kick where I was going to put it. I didn't do any research into John Lukic and the way he went.

It was a long, long time between the penalty being given and my being allowed to take it. I was standing on the edge of the box for ever. In your head, you can think, 'I'm going to put it there,' and then do the opposite, and you don't know yourself why you're doing it. Sometimes, the movement of the 'keeper can make you change your mind.

I used to whack it, and I missed a few, but not many. I took them top right, bottom corner, blasted straight down the middle, and I never knew from one day to the next how I was going to do it. A lot of mine were side-footed, unlike Killer's at Coventry, but if you side-foot them you still have to hit the ball hard because nine times out of ten, even if the 'keeper gets a hand to it, it will still go in the net.

Taking penalties is nerve-wracking but when I took one, I used to psych myself up by reminding myself what a massive area the goalmouth is. Other goals you score as part of the match and they are followed by this great adrenaline rush, but with a penalty the adrenaline rush comes beforehand. Zidane, against England, actually threw up as he put the ball on the spot. You think, 'I'm going to score, but I must make sure I do.'

You have to be a particular sort of person. A lot of forwards don't take them. You look at the Southgates and the Battys of this world, and you think that there should be others doing it before them. Penalties find people out. Some people never take them; some take one and miss, and never take another.

I missed one for Hibs in the UEFA Cup against Liege. It was live on the BBC, when we got led out by pipers. We drew. I went right through and was about to score when this lad brought me down. I took the penalty, and struck it identically to the one against Arsenal, probably struck it better and truer. But he guessed right and got a tiny finger-point to it. It took the ball onto the post, and it was passing me and going back to the half-way line before anyone could react. It made the difference when we went out 1-0 in extra-time in the second leg. After that, I said I wouldn't take any more. Why put that kind of pressure on myself? I did take a couple when I was back at Hartlepool. The first hat-trick I ever got was at Peterborough when we drew 4-4 and my third one was a penalty. I remember hitting that in the top right-hand corner, just knowing, 'Give me the ball, I want to get a penalty.' If you have gone for a month without a goal, it's tougher, but good forwards will always take penalties. That's why I like Alan Shearer. He is a proper forward, doing more than little bits. You should always want to put the ball in the net.

I had a big fall out with Barry Silkman at Orient. We were at home, and I hadn't scored for a while. I wanted to take the penalty, but he also wanted to. We

had a stand-up argument in the middle of the pitch, and the crowd had to wait.
He got to take it, and actually missed. Then we got another penalty, so I got hold
of the ball, and I was thinking, 'Fucking hell, I've got to score now.' I did.

The Arsenal manager, Don Howe, had spent £4.5 million on a team that
included stars like Tony Woodcock, Charlie Nicholas, David O'Leary
and Paul Mariner. Arsenal had been 8-1 joint second favourites to win
the Cup, York were 300-1 outsiders.

Don Shaw, the referee from Cheshire, had a long day. He had to be at
the ground at 7.00a.m. to pronounce on the conditions. With the help
of the public, the snow was shifted, the pitch cleared.

Football grounds have a strange intimacy in the snow. It's 'all hands
on deck' to steer the vessel through the straights. It took Lincoln and
Coventry a record seventeen attempts to do so in the FA Cup in 1963.
The thinness of the air, as much as the whiteness, draws the players and
their shirts into sharper relief. The cries are keener and more resonant,
the orange ball a tropical surprise. There is a making do with gloves and
Bovril, a sense that with all those breaths suspended in the cold you
shouldn't really be mucking about outside.

Shaw said:

> I am mentally shattered. It's been a long day. I had no doubts about the penalty
> because I was very close to the incident.
>
> The Arsenal player Williams pulled Houchen back by the shirt and then I
> saw both his hands go round his neck. I didn't have a single complaint about
> the decision from any of the players.

Hoodlums were quickly into action after the game, a gentleman who
had his window smashed likening them to 'wild rats'. There was a smash-
and-grab on a jewellers in the city centre, and a disabled man emerged
from the ground to find that his invalid car had been wrecked.

One local boy didn't make it to the match after being accidentally
knocked unconscious by a snowball, and the owner of Oscar's Wine Bar
fulfilled a promise to give the York players four salmanazars of champagne with which to celebrate.

Niall Quinn, in *The Guardian,* recalled the effect of the result on
Arsenal:

I was not at Bootham Crescent but I was an Arsenal employee… For the next few days the club was in a state of shock. Shock is a strong word but that's how it felt and, although Howe had not been in charge for long, it was the beginning of the end for him.

Arsenal recovered, and the Arsenal players too. Memories of the indestructible-looking figure of Keith Walwyn provide a poignant reminder of two tragic footnotes to the Arsenal game. Walwyn, from the Caribbean island of Nevis, later had to retire due to a heart problem. He went on to work as a community sports officer at a school near Blackpool, and also ran a sports shop. In April 2003, he died following a heart operation at the age of forty-seven.

The Arsenal centre-back Tommy Caton had been a prodigy at Manchester City but his game got stuck after his transfer to Arsenal. At Oxford United, on the slide from the First Division, he found that a serious foot injury required repeated surgery, and this induced depression alongside an alcoholic problem. He moved to Charlton Athletic, and played his last League game on New Year's Day 1991. In April 1993, a decade almost to the day before Walwyn, he died of a heart attack, aged thirty.

On the day after the Cup-tie, John Wallace, a resident of Dunnington near York, was moved by his muse:

The Blowing-up of Arsenal

'Twas on a cold mid-winter's day
When snow lay on the ground,
York City had a match to play,
The FA Cup Fourth Round.

But first the snow they had to clear
To let the match go on.
Two hundred came to volunteer
And soon the snow was gone.

They came with spades and shovels too,
With barrow, stick or hand.

York

They sweated blood because they knew
This game must not be banned.

The Arsenal, so strong and proud,
Had come to Bootham Crescent,
And when they waved back to the crowd
Twelve thousand fans were present.

The ground was packed from door to door
When City took the field,
But as they heard that mighty roar
They swore they would not yield.

Those lads in red were eager now
And first to every ball.
They fought to win, they would not bow,
And each one gave his all.

Then Butler charged without a stop
And Ford hit it well,
And Walwyn's centre we saw drop
But Pearce in anguish fell.

In midfield City ruled the park
And our defence marked it tightly.
They kept 'The Gunners' in the dark
And let no Stars shine brightly.

But as the half drew to an end
The Arsenal showed their cunning.
A goal right now our will would bend,
We thought we saw it coming.

But when the whistle blew at last
Our net was guarded still,
For seven halves no ball had passed,
The score remained nil-nil.

A Tenner and a Box of Kippers

The second half had scarce begun
When Astbury saved the day,
And Senior blocked off every run
Backed up by Alan Hay.

But as we chased and as we ran
The Arsenal grew rattled.
Keith Walwyn was a mighty man,
Before the goal he battled.

Ricky, John and Haslegrave
Supported each attack,
And Butler, arrogant and brave,
Provided Keith with flak.

Then Nicholas received a hurt,
He could not stand the pace.
But Tommy Caton held the fort,
They had to save their face.

Keith's lob was headed off the line
And other chances went.
'Oh God, just grant us one more time' –
That prayer was really meant.

Ten minutes left, and on the break
The Arsenal caused trouble.
If they should steal it, what a take!
Yes, that would burst our bubble.

Five minutes left and ten to one
We'd meet another day,
The score the same as when begun,
A Highbury replay.

Two minutes left, and Butler took
The ball on his right wing

York

But Williams, trying out his luck,
Struck Houchen coming in.

But Mr Shaw was on the spot,
A penalty he pointed.
Whoever dares to take the shot
Must needs be God's Anointed.

Keith Houchen missed one when before
He played in his first game.
Oh will this happen once more
Or will he gather fame.

The mighty din becomes a hush
While Houchen walks away.
He will not fret, he will not rush
While Arsenal delay.

He strikes it low unto the left,
Sends Lukic to the right.
Oh gallant foot so true and deft,
Oh what a glorious sight.

The roar was heard all over York,
They needed no loud-hailer.
And even in the Theatre Royal
'Twas heard by Berwick Kaler.

We sang and danced, we hugged and kissed,
We knew we had it won,
Another honour to the list,
We're second unto none.

Oh glory be to Denis Smith
And old Viv Busby too,
And everyone who did their bit
May also claim their due.

And when you're old and when we're grey
And only just alive,
We'll think back on that glorious day
In nineteen-eighty-five.

Mr Wallace sent a copy to Keith Houchen, 'for your kind consideration'.

In the fifth round of the Cup, York were drawn at home to Liverpool. An all-ticket crowd of 13,485 was fixed. As the club launched a voucher scheme, there was a gate of 10,948 for the game against Wigan, more even than for the Arsenal match. Houchen was injured, and subsequently missed the Liverpool game. The pitch was protected from the frost by a duvet of straw and polythene. York held Liverpool 1-1, with a goal by Ricky Sbragia.

Houchen was back for the replay at Anfield the following Wednesday, when the cards came crashing down with a 7-0 defeat. Exactly a year later, York reached the fifth round again, were drawn against Liverpool, drew 1-1, and lost the Anfield replay – but this time by 3-1.

The Minstermen finished eighth in the Third Division. Houchen's injury effectively kept him out of the team until the end of March, but injuries were to have a more serious impact on his game in 1985/86, when York went one better in the League.

Football knocks were the last thing on Keith Houchen's mind as the aircraft returning York players from an end-of-season trip to Spain dipped like Granddad easing his way into the armchair to the bottom of the steep descent into Leeds. The undercarriage groaned its preparation, distant shirtsleeves and the mopping of summer brows could be seen through the windows. It wouldn't be too much of a shock to the system or the sun tan after a week spent on sultry links or at the pool-side with a cerveza. A gentle Yorkshire breeze would be welcome. But suddenly, with the runway coming up to meet them, there was a violent jerk and a strangulated squeal of the engine. The pilot was trying to take the plane up again, but he was too late. This enormous body was about to do a belly flop.

The next few seconds were a cascade of terror, with the senses caught between two worlds. It was like being in a film, *Airplane* even, but without the suave reassurance of Leslie Nielsen. Then came the thud of a collapsing wheel, the grinding helplessness, and imminent horror as the aircraft cheerily whirled around on the grass as if at a funfair. The lockers, carefully secured by stewardesses stretching in their uniforms at the start of the flight, mockingly disgorged intimacies and mementoes into the cabin. Saved up pesetas-worth of Gordon's and Marlboro flew through the air. Keith was sitting next to Denis Smith by the emergency door over the wing. It was Denis's idea to take the players away. He had been regaling Keith with blasé recollections of his flying experience; now he was curled up in 'the protective brace position'.

Some of the Lincoln City team were also on board:

Their manager had this tick. It was working twenty times over that day. For a few seconds, it was deadly quiet, and then the screaming and panic set off.

Down went the chute, and down went Denis and Keith.

The young cabin crew asked us both to stay at the bottom of the chute and help out. There was pandemonium in the doorway with people trying to get out. We caught at least two toddlers who were dropped over the adults and onto the chute.

The huge engine was whirring right next to us. I was wondering whether it was going to explode.

It only occurred to them how sullen and smoking the danger was when people started to run, anywhere, anyhow. The cries were like the silence of the grass at school, a curiosity in the desperation of the moment.

On the trip, Keith roomed with Bryan Foster, the popular grounds-man who first joined the ground staff at Bootham Crescent in 1958. Fozzie had been temporarily distracted from the concerns of re-seeding and his customary advice from the *Sporting Life*. Gripped in his hand as he surveyed the scene behind him was a box of perfume, an expensive one at that. He was determined to bring it home to his wife, air disaster or not. Such gifts were beyond the normal remuneration bestowed with a mower or guaranteed by the *Life*. But as Fozzie cosseted his trophy, someone gently pointed out that the scent had seeped out as he sped from the scene. Fozzie's missus, no doubt, would show her understanding. Everyone, thank God, had survived.

Injuries cast their pall over Houchen during the 1985/86 season. He had a run of appearances in the autumn, with a brace of goals against Bolton and a singleton in a 7-0 win against Darlington, and then a ten-game stretch that saw him through to February. He came on as sub in the Cup replay at Liverpool but, aside from the return at Darlo, he was done. Scunthorpe beckoned.

Keith would take the Arsenal match with him, but a gentleman from London E16 was less enthralled than Mr Wallace at the outcome of the game, and wrote to Houchen to give him the benefit of his wisdom:

Dear Keith,

As one of the many dejected Arsenal supporters who helped clear the pitch last Saturday (my big mistake) may I first of all be man enough to offer my congratulations to you and your team, and wish you all the luck against Liverpool.

I however cannot understand why you appeared so churlish in the London Press, especially with your remarks against Williams and Nicholas. After all, most sportsmen try to be magnanimous to their defeated Opponents who have suffered enough, and do not kick them when they are down.

Your remarks on the pitch being the same for both teams was only figuratively right as you well know.

The FA Cup is all about luck, proving that every year the top 8 clubs in the First Division do not monopolise it, and in your tie with Arsenal, your club got everything that was going.

First of all, you got the HOME advantage. Then as the most inferior team you got the dicey pitch you were praying for, so that the difference in ability and skill would be nullified, and the match would be like a game of Russian Roulette. Thirdly, you had a benevolent Referee who had a rush of blood, and for an incident that Referees decide to overlook so often, as you yourself admitted, he awarded a penalty. The point was brought out by Jimmy Greaves on TV on Sunday, after the Referee failed to give Spurs a penalty in their match with Liverpool. He said 'If that was not a penalty how could that idiot give one to York yesterday'.

Now, re your match v Liverpool. I really do wish you all the luck, for you are certainly going to need it. Luckily you have got HOME advantage again, but this is where the luck I feel will finish. You will certainly have no ice or snow to help you, and it does not matter how much help you might get from the Referee, it will have no effect whatsoever. Believe me now, for if not, you will have to believe me at 4.40p.m. on the day.

After all, class tells in the end, and good teams are not found half-way down the Third Division. Yours sincerely,

The correspondent added a PS:

Ironically, that berk of a Referee, apart from providing you all with a few moments of ecstasy, did your club no favours at all. Just consider. Little minnows like you cannot survive on Glory and moments of heaven. What clubs like York hope for in the Cup is Cash, and plenty of it. Had the Referee not made that diabolical decision, the club would have shared in a 30,000 plus gate in the replay at Highbury, win, lose or draw. But now all they will get is the same share of a 10,000 gate and certain exit.

When you really digest this letter, I am sure you will conclude that it is not written on sour grapes, but is absolutely logic.

5

Scunthorpe

Houchen's second full season at Bootham Crescent had been depressed with injury. Scunthorpe United offered York £40,000 for him to drop down to the Fourth Division, and he signed on 28 March 1986. The Scunthorpe board was prepared to match Houchen's wage of £250 and provide a bonus scheme that, unusually, included a crowd bonus based on attendances of over 2,500. Life as a professional footballer had been a financial struggle and Keith and Yvonne wanted to be able to cultivate their life together and support a family.

It was the only time I ever gave up. I'd gone to Orient hoping it was a stepping stone, and it was the same at York. I remember actually thinking, 'I've got to make a living and play for as long as I can at this level. It's not going to happen for me at the very top so I might as well sign for Scunthorpe.' They gave me a £10,000 ex-gratia payment, which was an absolute fortune. I got that tax free, and a club car, brand new. I'd never had these things.

It wasn't the right club because it wasn't going anywhere. But I was getting older, I couldn't keep chasing this impossible dream. I said to Yvonne, 'I'm just going to take the money and then see what happens from there.' And Yvonne has always been really, really supportive, whatever I wanted to do.

No big clubs came in, but at that level I was probably the most sought after player in the Third and Fourth Divisions: Preston offered me the most and Martin Dobson good money to go to Bury. I remember ringing him and he took a right hump, 'Signing for Scunthorpe are you, are you fucking right?' I told him it was my decision and he said, 'You're fucking making the wrong decision,' and put the 'phone down on me. John Rudge was desperate to sign me at Port Vale. He had wanted to sign me since I was a kid. It was funny how I finished up at Port Vale and then never got on with him when I did get there.

We were settled in York. It was a lovely city. I could travel over to Scunthorpe every day. I knew Frank Barlow because he was my coach when I was a trialist at Chesterfield. He was a nice man, I got on with him, and I knew big Bill Green who was his assistant.

They were trying to build a side to go up a division or two. I remember standing there, a jigsaw piece, the one they were going to throw a bit of money at.

Within a week, I was saying to Yvonne, 'I've made a mistake. I hate it, absolutely hate it.' I hated everything about it. The set-up was so lower league, the whole thing lower league, very, very lower league. The Old Show Ground was shabby, depressing, horrible. And the smell, I couldn't stand the smell.

We had a bad side, I could tell that. You get a feel for the place, and the supporters were miserable, moaning gits. I had only been there for a couple of games and I felt 'Give us a chance.'

I thought I'd made such a big mistake but I'd just stuck a £10,000 cheque into the bank and I'd never seen anything like that. I said to Yvonne that I wished I could have the money and not the club. But Frank was a lovely fella, as was Bill.

I only lasted nine games in the end.

Many of the locals had plenty of time to moan – one in five was out of work. As with the 'five towns' of the Potteries, Scunthorpe evolved from a pudding of parishes. Crosby, Scunthorpe, Frodingham, Brumby and Ashby were welded as one by the steel industry a century ago, and when the foundries floundered the community suffered.

In 1954, some years after Yeovil and Petters United in the opposite corner of the country had become Yeovil Town, a change of title was formalised in Lincolnshire. Lindsey, which lends its name to a prominent society for the blind, ceased to share in the name of Scunthorpe and Lindsey United, although the use of the title – like that of the Milan Cricket and Football Club – had long since fallen into abeyance. This mouthful of a club had graduated from the Midland League to the Football League in 1950 when membership was increased with the election of Colchester United, Gillingham, Shrewsbury Town and Scunthorpe. Scunthorpe got in only on a third ballot.

A 1-0 defeat at Hereford United in the fourth qualifying round on 11 November 1950 distinguished Scunthorpe with becoming the first and only Football League club ever to be eliminated from the FA Cup before the first round. The four newcomers were scheduled to play in the qualifiers before news of their elevation was confirmed. Shrewsbury, piqued perhaps that Gillingham were nonetheless exempted, scratched from the competition. Delusions of grandeur were red on their faces the following year when they were tipped over at the first hurdle by the amateurs at Leytonstone.

Scunthorpe's new nickname, the Iron, was vindicated during their debut season by an extraordinary home record – only 9 goals were conceded in the 23 matches.

> Any old Iron, any old Iron,
> Any any any old Iron,
> You look sweet walking down the street,
> Hammer in your hand and boots on your feet,
> Dressed in style, always a smile,
> We sing up the Iron,
> Oh we don't give a damn
> About Donny Rovers fans,
> Old Iron, old Iron.

In 1958, at St James' Park, Scunthorpe knocked Newcastle out of the FA Cup, although the hosts' poor form that season made Hartlepools' brave showing against Manchester United the previous year appear more tantalising. In the Second Division in 1961/62, with Barrie Thomas scoring thirty-one times in the first twenty-four games, Scunthorpe finished behind only Liverpool, Leyton Orient and Sunderland.

The sale of Thomas to Newcastle signalled such a decline that when Scunthorpe scraped the bottom of the table in September 1963 a Baptist minister, David Mansfield, announced his intention of praying for the team, saying, 'After what I saw on Saturday, I am convinced that they need theological help.' In the early eighteenth century, you might have solicited spiritual assistance at the Old Rectory in nearby Epworth. This was the boyhood home of John and Charles Wesley. The Old Show Ground, once the venue for the Scunthorpe and District Agricultural Show and until 1988 the first and only home of the football club, is now most frequently invoked for being the starting ground for Kevin Keegan, Ray Clemence, and even the brief footballing career of Ian Botham.

Scunthorpe is in North Kesteven which looks across the Humber to the East Riding. It is the part of England where the Pilgrimage of Grace fermented in 1536 against the repressive measures of Henry VIII. The Crown's revenge was ruthless: over 200 people were executed and Robert Aske, the leader of the rebellion, was hanged, drawn and quartered.

In *Foul Deeds and Suspicious Deaths in and around Scunthorpe,* Stephen Wade relates the violent legacy that lingered in the locality. In 1847, Mary Milner applied a fatal dose of arsenic to Hannah Jickels's pancakes. In an enterprising initiative in forensic science, a GP from Brigg traced the remnants of the pancakes to places where Mrs Jickels had been vomiting. Milner had not been entirely successful with her mop although some of the sick was uncovered on a dung hill. Dr Moxon discerned a level of arsenic sufficient to have done for a whole household. Milner denied the many punters at Lincoln Castle the spectacle of her public execution by stringing herself up by a handkerchief in the Green Room as she was about to be called.

In 1891, Arthur Spencer, a young man spurned by a mature widow, was less successful at pre-empting the performance of execution. Having blasted the lady at close range, he addressed the muzzle to his own mouth at an inadequate angle. The bullet passed through his neck and into the wall. He lived to tell the jury.

During the following year, it was reported that a Mr Pryce was abused in a saloon simply on account of being Welsh. He responded, rather aptly, by hurling a spittoon at one of his attackers, although it is not clear at what stage of the evening.

There was always a good demand for executioners in the area. Wade writes:

> Hanging was certainly not a fine art: Calcraft often had to scuttle down to the lower level and tug the legs of his clients to hasten death. Some may have thought him a man who botched the job, but evidence is not reliable. One witness noted that he was 'a kind, benevolent and reserved old man' who wore a skull cap when doing his trade… But the Lincolnshire man, William Marwood, was a different type. He saw the post of executioner as being highly skilled and professional, and even made his own business cards. He conceived of the 'long drop' which was a more humane way of handling a hanging… He was sarcastic about Calcraft, saying, 'He hanged them – I execute them!' Marwood insisted that he had improved everything done in that line of work:

'I believe that I spare suffering better than anyone else. The old plan was to kill by strangling: mine is dislocation.'

Syd Dearnley sat down at Lincoln Prison in 1948 for a job interview as Assistant-Hangman. The Governor, Brigadier Paton-Walsh, enquiring about his hobbies, noted that Dearnley professed a predilection for pheasant shooting.

At the Baths Hall in Scunthorpe, the annual performance of *Messiah* would take place with some gentlemen loath to be parted from their caps even when they stood up for the *Hallelujah Chorus*.

Down at the Old Show Ground, on 28 March 1986, Keith Houchen started his ninety-seven day stint as a Scunthorpe United footballer. Jack Brownsword, an ex-miner who played in Scunthorpe's first League game in 1950, stuck it for fourteen years, making 595 League appearances before retiring at the age of forty-one when Scunthorpe lost their Second Division place to Coventry.

'The Iron' were coming to the end of a season with little left to play for. Frank Barlow had quietly turned things around with a distinct improvement in form since Christmas. The introduction of other new faces such as on-loan midfielder Kevin Dixon from Hartlepool was a help. On April Fools' Day, Houchy made his debut, at Hartlepool. Scunthorpe's all-time top scorer Steve Cammack scored the second-half winner. Preston – in their least invincible season ever – won 3-1 at the Old Show Ground, but 'the Iron' drew against Swindon and Colchester. Houchen opened his account in the sixty-fourth minute of a 3-1 home defeat of Rochdale and scored again in a victory against Burnley at Turf Moor. Steve Cammack's spectacular diving header in the last game against Chester helped propel the team into fifteenth place.

On the face of it, it had been as odd a move as the Orient one. For Houchy, the season was not yet over – not quite. Frank Barlow had a request, 'We've still got two reserve games left, lads, and not enough to make up a team. Houchen, will you play in one of them?'

Houchen opted to play in the first.

'Who's it against?'

'Coventry City. It should be a decent match that one.'

Neither of the towns' local newspapers bothered to send a reporter. An obscure paragraph in each was enough to record the facts: Coventry, who had already won promotion from the Second Division of the

Central League, lost 3-1. Houchen scored a couple for the home team with Julian Broddle adding a third. Kenny Hibbitt netted a penalty for the visitors.

I had a fantastic game. Graham Rodger was marking me and Sedge and others were playing, but I was on another level. The thing is I was an experienced player. John Sillett said I made his players look like amateurs. It was a lovely, sunny day, the end of the season and holidays coming up. I really enjoyed it.

A year and ten days later, the press box would be overflowing. The 'impossible dream' was about to come true. For now, back home in Middlesbrough at Newport & District Working Men's club, Houchy watched the Cup Final on the television.

6

Coventry

George Curtis's handshake was warm and whole-hearted. Curtis was a Coventry icon, and had led the team from the Fourth Division to the First during a record 534 games for the club. Houchen was twenty-six and had yet to really indulge in the facilities of a First Division club. Curtis took him upstairs to the restaurant. He was a genial man, with whom Keith still feels at ease. The Grandstand Restaurant was exceptional by most standards – it was one of the very best in the Midlands and was in the Michelin Guide – but the salvers and starch and opulent air were a new experience for this Fourth Division footballer.

They stepped through to the directors' box in the Main Stand and looked out onto the pitch. Curtis then drove Houchen round the sights of the city. The training ground was a revelation, the huge car plant at Ryton less contentious a backdrop than a nuclear power station or a lunatic asylum. The club put Keith and Yvonne up in the Leofric, the best hotel in town.

It came when I least expected it. It was as if fate had decided, 'Alright then, alright, we'll give you your break.' The weird thing is that the next move could have been to Port Vale or Bolton, but suddenly there were two First Division clubs who wanted me. Bryan Hamilton had tried to sign me at Tranmere and Wigan.

This time, Hamilton had Leicester City's cheque book in his hand. However, the next day Keith Houchen became a Coventry City player.

Yvonne and I were in the hotel. I said I couldn't believe it, the choice of two big clubs and we are sitting here drinking champagne. 'We'll stay here,' she said, 'I like it. They've been really nice to you, haven't they?'

George Curtis and John Sillett had been confirmed as the new management team after successfully pulling the rabbit out of the hat when Coventry, yet again, cheated relegation at the end of the 1985/86 season. Keith went to see them the following morning. The signing-on fee was £10,000, to add to the £10,000 from Scunthorpe, on top of a basic of £350 a week and £50 an appearance. It was more than young professionals like Graham Rodger were getting but nowhere near as much as the senior pros.

I was thinking probably £500 or £600. They were paying Scunthorpe £60,000 for me, which was decent money. Jesus, I thought, the only person never getting it is me!

   I said to Yvonne that I was definitely signing for them, and she said alright. I told George that I wanted to sign but I was supposed to be going to Leicester in the afternoon. When I asked him for £450 basic, he told me that I could take the £350 or leave it and walk out of the door now. Was he bluffing, who knows?

Would George have let Keith walk out? The two clubs had agreed the deal and they were paying most of the other players far more. Keith flushed like a boy chastised by the certainty of an adult's retort. He took the offer, and saved face with a quip about giving him loads of money if they won a major trophy. Coventry never won major trophies, and what would he need with the lavish lifestyles of some of the players he might be playing against?

   The 'Basic Wage' was for £350 per week, rising to £400 on 1 July 1987. Under 'Any Other Provisions', the schedule stipulated:

> In the event of the player scoring 14 goals in 1st team competitive matches during the 1986/87 season, the club agrees to pay a bonus of £5,000. Should the player go on to score a total of 20 goals in 1st team competitive matches during the 1986/87 season, then a further payment of £3,000 will be made.
>
>   In the event of the player scoring 14 goals in 1st team competitive matches during the 1987/88 season, the club agrees to pay a bonus of £5,000. Should

the player go on to score a total of 20 goals in 1st team competitive matches during the 1987/88 season, then a further payment of £3,000 will be made.

It is agreed that the appearance bonus of £50 which appears in the Incentive Schedule will only apply during the 1986/87 season, after which time it will revert to Nil.

The contract was signed for the Club by the secretary Graham Hover, and one of the directors. The 'Incentive and Bonus Schedule for Insertion in Players' Contracts' read as follows:

CANON LEAGUE

A bonus of £40 per point will be paid to players nominated by the Team Manager for all matches played in the First Division of the Canon League.

In addition, the following Final League Positional Bonuses will be available for distribution amongst players on a pro-rata Canon League appearance basis:

1st – £150,000 : 2nd – £75,000 : 3rd/6th – £50,000 : 7th/11th – £25,000

These amounts will reduce by 50% should the club, at any time during the currency of this agreement, be playing outside the First Division of the Canon League.

FOOTBALL ASSOCIATION CHALLENGE CUP

The following win bonuses will be paid to first team players nominated by the Team Manager for matches in the FA Cup Competition. 50% of the bonuses will be paid in respect of any drawn match.

3rd Round £200 4th Round £300 5th Round £400
6th Round £800 Semi-Final £1,000 Final £2,000

In addition, an appearance bonus will be paid to a maximum of 12 players, as follows:

Semi-Final £500 Final £1,000

MILK CUP

The following win bonuses will be paid to first team players nominated by the Team Manager for matches in the Milk Cup Competition. 50% of the bonus will be paid in respect of any drawn match from the 3rd to the 5th Round and the Final.

2nd Round £100 for winning the tie (£50 for playing in only one leg)
3rd Round £150 4th Round £200 5th Round £500
Semi-Final £1,000 for winning the tie (£500 for playing in only one leg)
Final £2,000

In addition, an appearance bonus will be paid to a maximum of 12 players, as follows:

Semi-Final £500 per match Final £1,000

APPEARANCE BONUS

The player will be entitled to an appearance bonus of £50 for each first-team competitive match in which he plays or is nominated substitute.

FOOTBALL LEAGUE FULL MEMBERS' CUP COMPETITION

The club agrees to pay to the players 20% of the Club's share of the Net Gate Receipts. This amount will become payable immediately upon the Club's exit from the Competition and shall be distributed on a pro-rata appearance basis.

To put this in perspective, each of Tottenham's players, come the Cup Final, was on a £10,000 bonus, win or lose. Keith Houchen, during the whole of that successful first year for Coventry, earned less than £28,000. Twenty years later, many footballers playing at the same level earn more than that in a week, and that's before they've even put on their boots.

Houchen signed for Coventry on 19 June 1986, in the middle of football's domestic holiday. India were batting in the Second Test Match at Headingley. *Wisden* opened its report as follows:

Hammonds Sauce Works Band, playing in front of the Football Stand, was the indisputable success for England during a match which India won by a resounding margin in under three and a half days. This victory, their first in England outside London, gave them a decisive 2-0 lead in the three-match series. Summing up England's performance, their chairman of selectors said: 'We were outplayed in every department.'

Groundsmen were making the final preparations for the Centenary Championships at Wimbledon, with players and officials being asked to undergo drugs tests for the first time. Meanwhile, in Mexico City, 'The Hand of God' was readying itself to intervene three days later in England's World Cup quarter-final against Argentina.

A month after signing for Coventry, a letter arrived at the Houchens' home at Rawcliffe, near York, from Graham Pearson, one of the Scunthorpe directors:

> We are now in receipt of the money from Coventry City regarding your transfer… On a personal note I would like to take this opportunity of wishing you every success with your new Club and trust that you will have happy memories of your short stay with United. Would you also pass on my regards to your family. Should you ever wish to visit our Club, please do not hesitate to contact me.

Scunthorpe had done their best, but it had been a strange interlude. Houchen relished a sense of involvement with the clubs he played for but, having been at Scunthorpe for such a short time and having not moved home, he felt strangely detached from the whole experience.

Houchen was joining a club that had led the way in the 1960s in innovating ways to market itself. Despite a down-trodden record in the First Division over the years, Coventry were in a truly different league to anything Houchen had hitherto experienced. Jimmy Hill and John Camkin penned a *Sky Blue Song* to the tune of the *Eton Boating Song*:

Let's all sing together,
Play up Sky Blues,
While we sing together,
We will never lose.

Proud Posh or Cobblers,
Oysters or anyone,
They can't defeat us,
We'll fight till the game is won.

For thirty-four years, *Tottenham or Chelsea, United or anyone* was the rarefied modulation. Reasons of grisly scansion apart, the choir at Coventry's new Ricoh Arena refuses yet to yield to the reality of *Proud Pilgrims or Canaries.*

Even that season wasn't all plain sailing. I was jogging on an old airfield near York – it's all built up now – when I stood on some glass. My foot flared up and I was rushed into hospital for a week pre-season. They had to take all this glass out of the bone in the foot and drain it off. I was off for several weeks. I then lost two weeks to a stomach bug.

Another dour season was in prospect for Coventry when they ran out at Upton Park for their opening fixture. Fans had heard of David Phillips, a Wales international midfielder signed from Manchester City. But where were the goals going to come from? Supporters' only recollection of Keith Houchen was his penalty for York on *Match of the Day*, their most frequent question: is he Whochen or Howchen?

Houchen and Phillips shared a house during their early months at Coventry. David Phillips recalls visiting Houchen at the Walsgrave Hospital when he had his foot up, to be greeted by a doleful pair of eyes. It had been a bad day on the stock market. Houchy was a thrifty Tyke, if ever there was one, and Phillo wondered whether to feel sorrier for the depressed investor or his wounded trotter. However, Houchen's main concern at the time was to help his dad secure the tenancy of a pub in Stockton.

Ian Painter was to be as afflicted by fitness problems as the outgoing Alan Brazil. The young Stoke striker never managed to ingratiate himself with Sillett. It didn't help matters when, on one occasion during training, he felled Sillett by kicking the ball hard at the back of his head.

I never expected to play in the West Ham game – you could have knocked me over with a feather. One player who took a right hump that day when he wasn't included was Micky Adams. He just went and sat on the side and wouldn't talk to anyone. I don't think he and Sillett really hit it off.

Defeat at West Ham was followed by a home win over Arsenal. In the third match, Houchen slid into Bobby Mimms in the Everton goal and broke two ribs, which set him back a month. He spent the autumn in that frustrating cycle of niggling injuries that so often blight a footballer's routine. It was worse still for one trying hard to impress his new manager and new supporters, striving to colour the few lines that formed the bunting on his arrival and to build on the profile in the match programme which highlighted his hobby of water skiing. It didn't help when, in doing David Phillips a good turn by chopping some wood for his stove, he whacked himself over the knuckles with the axe. However, a run of appearances in the Central League side, with three goals, began to restore his fitness and confidence.

In October, Dean Emerson – a tigerish and talented midfielder – was signed from Rotherham, having done well in his side's two second round League Cup matches against Coventry. Few City players down the years have been so quick to impress. He was soon joined from Rotherham by centre-back Kevan Smith. Smith's career at Highfield Road was benighted by injuries, but 'Smudge' was a very close friend of Keith Houchen. The two of them had played in the same County side whilst at school.

Curtis and Sillett made two major tactical adjustments. Cyrille Regis had scored only fifteen goals in his first two seasons at Coventry, and five of those were in a Milk Cup-tie against Chester. Regis persuaded Sillett to release him from his target-man role in order to make fuller use of his control, acceleration and penetration. It became Sillett and Curtis's most significant decision. The dribbling and shooting skills of Dave Bennett were then maximised by playing him alongside Regis in a 4-4-2 formation.

Handing Curtis and Sillett the reins had struck some Coventry supporters as little more than a parochial convenience but results began to suggest that, come the end of the season, the two men could be paraded for doing a little bit more than just keeping the team in the First Division. The side was a buoyant sixth in the table as the leaves continued to fall and a trip to Hillsborough beckoned at the end of October.

Someone who scores once, and only once, during a career of well over 700 senior games is almost certain to be a goalkeeper. Goalkeepers are as likely to score as cricketers to be dismissed for Hit the Ball Twice or Handled the Ball – Len Hutton was given out in a Test Match for Obstructing the Field. When it happens, it is either from a flukeish punt or in a kitchen sink role when everything needs to be thrown at the opposition. Jimmy Glass famously saved Carlisle from dropping out of the League when he manifested himself like a phantom in the Plymouth penalty-area. In January 1984, the Watford 'keeper Steve Sherwood scored against the Sky Blues, his kick taking Raddy Avramovic by surprise in the high wind.

Hillsborough lies in a valley and on the day of the game the wind was sweeping down from the Wadsley side of it. It was also raining hard. Ogrizovic was six to eight yards off his line as he stood clasping the ball at the Leppings Lane End. At the other end, Martin Hodge was standing well off his goal-line. You could see the strength of the wind at that moment from the angle of the rain under the floodlight in the left-hand corner. Oggy aimed a huge kick. The ball pitched in front of Hodge and took off over his head, brushing the inside of the left upright. It trickled unassumingly across the line and into the opposite corner of the goal. For a moment there was an eerie silence – 'Was it? Wasn't it?' – then the realisation. Poor Hodge stood with his head bowed. From then on, Coventry fans in the cages at the Leppings Lane End shouted 'Shoot, Shoot!' every time Oggy had the ball.

The Sky Blues visited Hillsborough twice more that season. Keith Houchen would be in the team for both matches.

This was the start of an *annus mirabilis* for Ogrizovic. It was fitting that the likes of Diego Maradona and Michel Platini should have the opportunity to play against him when he was selected for the Football League against The Rest of the World at Wembley the following August. His skill, sportsmanship, loyalty and professionalism place him amongst the very finest players ever to have represented Coventry City. His record of 601 first team appearances, 246 of them consecutive, is unlikely to be surpassed. Dion Dublin described him as 'the hardest working single professional I have ever worked with'.

The attractiveness and finesse of Coventry's football found its maturity at Highfield Road that Christmas. In an outstanding match that emulated any festive puff of panatelas, the Sky Blues twice came from behind to beat Tottenham. It was some game in which to score your first goal in the First Division. A year before, Keith Houchen was a member of the York team that had just lost at home to Donny Rovers.

Houchen scored Coventry's first goal with a header from a high right-wing cross from Emerson, and Regis made it 4-3 with the last act of the match. The spirit and excitement were a portent of the extraordinary weeks to come, but there was more frustration for the forgotten forward who had unexpectedly returned and made his mark.

We lost at home to Luton on New Year's Day. Low and behold, Sillett gave me a bollocking, and dropped me. I actually went home and cried. I had said to Yvonne, 'I bet you any money that if we lose the next match he will leave me out.' I couldn't believe it. I had waited all that time.

On 30 August 1986, an annual saga began all around the country. Meanwhile, at Folkestone's Cheriton Road, Essex went in to bat against Kent. 'A masterly innings by Gooch, with fine support from Fletcher, kept Essex going against the spin of Underwood', wrote *Wisden*. Just down the road at the Crabble Ground at Dover, where – almost to the day in 1935 – W. H. Ashdown smote an unbeaten 282 on the opening day of Kent's match with Derbyshire, Dover Athletic were playing out a goalless draw against Tunbridge Wells. It was the preliminary round of the Football Association Challenge Cup. The attendance, the fifth highest in 131 Preliminary Round matches, was 308; Coventry Sporting's official crowd for the visit of Racing Club Warwick was 32, the second lowest.

Dover Athletic scored three more goals in the Cup that season than the eventual winners. It was the centenary year of the original Tunbridge Wells club, whose percentage of wins per games played, has only recently been surpassed by King's Lynn as the highest in all-time FA Cup results.

Top scorers that day were Metropolitan Police who chalked up an 8-1 win at Chesham United. The most bizarre episode of the round occurred later at Ringmer where the referee called off a replay in extra-time due to bad light when Arundel were leading 3-0. Arundel repeated the score when the match was played again, but in just ninety minutes.

Over 160 of the 504 FA Cup entrants had already been eliminated by the time Essex won the County Championship on 16 September. Caernarfon Town had won the first of six ties. Only one other team would win as many.

On 10 January 1987, the First and Second Division clubs entered the fray. At Highfield Road, Coventry City entertained Bolton Wanderers. Bolton – Cup winners as recently as 1958 – would find themselves in the Fourth Division in a few months time, with Wolves, another fallen giant, among their opponents.

Supporters had only just begun to trust that something rather special was developing. There were still only 12,044 at Highfield Road for the Bolton game. Bolton's manager Phil Neal had dropped himself. Houchen was on the bench for the home side. Greg Downs, from twenty-five yards out, opened the scoring from Brian Borrows's free-kick. Further goals, from Regis and Bennett, gave the Sky Blues a 3-0 victory.

Being drawn at Manchester United in the fourth round would certainly have guaranteed the excitement of the bank manager, but many people also felt that a good result was within City's reach. United had already lost four League games at Old Trafford. Alex Ferguson was the new manager, Gordon Strachan and Terry Gibson two of his team. George Curtis returned with his players from a week in Spain and blithely announced to the cameras, 'Our name is on the Cup.'

Keith Houchen gave credence to his words. He was only playing because of injury to Bennett, but twenty minutes into the match, with the ball bobbling as if on a ping-pong table, he stabbed home the only goal of the game from a yard out.

I felt that this was a big, big game, I've got to perform in this. I knew I could do it and it was one of my better performances for Coventry up to then.

This time, the draw was a little kinder with an away tie at Second Division Stoke City. Twelve First Division clubs had already fallen and the draw guaranteed that another three would fall at the next hurdle. It was hardly a case of Foinavon in the Grand National, but the realisation was growing that this closely-knit Coventry side were a good bet for the Cup.

Memories of City's desperate win at the Victoria Ground two years before were still fresh in the mind. On a previous occasion, the shouts of someone accidentally locked in the Gents had gone unheard until the end of the game. Maybe he was still on the throne when they came to demolish the ground.

Stoke had crashed 4-1 at the Hawthorns a week before, ending a fourteen-match unbeaten run that included a 7-2 victory against Leeds. Coventry were without the suspended Emerson for the first time but won with a seventy-second minute goal from Michael Gynn. The jazz-loving Gynn, dipping and scudding with nervous energy and with something of the Chaplin in his face, was improvising to increasing effect and proving himself worthy of more than his usual walk-on role. The unmarked Phillips could not properly control Nick Pickering's cross but Gynn was there to put it away.

A Lloyd McGrath goal gave City an inspiring League victory in atrocious conditions at home to Sheffield Wednesday a week before the two teams met in the Sixth Round. But victory was expensive. The injury sustained by Emerson as a result of a bad tackle by Megson was to keep him out until the end of October. At least, Coventry could recall Bennett.

There had been 4,000 City fans at Old Trafford, 8,000 at Stoke; 15,000 would take over the Leppings Lane end at Hillsborough. The excitement of the Cup run was sweeping the city.

The most recent of Coventry's four previous quarter-final appearances had been in 1982 when Cyrille Regis scored a superb goal for West Brom. City's only win in three FA Cup ties at Hillsborough had been in 1911. The Owls were unbeaten at home in the FA Cup for fourteen years.

There are abiding memories of Cyrille Regis at Hillsborough, casting a cross-field ball like a yo-yo or feeding his team with that obstinate skill and determination, but especially of his goal. Those looking down from the Leppings Lane End had the perfect view of it. Bennett unleashed him and Regis drew the eye, the perfect vision of a centre forward bearing down on the far goal with the field his own. Hodge advanced and the goal magnified with Cyrille's deadly finish. What made the goal possible, though, was Houchen drawing the centre half to the touchline. This created space in the centre circle where Bennett received the ball via Downs.

A Sheffield Wednesday equaliser finally arrived in the sixty-seventh minute when Gary Megson forced his way through to score. Houchen remembers the enormous wall of sound from the opposition supporters, like a profound explosion. For a time then, Wednesday were on top.

With twelve minutes to go, Sillett was about to make a substitution, pulling off Houchen and pushing Bennett up front. In the very next attack, however, Houchen made himself irreplaceable when he scored with a deflected left-foot shot from just inside the area. It was the greatest substitution that never was. Five minutes later, Houchen scored again. A headed clearance caught him right in the face, bringing tears to his eyes as he struck the ball sweetly into the far corner from almost the same position as his first goal.

Houchen was not the only one in tears:

I could see men crying, I could actually see them crying.

The hero had dropped to his knees, fists clenched, in front of grown men for whom it was all too much. The following week, a letter arrived from the bank manager:

As always, I was a bit worried about what the contents might be. But it turned out to be a personal letter congratulating me and the rest of the lads on reaching the semi-final.

The pilgrimage swept northwards in the Sunday morning sun. Cars crammed the M1 with a sea of scarves swirling from every window to match the brightness of the sky.

At the Sheffield exit, the traffic ground to a halt. Passengers, full of tea no doubt, leapt from their coaches. Travellers were relieved that the 12.15p.m. kick-off had been put back a quarter-of-an-hour, although it would stretch the nerves of the players. What a tragedy such a decision would not be taken two years later.

This was the draw everyone at Coventry had prayed for as they huddled round their radios. The Sky Blues had certainly earned it, on the road at Old Trafford and Stoke, and already at Hillsborough in the quarter-finals. Watford were Tottenham's opponents in the other semi-final. Spurs crushed them 4-1 but they went on to finish ninth in the League. Leeds were Second Division, with half an eye on what was to be an unsuccessful play-off.

It is a cliché to say that semi-finals rarely live up to expectations and this one may have been the exception that proves the rule.

David Miller, in *The Times,* commented:

Here was a day when English football could be proud of an outstanding, traditionally hard, but fair cup tie.

Coventry and Leeds produced a semi-final of rare excitement and action, one of the best the competition has seen in the past 20 years or so. For two hours the game galloped along in a fever of incident and uncertainty, the epitomy of the English game which is so widely appreciated abroad as well as, though less so nowadays, at home.

It was a match as dramatic as Saturday's at Villa Park was bland. Hillsborough's south stand, though blotting out the backdrop of South Yorkshire landscape with its bleak aura of industrial revolution, has given the stadium an added sense of theatre, and both teams responded with a predominantly sporting and adventurous attitude which semi-finals so rarely generate.

Leeds looked anything but Second Division in the opening fifteen minutes as the Sky Blues were gripped by stage fright. These were the most uncertain moments of Coventry's whole Cup run. It was Steve Ogrizovic, playing the game of his life, who kept Coventry in the match. How Watford could have wished for him the previous day at Villa Park when their stand-in 'keeper Gary Plumley – son of the former Coventry secretary – was deemed to have cost his club dearly.

It had been little surprise that Leeds, who were dictating the early pace, took the lead after fourteen minutes. David Rennie, later to play for Coventry, headed in a corner from Micky Adams, whom Leeds had bought from City at the beginning of the year.

Oggy, who had beaten out a close range header in the second minute, made a superb point blank save to keep Coventry in the game minutes after Leeds scored. Gradually, the Sky Blues steadied themselves. Regis, who had twice been a loser at the semi-final stage, made three glaring misses in a nine-minute spell. He later conceded that his failure to cut out Rennie's header was playing on his mind.

In the dressing room at half-time, Lloyd McGrath, for whom the expression 'quietly spoken' could have been coined, burst into a rendition of 'Here we go'. Soon, he was joined by all his team-mates. The Coventry players emerged with their confidence reborn.

It was the introduction of Gynn fifteen minutes into the second half in place of the injured Pickering that saw the game begin to turn. Minutes afterwards, the Leeds defender Ormsby attempted to allow the ball to run over the line for a goal-kick, only to be left stranded as Bennett determined to keep some of the ball on the chalk. Having pursued this seemingly lost cause, Bennett crossed to Gynn who had enough space in which to finish off with a flighted, not to say slightly fluffed, shot. There were 27,000 City fans who hit the roof. This was the moment when Coventry, in Trevor Peake's words, 'rescued the result'.

Nine minutes later, there was another eruption as Houchen put the Sky Blues in front. Gynn's run created panic in the Leeds defence.

Houchen coolly collected the ball and rounded his old Orient colleague Mervyn Day before finding the net with a low left-foot shot. The hero was buried by his team-mates, who echoed the roar of the gigantic bank of sky blue in front of them, shouting, 'Roy, Roy.' It was Melchester Rovers, and this was the front page. It took a few moments to stem the flow of tears on Roy's cheeks.

Bob Bradshaw, a Coventry supporter, recalls:

> We all went berserk. I threw my arms in the air as the ball hit the net only to discover, when I ceased celebrating and looked to see how long there was to go, that my wrist watch (twenty-five years service presentation watch) was no longer on my wrist. I shouted to my mate next to me and the crowd in general, 'My watch has gone, anybody seen a watch.' A shout came back from a man some ten or twelve steps behind me, 'Here you are mate, I caught it as it flew by,' and my watch was passed down through several pairs of hands to me. What a lucky omen!

Coventry were nearly there. But the game took another unexpected turn seven minutes from time when Downs and Gynn failed to stop the tireless Andy Ritchie from putting in a great right-wing cross. Substitute Keith Edwards headed home from close range with his first touch of the ball. 'A match that was always memorable has now become wonderful,' enthused Martin Tyler from the commentary box. Roger Milford blew for full-time. One or two Leeds players, with the excitement of the equaliser, had forgotten that there would be extra-time. How galling that must have been. Coventry, too, had been so close but yet so far. This was no longer from the pages of a comic. John Sillett's pep talk would be crucial.

Ten minutes into extra-time and it was 3-2, 3-2 to Coventry. Adams fouled Bennett and Gynn's free-kick was headed into the crowded goalmouth by Regis. Houchen's left-foot shot was blocked. Bennett pounced. It proved to be the winner and it was appropriate that Bennett should be the scorer. He had taken the laces out of Adams's boots that afternoon, making the first goal and so nearly several others.

There could have been another twist as extra-time ebbed away. Ogrizovic, arms outstretched in front of him, dived full length at the feet of Edwards. Just as Oggy had kept City alive in the early minutes, it was this absurdly brave save that ensured that Coventry City would be playing at Wembley.

Gordon Banks, writing in the *Daily Mirror,* was effusive in his praise of Ogrizovic:

> On this season's form he is the best 'keeper in the country... he has taken on a coating of extra-special skill and brilliance that separates the great goalkeepers from the good ones.

It had been a semi-final of rare quality, of fluctuation and skilfulness, of high resolve but sportsmanship. Coventry City had booked their place in the wider public consciousness. Derek Hodgson, in *The Independent,* reflected:

> What was billed as the unfashionable, down market semi-final crackled into two hours of passion and poise as Coventry defeated a daring Leeds to reach their first FA Cup final in 104 years before an enthralled 51,372 spectators at Hillsborough yesterday. The sight of the new £1 million Sheffield Kop as a mountain of sky blue and white in the habitual victory salute of the scarves will stay in the memory.

The sun and warmth suggested summer. Billy Bremner, wrapped in a fawn-coloured coat, offered John Sillett his hand. One of Leeds's greatest players, he was sacked as manager the following year. He died prematurely in 1997.

It had been a joyful occasion, beautifully organised and policed. How incomprehensible that the semi-final at Hillsborough two years later could result in such horror. On this occasion, as the fans collapsed into their coaches, it was with mere exhaustion.

The *Coventry Evening Telegraph,* in its leader on 13 April 1987, commented:

> The City feels young again today. It has a skip in its step, a smile on its face and a tear in its eye. It has dreamed the impossible dream and woken up to find it reality. Coventry City at Wembley... the boyhood ambition of so many fans long ago and now realised in their dotage. Nobody was talking about anything else today. And how marvellous that is for the city. Not since the sixties has a Midland team got to the Cup Final. The prosperous place it was then is very much different now for Coventry as for the rest of the region. The Sky Blues' lusty victory on a glorious spring day in Yorkshire will give

people something to cheer and be proud of. Yet the city is just starting to believe in itself again and soccer success can symbolise it. The people's game has the power to do that as anyone who's been in the factory on the Monday after a big result will testify. George Curtis, John Sillett and their players have lifted the city's morale sky-high. What was possible for them against all the odds is possible now for us all.

Seven days later, on 19 April 1987, Keith was at Yvonne's side as she gave birth to Ross. Some fans were determined that the Houchens should call their son Roy.

I've described a few things this season as the greatest moment of my life but there's nothing compared to seeing your son born. It puts everything else into perspective and you suddenly realise that you tend to exaggerate a little when you are talking about scoring goals.

7

Wembley

'The day will come when everyone will be famous for fifteen minutes,' said Andy Warhol. Quite what Warhol meant, and quite why we should quote him, is not clear. When Myra Hindley, even now, is regularly thrust in front of us without any apparent justification, we are nonetheless well aware of what she represents. Warhol's face is one of the most immediately recognisable images of the last century, but for what reason? What is fame, and does fame matter?

Warhol, who once made a photographic study of Pelé, died from a heart attack following gall bladder surgery only twelve weeks before Coventry won the Cup. On that May afternoon at Wembley, the stadium's capacity had been shorn by a couple of thousand. For years, the purity of the traditional figure of 100,000 had brought summation to a domestic season in which attendance figures have always enjoyed a mysterious fetish. Even football fans would have been surprised to find Kenneth Tynan's theatre reviews, for instance, published alongside the 'gate' for the show.

At Wembley, there were more than just the 98,000 pairs of eyes looking on from the touchline. And there were more even than the millions of viewers watching the live coverage on BBC and ITV. Around the planet, not just in Scandinavia where they are traditionally treated to English football on a Saturday afternoon but live in sixty countries, there was a vast television audience. Across swathes of Europe, the subcontinent, the Far East, Australasia, through parts of Africa and the Americas, whether as chatter in the corner of a bar or a familiar reassurance in the hiatus of another day, focused through rapt attention or in a last blink from a hospital bed, what suddenly happened caught the breath of the world. And in the succeeding minutes, that moment excited more comment than anything in life, and the man at the heart of that moment, briefly – only briefly – became the most talked about man on earth.

In the days before Television considered it necessary to smear all documentary programmes in background music, John Betjeman made a glorious film for the BBC called *Metro-Land*. Striking north from Baker Street on the Metropolitan Line, Betjeman punctuated the spontaneous sounds of his journey by alighting on the quaint and quintessential along the way.

The entrepreneurial vision of Sir Edward Watkin – like Queen Victoria he lived from 1819 to 1901 – was that the Metropolitan Line should extend into the Midlands as part of a connection between Manchester and Paris. With inimitably puckish delight, Betjeman described Watkin's grandiose plan to erect a rival to the Eiffel Tower. A competition was mounted and various weird and wonderful plans submitted. Work started and the structure rose to a treetop platform. The public, however, did not respond to such fantasy and 'Watkin's Folly', as it became known, was abandoned to rust above the branches. The Metropolitan Line itself later ran out of puff at Brill and Verney Junction.

Betjeman addressed the camera, 'This is where London's failed Eiffel Tower stood… here on this Middlesex turf.' 'Since then the site has become quite well known,' he insouciantly added, at which, with a coup de theatre to match the litotes, the lens shrank to reveal Betjeman standing aside a sprinkler on the edge of the centre circle in Wembley Stadium.

The Metropolitan Railway Company had acquired the Wembley Park estate in 1889 as the site for a leisure centre for northwest London. There was an early smidgeon of sporting recognition when the Australians played a match against Wembley Park during their 1896 cricket tour of England. The game finished on the second afternoon with the visiting captain, Harry Trott, rolling the hosts over with his leg-spin.

Trott died in a mental institution. His younger brother Albert was the first and, to this day, the only person ever to hit a six over the pavilion at Lord's. Albert settled in England and predeceased Harry by shooting himself in the head in a room in Harlesden, two stops down the Bakerloo from Wembley. His landlady discovered the body, along with a will scribbled on the back of a laundry ticket bequeathing her the wardrobe.

The Wembley Park side, incongruously, included 'The Demon' Spofforth, the legendary Australia fast bowler. Spofforth had long since withdrawn as the scourge of England batsmen but *Wisden* commented on his 6 for 49 that he could 'still be deadly on a treacherous pitch'.

In 1924, a local estate agent commended the Chalk Hill Estate, 'Adjacent to Wembley Park Station, and The British Empire Exhibition in a picturesque and healthy locality, within close touch of London, yet in the open country beyond the recognised suburban area'. Its high-rise successor of the 1960s became so notorious for crime that it had to be pulled down.

On the other side of the road stands Brent Town Hall. For years, companies such as Philips came there to record the LSO and other great orchestras in its main hall. One day, the ceiling collapsed during a flood. Repairs were made too hastily and the precious acoustic was lost for ever.

Now and again, the corridors of the Town Hall still echo to the caricatures of *Peter Simple*. Try not to place too much emphasis on the word Christmas, and beware of councillors' arms raised as high as the building plans they pass – even the wilderness above the railway embankments allures developers' eyes. The busy High Road boasts several good shops, but the authorities completely ignore the threat to shoppers from cyclists illegally riding its pavements.

Wembley continued to grow. Walter Citrine, general secretary of the TUC between 1926 and 1946 and siphon of popular opinion relied upon by Baldwin during the Abdication Crisis, later chose to be ennobled as the 1st Baron Citrine of Wembley.

As a reminder of Wembley's parochial past, rural lanes still lead to the Welsh Harp, the Brent reservoir which is used for sailing and water sports. On its banks there was once a greyhound track at which, in 1876, a mechanical hare was tested for the very first time.

The Hare Controller became an indispensable figure at greyhound meetings, enjoying pride of place on the printed programme. At Wembley, dog racing generated the stadium's steadiest income, more than pop or the Pope, let alone the Olympics or the World Cup. For all that, on a winter's evening, there might be only a few score people clustered on the small piece of terracing open under the Royal Box.

Sometimes, the immortal rabbit would overrun the finish with the dogs still giving chase. 'C'mon FIVE, C'mon THREE,' punters might shout, betting slips shrivelled in their empty hands. Once in a while, a dog would escape through the fence, the dark wastes of terracing echoing to its misty cries.

One June night in 1963, the dogs – and the bikes of the Wembley Lions – gave way to Henry Cooper and Cassius Clay:

> I'm going to whup him like I'm his Daddy. I'm going to whup him like he stole something.

For a leap second in the fourth round, as Clay crumpled to the ground, the assertion appeared uncertain. However, Cooper's eyes – never as resilient as his left hook – had already begun to gush.

Cyrille Regis, a child in Stonebridge – between Wembley and Harlesden – was once turned down for a job as a porter by the hotel next to the stadium. The particular form of abuse that had greeted Cassius Clay was still prevalent when Regis abandoned his electrical skills for a career in football.

Across the hill from the stadium, Regis grew up playing in King Edward VII Park under the spire of Harrow-on-the-Hill. That gravity of balance, that ability to strew opponents like a scythe, took shape in this early haven.

Neatly-trowelled flower beds flaunt Lady's Mantle, Phlox and September Charm. Groups of brave brats may harangue the unsuspecting, while some kids slope off into the bushes to play with drugs, but King Edward VII Park is predominantly a peaceable Babel – of Tamil, Gujarati, Polish, Arabic, and more. A demure procession of saris, the occasional skritter and skreak of a flock of parakeets – yellow breasts burnished in the sinking sun, and the bobbing caps of distant bowlers scuttling up the green, chaperone al fresco games of cricket into the cowl of the evening. And an Asian gentleman at gully, contemptuous of any earnest running, shuffles off his shooting-stick to dispense one last class in batsmanship.

The new stadium has arisen. In the nearby Arena, once the Empire Pool, you pass dressing room signs redolent of Ice Hockey, Jack Kramer's tennis circus and the World Professional Tennis Tournaments of fifty years ago, the sign writing as much of its period as the Van Allen Simplified

Scoring System. Outside, the Horse of the Year Show was groomed from temporary stables set down like a caravanserai around an oasis. On this site, overseen by the facades of the old Pavilions, was the lake of the Empire Exhibition, close to the Toy Railway where newsreels captured Queen Mary, inseparable from her toque, and the bowler-hatted King George V crouched for the ride.

Across the fence from the Arena is the dust of CTS Recording Studios. All of us, at one time or another, have been surrounded by music that was recorded there. Wait for the fruit parfait girl to switch on the lights before rising from your seat in the cinema and you will see the studio's name on the credits of hundreds of British and American movies, from *Gandhi* to *007*, *Batman* to *Superman*. Look too at the small print on the back of your CD collection. CTS – like the Twin Towers – was turned to rubble, but its sounds survive beyond bricks and mortar.

The restored bells of Coventry's bombed cathedral rang out for the first time in a hundred years. The bells had fallen into disrepair before the turn of the century and had been recently restored with a £100,000 grant from the late Sir William Lyons, founder of Jaguar.

The bells were due to be rung for the first time on 25 May 1987 to mark the twenty-fifth anniversary of the consecration of the new cathedral.

Provost Semper said:

> I decided to pre-empt it. To people outside Coventry this may seem a pretty
> trivial event, but to us it is not. What this football team has done is to give us
> hope of a new resurrection in Coventry like the one we had after the war.

At the end of Morning Service, the congregation applauded and cheered as choirboys donned sky blue scarves over their surplices and sang out in exultation. At St Thomas More Church in Cheylesmore, an anonymous member of the congregation left £100 in the collection plate with a note attached: 'For the poor, from a City fan'. Later in the day, nearly a quarter of a million people – most of the population of Coventry – crowded into the Sunday drizzle to rejoice.

The De Vere Hotel overlooking Pool Meadow had been offering a special deal for people wanting to avoid the Cup Final. Not surprisingly, there were no takers. For this was more than just a football match, a great one at that. It was more than romance over the triumph of the underdog, more even than civic pride at the greatest day in the local football club's history.

This was about a spirit of community in an age of less and less certainty. For a moment, football transcended its many problems, problems overseen at the time by a government intent on holding the game to account for the wider social evils that bedevilled it.

It was a human allegory, the story of years of getting by and hanging on, of everything then coming together in a marriage of circumstances, personalities and talents – in one extraordinary achievement.

It was the story of Keith Houchen launching himself across the turf to score one of the most spectacular goals ever seen at Wembley Stadium. It was in that moment, as Houchen's head made contact to level the scores at 2-2 that the sea of Sky Blues supporters behind the goal – and probably the Tottenham contingent too – realised whose spirit was going to prevail that afternoon.

George Curtis and John Sillett, jigging and gallumphing together with the trophy, personified the balance of contrasts and coincidences so vital to success. It was a triumph for 'Schnoz', who had returned to the club he had once played for and from which more recently he had been sacked as youth coach. From the moment of the fourth round win at Old Trafford and being drawn at Stoke, from having the 'Our name's on the Cup' feeling for the first time, the two men devotedly and enthusiastically kept their team bubbling.

That elusive chemistry of character and ability had been taking shape over many months. More than anything, Sillett and Curtis fostered an unquenchable team spirit. They recognised, too, how important it was to involve the wives and partners in this, so that social events became more than just 'Boys' nights out'.

When it came to the Cup ties, the boys and their masters relaxed and prepared for each hurdle at the same Dorset hotel. Not far into the adjoining county, Sillett had grown up in the hamlet of Nomansland in the New Forest, just south of Salisbury. His parents had moved there to keep a pub when he was six months old.

Jake Findlay, Coventry City's reserve goalie, went fishing in Cup Final week. There was not much else for him to do – Oggy had not missed any of Coventry's 148 games since joining the club. Findlay, a more than able fisherman born at the centre of a raspberry-growing district at Blairgowrie, presented Houchen with a trout. It poisoned him, and Houchen was laid low throughout the week. He even had to miss the visit to the stadium on the day before the Final. A few weeks earlier, he needed stitches around the eye after a head injury at Luton, and was also injured in the home match against Liverpool, causing him to miss the last three League games.

Tottenham, like Coventry, had enjoyed an improved season. In the League, they rose from tenth to third, finishing fifteen points behind Everton, six behind Liverpool, and eight ahead of Coventry in tenth place. Tottenham lost a semi-final replay to Arsenal in the Littlewoods Cup. In the FA Cup, they were favoured with home draws in their first three ties, beating Scunthorpe United 3-2, Crystal Palace 4-0 and Newcastle United 1-0. In the quarter-finals, they won 2-0 at Wimbledon who finished fifth in the League, before sweeping aside Watford.

On the Coventry side, only Dave Bennett for Manchester City against Tottenham in the 1981 Final, and Cyrille Regis a couple of times for England, had any comparable experience to the Tottenham players of playing at Wembley, although Oggy had been on the bench three times for Liverpool. Aside from Clemence, Hughton, Ardiles and Hoddle who were survivors from Tottenham's 1982 team (Tottenham were also finalists in the League Cup that year), Glenn Hoddle, Ray Clemence, Gary Mabbutt, Steve Hodge, Gary Stevens and Chris Waddle could boast fifty-eight Wembley caps between them. Richard Gough (Scotland) and Chris Hughton (Republic of Ireland) were established internationals and Clive Allen, too, had played for England. Ossie Ardiles (Argentina) and Nico Claesen (Belgium) were major international stars. On the other hand, aside from Regis and Pickering (who had one England cap), Coventry's only international player was David Phillips of Wales. The Tottenham team had cost £4,045,000, Coventry's £972,500.

Tottenham first won the Cup in 1901 when they were a Southern League club. There was a crowd of 110,820 at the Crystal Palace to see them beat Sheffield United. They won again in 1921, 1961, 1962, 1967, 1981 and 1982, and had never lost an FA Cup Final. Only Aston Villa, whose most modern victories were in 1920 and 1957, had won the Cup as often. With number conundrums becoming the fashion on the puzzle pages, North London newspaper readers were quick to identify a potential sequence with 61,62,67,81,82...

It was Keith Houchen's first season at this level – 'just to go to these places and be in them was incredible' – and for most of the Coventry team it was a thrill simply to be playing in Wembley Stadium. However, it was not a moment for feeling humble – they were not at the Palace for a Garden Party. It had been a massive turnaround for everyone at Coventry City – a lot of the team had spent the last three years struggling against relegation – so they wanted more from Wembley than merely to autograph their experience with the privilege.

Realising how few of the Coventry team had played at Wembley, John Sillett got the permission of the groundsman to train there.

Sillett said:

> The ground staff even provided piped crowd noises to give us a sense of the atmosphere. The visit was to protect the players so none of them would be surprised on the day. I think that played a very important part in our winning.

Sillett ensured that the preparations for the Final were perfect:

> We had a superstition that if we saw a bride on the day of the match we would never lose. We were staying in Marlow, and there was a church on the opposite side of the Thames. So on the morning of the match I organised a boat to bring a bride across the river, and she met all the players.

At dinner on the night before the Final, there were little presents by the plates. All the management and staff were there. The players thought that they might get a special memento, an engraved watch maybe – something to wear for ever – to commemorate the achievement of playing in the Cup Final. There was nothing like that, at least not on the players' tables.

I loved the chairman, John Poynton. He was a fantastic, really lovely man, but all we got was a funny sort of pen.

The players drifted away from dinner, some to rooms around the hotel, some for a beer.

We were not one of those clubs where you couldn't have a drink. One or two of us might have a pint or a half or something.

I slept, but I woke up at about five or five thirty and I wanted the match to start straight away. Before big matches I used to get this really serene feeling and

I was just ready for it. I'd walk out on the pitch and feel that I was not actually touching the floor. It felt really strange.

I was rooming with Dave Phillips as usual, so I got up and put my kit on and went running. I was jogging around the grounds of the hotel. It was dawn, the hotel was asleep and there was a bit of mist coming off the river. I was just jogging. I remember thinking, 'Are we going to lose it, how's it going to finish up?' So, I imagined what the match itself was going to be like. I hadn't been on the pitch like the other lads.

Knowing Dave Phillips, he wouldn't have been asleep, he would have been sat up doing something, but he didn't come jogging. We were first down to the canteen. Slowly, all the lads came down. You could start to feel the electricity, and there were reporters around.

It remains a tradition, unusual in the entertainment industry other than in sport, for players to share rooms. David Phillips recalls another occasion when he and Houchen were rooming together:

Years ago we were with CCFC in Majorca, lapping up the sun, sinking liquid refreshments as we did, all day every day. On about the third day, Houch disappeared up to the room at about 8.30p.m. after a long day. I followed half-an-hour later.

As I entered the room I could hear Houch sleeping. I had a quick shower, got into my trunks, turned on the lights and shouted at Houch to get up as everyone was down at the pool waiting. In his sleep he got out of bed, went into the shower, washed and came back into the room with his trunks on. 'Come on then,' he said. 'What's the time?' 'Just after 9.30,' came the reply. He opened the curtains to see it was pitch black outside. 'What's going on here then?' The next few words were unprintable…

It is the only occasion Phillips can remember his pal getting really stitched up although, keen drivers as they were, Houchen once responded to Phillips's challenge to race him home, only to be greeted by Phillips at the front door holding two mugs of tea.

Houchen had clear memories of early visits to Wembley when he was a Hartlepool player:

I went to the Cup Final in 1978, when Osborne scored for Ipswich. We always got tickets at Hartlepool, and Trevor Smith and I drove down. We slept in the car-park at South Mimms in the Ford Escort – we had big sheepskin coats on. In the morning, we drove as close to Wembley as we could get. We were where all the Ipswich fans were gathering so we joined them and sat in the pub and had a few drinks.

Then we came round the corner where the tube station is, looking right down Wembley Way. That was the first time I saw it.

I nearly got arrested. I was so fascinated by the players on the bus, seeing them looking out of the windows, that I was leaning over the parapet as the bus disappeared underneath. He was a young bobby. He grabbed a hold of me and said, 'I've told you once, do you want me to arrest you?' It all came back to me when I was sitting on the coach.

We stood right at the back of the goal. I was watching the players walking around with their suits and thinking, 'God, that must be fantastic, you've got the best, you've got your lovely suits on, it's a lovely sunny day, the crowds are coming in, you're about to play in a Cup Final.' I thought, 'Oh God, I would love to do that, I really would.' That's what I really, really wanted to do.

At 12.45p.m., the coach eased out of the car park at The Compleat Angler, at the start of its hour long journey to Wembley. As it reached the other end, it began to grind slowly through the crowds like a ship cutting through ice. The figures within froze into smiles and waves. The huge towers, like icebergs, swung into view. Hands were thrust towards the windows from a sea of heads, some spanking their encouragement on the bodywork, others snapping their cameras as if at a family wedding. There were more and more scarves, and an occasional not-so anonymous face recalled from a social club or the paper shop. Some people were rooted to the spot by burgers, favours and souvenir programmes, while chants and shouts and noise – ever-increasing noise – carried the coach on its way.

Not everything in the lead up to the Cup Final went entirely smoothly. At the end of the last game, fans took to the pitch to demonstrate their support for the team. The police sent on the horses. For a few moments, we looked on aghast from the stands at a potential catastrophe.

A leader in the *Coventry Evening Telegraph* commented:

It was an unforgivable over-reaction... The result of what the police did badly frightened a lot of people and offended many more. More seriously, two disabled lads were knocked to the ground and a pregnant woman kicked in the back. For them a pleasurable day ended in terror. Because a policeman couldn't tell the difference between a riot and a carnival.

The club made a cock-up over the sale of tickets, but Frank Keating, in *The Guardian*, was able to congratulate Coventry on a Scrooge-like change of heart over its choice of charabanc:

> To their great credit, having won that vibrant semi-final so chivalrously, Coventry's players and management sat down to rethink their attitude. They came to the conclusion that they wanted to share the club's day of days with the world and its wife. Their journey up Wembley Way, they decided, would be spiritual not temporal, and based on emotion not Mammon.
>
> It was a heartening change of tack. A national bus company offered the players' bonus pool an incredible £18,000 just to have them use one of their coaches… No thanks, said Coventry, we're using our own team-bus driven by Dave Bacon, who's got this far and why should we ruin his day for a bundle of booty?

Harry Shaw, the local firm, had supplied a £105,000 new coach. The aloof alertness of Dave, a cockney and former London bus driver now living in Binley, waited as if on a pass. The gear stick was goaded like a woman's knee and the window wound down for intimate directives from uniformed officials. Outside the other window, a horse casually raised its tail. There was a camera crew on board to bring communion to the front room, and convey the lads' reactions as they drew near to the shrine.

The intimacy of the coach was about to be turned inside out. At the side of the ground at the top of the industrial estate, Houchen watched Dave cross his hands over the wheel and coax his vehicle through the gates. The huge doors of the stadium were open, awaiting them. It was like driving into the cavern of a cross-channel ferry.

The players rose, newspapers abandoned behind them. Had any of them read James Lawton's piece in the *Daily Express* about Coventry's prospects?

> …they play the game honestly and with an understanding of where its beauty lies.
>
> It is not in the kick-and-rush of Wimbledon, the sterile long ball of Watford and Sheffield Wednesday and all those other imitators of football whose doctrine yields limited success at the cost of prolonged brain damage.

Coventry shouldn't really live with Spurs. But I think they will… even to
the point of nicking it, perhaps by the odd goal in five.

Lawton was not the only one to choose right. Jimmy Hill, sitting beside
John Motson in the BBC Television commentary box, congratulated his
colleague on correctly forecasting the score, and Neville Foulger, about
to sign off as the *Coventry Evening Telegraph*'s chief football correspondent,
had splashed 3-2 over the centre pages of 'The Pink' the previous week.

As the players got off the coach, the mayhem seemed to have subsided.
The high ceiling in the passageway was enough to dwarf any aspiring giant.
Beyond the shade and the reassuring intimacy of smiles and familiar laughs
and handshakes from members of the Highfield Road staff – even the
most informal of them adorned in fresh suits – was the sun and blue sky at
the top of the tunnel. The atmosphere was informal, the noise of chanting
distanced by business-like words of supervision which echoed around the
players as they were ushered into the dressing rooms. Only Dave seemed
completely relaxed, his job done, a cigarette cupped in his hand.

Coventry City were in the North Dressing Room. Teams were allo-
cated the dressing rooms on an alphabetical basis with the first-lettered
team always going in the North Dressing Room. There was only one
occasion when this did not happen, in 1964 when Preston played West
Ham, and Preston were given the wrong dressing room by mistake.

The kit manager had got there early to do his homework. He had
acquainted himself with the layout like a prospective home buyer, 'Down
there lads. Toilets on the right. There's a lounge at the end.' Having been
resting his stomach the previous day, Houchen was the only one who
had gone to bed without an image of the room where he would be peg-
ging his hopes.

The players' pool could have been turned into a very nice jackpot
indeed, had Coventry accepted the £25,000 from a kit manufacturer
who was all tooled up to roll out a brand new design for the players to
model at Wembley.

John Sillett said:

We stick to the original kit and colours we've used all season. Why should we
join in the con? There's a lot of unemployment around here, and I know parents
coughed up to buy kids our kit for Christmas. Why should they be badgered to
fork out for another set, just because Coventry City want to get rich quick?

So, the kit was laid out as normal, little considerations taken care of. There were familiar hold-alls, embrocations, bandages and tassels, and more than anything the banter of familiar voices. It was a temporary home, but full of the usual habits and routines.

The dressing rooms were massive and they had a waiter working there bringing you teas and whatever you wanted.

I put my suit on to walk on to the pitch. We walked along the tunnel. It was long and dark. It's like a big television screen at the end, black and white, and colour.

Where were the Tottenham team? Was it the same for them? It was different from being in the dressing room at Highfield Road, or anywhere else for that matter. Others had been there before but there wasn't the common ether of a club dressing room. This was big and bare and impersonal, an uncharted territory, out of which the resilient or the fortunate had stitched themselves into scrapbooks but from where some had emerged with the desolation of an Oates. Houchen recalled the mail on the floor of the club house at Woodford the night he signed for Orient. Who had been there before him, and where were they going? At the top of the tunnel waited the flicker of cameras, a shimmer in the world's awareness, perhaps, or a stain to be rued for ever.

Doubtless, onlookers would be searching for signs of 'pressure' and 'tension' – surprised that anything could be more stressful than sitting in the armchair peeling open a six-pack.

Yes, you get nervous before a game, your legs feel like lead for about five or ten minutes. Once you are out playing it's different, but I think if you do get nervous the nervous energy tends to drain the strength out of you and you get very heavy-legged. I did get it a few times when I was under pressure, probably at Hibs more than anywhere.

But I used to get this feeling before a big match when the hairs on the back of my neck prickled up and I was just ready for playing. It wasn't nerves at all, just this really strong sensation.

The players began to change, their kits sparkling from the aura of the training ground washing machine and its attendant, Mrs Joyce Hirons.

There were final visits from outsiders, absolution from the lips of Sillett and Curtis, one last piss, and a reassuring glance at the mirror.

In the distance, the cheering dulled as *Abide with Me* cranked up. In older days, abandoned song sheets swept across the terraces as cleaners came to clear up the mess. But now, the song sheets had been swept away for ever. The England manager, Bobby Robson, could be seen forlornly scouring his match programme for the words. The nearest he would have got to them was an article concerning the rather different musical preferences of the players. At least the Massed Bands of HM Royal Marines could lend gravitas to W.H. Monks's *Eventide* tune. People know the words of the National Anthem, like some even know the Lord's Prayer, but, as with *Land of Hope and Glory*, most need prompting with *Abide with Me*.

The time had come. Cyrille's chest resembled an armoured breastplate while Oggy, even taller than Houchy, clutched his gloves like a powder puff. A jaunty smile lit up Lloyd's sheepish eyes and Killer, enthused by his breakfast kipper, emerged from beneath luxurious locks of hair.

The contestants seeped into the tunnel, all of a sudden confronted by their adversaries. But for the colour of the kits, there was little to tell them apart. In a lonely excitement, with a little chatter and the odd laugh, the players paused before the illusion they had come to create, troops caught in a Christmas armistice. With practice balls popping around the tunnel like balloons, and boots primed against the concrete, Wembley provided no real rehearsal, just the real thing.

All at once, like boxers skipping, victims and masters were venturing forth, their studs leaping and repeating along the vault. Now they were in line, managers at the front, captains behind, except that Coventry didn't have a manager.

The Coventry secretary, Graham Hover, had appealed to the FA to allow both George Curtis and John Sillett to lead out the Coventry team. Anxious to avoid setting a precedent, the FA declined, but Curtis had already offered to stand aside.

Houchen recalls standing close to Ossie Ardiles in the tunnel:

He used to get a shy, diffident look on his face, a world-class player at that. I think he was dying to shake my hand but he was a bit wary. In the end we did. I thought that was nice.

1 Houchen family holiday *c*.1964: Patrick, Jackie, Mum, Jimmy, Dennis, Keith.

4 Keith (holding Albert) and Mr Houchen sitting on Keith's Ford Capri outside the family home in Orwell Street, Middlesbrough.

Opposite above: 2 Scottish holiday: Jackie, Dennis, Jimmy, Keith, Patrick (clockwise).

Opposite below: 3 Dennis, Jimmy, Jackie, Keith, Dad.

Above: 5 Jackie, Keith, Mum, Dennis, Jimmy (clockwise).

7 Sacred Heart Football Team 1970/71 (Keith is second from the left in the bottom row) with Mr Turnbull.

Above: 8 Hartlepool United *v.* Aldershot, 1 September 1979.

Opposite below: 6 Illicit anglers: Keith, Dennis, Jimmy.

9 A scrawny teenager…

10 ...begs to differ

11 Keith Houchen's first League goal, Hartlepool United *v.* Barnsley, 24 March 1978. The goalkeeper is Peter Springett.

12 Seaton Carew, 17 July 1982: Trevor Smith (best man), Billy Ayre, Mark Lawrence, Mr and Mrs Houchen.

13 A rainy day at Brisbane Road.

Above: 14 York City,
Fourth Division Champions
1984, Keith Houchen
standing behind Keith
Walwyn.

Right: 15 York City *v.*
Lincoln City, 20 April 1985.

16 Last minute penalty, York City *v.* Arsenal, 26 January 1985.

17 A split-second before the crowd reacts.

Right: 18 Keith Houchen and Cyrille Regis.

Below: 19 Cup Final breakfast: David Phillips and Keith Houchen.

20 John Sillett leads out, from right to left: Brian Kilcline, Steve Ogrizovic, Greg Downs, Cyrille Regis, Lloyd McGrath, Trevor Peake, Dave Bennett, Keith Houchen, Graham Rodger, Nick Pickering and Steve Sedgley. Michael Gynn and David Phillips are hidden. On the right is Ray Clemence.

21 Coventry City *v.* Tottenham Hotspur, FA Cup Final, Wembley Stadium, 16 May 1987.

22 Coventry City 3–2 Tottenham Hotspur.

23 'You'd be very welcome here Gary, but I don't think that's what they meant by sending you to Coventry.'

Above: 24 Hibernian *v.* Dundee United 1989, with the Easter Road crowd close to the action.

Opposite above: 25 Hibernian *v.* Celtic, Scottish FA Cup Semi-final, Hampden Park, 16 April 1989.

Opposite below: 26 Hartlepool United 1996/97. From left to right, back row: Chris Homer, Ian Gallagher, Graeme Lee, Denny Ingram, Sean McAuley. Middle row: Joe Allon, Jamie Allinson, Stephen Howard, Paul O'Connor, Glen Davies, Stephen Pears, Ian McGuckin, Chris McDonald, Billy Horner (Youth Team Coach). Front row: Gary Hinchley (Physiotherapist), Chris Beech, Stephen Halliday, Mick Tait (Assistant Manager), Keith Houchen (Manager), Mark Cooper, David Clegg, Brian Honour (Reserve Team Coach).

Left: 27 Keith and Ross.

Below: 28 Cara, Yvonne, Ross, Keith.

The instructions in the Football Association's *Programme of Arrangements* were specific and well-worn:

2.48p.m. The players must be ready to leave the dressing rooms. Mr H.N. Bird, FA Deputy Secretary will inform the players, referee and linesmen when to leave and will conduct them to the entrance of the playing arena. They will enter the arena side by side on receipt of a signal from Mr A. Duinkerk at the arena end of the Royal Tunnel and will proceed across the field of play and take up their positions at the flags opposite the Royal Tunnel in two lines facing each other for presentation to Her Royal Highness The Duchess of Kent, the Coventry City team at the blue flag and the Tottenham Hotspur team at the white flag. The referee and linesmen will take up their positions as indicated in the diagram below. Mr Bird will supervise these arrangements. Photographers must wait until after the teams are in position before they enter the playing field.

The two lines were on the move. The din grew louder and louder, the mouth of the tunnel wider and wider. Freshly laundered creases on their kits and hair neatly parted as if for a school parade, the players strode out. As the gladiators emerged, the roar was immediate and engulfing.

When you break, it's like nothing you can describe. There is this crescendo of noise bouncing off the middle and the colour just hits you. I remember that very, very vividly. I knew where my family were sitting because I had seen them when we went out there in our suits.

When I was wandering around with my suit on, I remembered what I felt when I came to watch in 1978. I picked out my mum and dad and people in the crowd.

For Keith Houchen, the noise was a reminder of the enormous wall of sound when Sheffield Wednesday had equalised in the quarter-final. Ahead of him, heaving from ear to ear behind the mouth of the far goal was a vast terrace saturated in a blue as intense as the sky itself. For some players, it was a relief to walk into that noise, into the cauldron of the moment, the hubbub of the occasion. Others needed to test the water, look to where they knew their family and friends were sitting, and ingratiate themselves with the experience.

John Sillett glanced behind him to make sure that Kilcline and the others were following. He could recall running out onto the pitch as captain of Plymouth Reserves only to discover that he had left his team-mates behind in the tunnel.

One piece of news was kept from Sillett at Wembley. It was the fact that his brother, Peter, had just been taken very ill and was on a life-support machine.

As the players walked out to the generous and sunny reception, John Motson told BBC TV viewers:

> If anybody doubts the validity of Association Football's continued claim to be the national game, let them take in this scene.

The words, no doubt, were scripted, but nobody could have anticipated how aptly the sentiment would be realised by the wonderful match shortly to unfold, and the very real impact that it would have in restoring some joy and self-confidence to the English game.

Oh, to feel the studs in the soil. It was no longer the sound of storm-troopers echoing from the tunnel, more like Oxford and Cambridge dipping their boats into the water. At last, it was time to stretch, lick the ball around the boot, design a pass, and take a shot or two.

It was a football pitch like any other football pitch, but the onlookers were no longer the isolated clumps of shivering humanity that Houchen had grown up with at Third and Fourth Division grounds, but banks of thousands backing their precious tickets on the biggest dream of their lives. This was not a trip to Torquay on a winter's night, trying to gee yourself up without any help.

On the evening before the final, Houchen had felt a kind of weight-less wave coursing through his body in a frisson of excitement at the game ahead. He had experienced the same sensation before both the quarter-final and the semi-final. He also had a keen sense of the history, of Matthews and Moore and others walking out of the tunnel before him. 'This could be the last time I ever play in an FA Cup quarter-final,' he had thought when he ran out against Sheffield Wednesday, the last time in the semi-final, and now, as fate narrowed its aim, the last time in the Final. Houchen was determined not to squander his good fortune.

I felt really proud after all those years of scuffling around.

It was a chance to reward the confidence of those who had invested in his future. A year before, he had been watching the Final on the telly at Newport Working Men's Club. This year he had received a letter from the secretary 'hoping you win the Cup'. He was going to make the most of his opportunity, and particularly for the sake of those who had wished him good luck. Telegrams – or telemessages as they became known in their dying days – greeted him in the dressing room:

DEAR KEITH HERE'S WISHING YOU THE BEST OF LUCK IN WHAT I AM SURE WILL BE THE BIGGEST THRILLER IN YEARS. ONLY ONE TEAM CAN WIN BUT EVERYONE WHO TAKES PART IN SUCH A POTENTIALLY MAGNIFICENT FINAL SHOULD FEEL HONOURED JUST TO BE THERE. YOU WILL ALL BE WINNERS TO THE FANS. ONCE AGAIN GOOD LUCK FROM DAVE EDEN – FOOTBALL FAN.

WISHING YOU ALL THE BEST ON YOUR BIG DAY. WATCH THE BIAFRAN! FROM ANNE AND SALTY

GOOD LUCK AND VERY BEST WISHES FROM ALL YOUR FRIENDS AT SCUNTHORPE UNITED

And, perhaps, most importantly of all, from the man who had nurtured and cajoled him at Hartlepool:

ENJOY YOUR DAY. BEST WISHES BILLY HORNER

At 2.53p.m. Her Royal Highness The Duchess of Kent will proceed to the playing pitch accompanied by Mr F.A. Millichip, Mr L. Smart and Mr E.A. Croker. On arrival at the touchline, the National Anthem will be played. The party will then meet the players, Mr F.A. Millichip will present the Captain of Coventry City who will, in turn, present his players and manager. Mr Millichip will then present the Captain of Tottenham Hotspur who will then in turn present his players and manager. The Referee, Mr N. Midgley, the Linesmen, Mr R.F. Nixon and Mr J.C. Hodson, and the Reserve Linesman, Mr D.A. James, will then be presented following which Mr Millichip will conduct Her Royal Highness to the Royal Box.

The Duchess of Kent emerged in stylish pink. There is, presumably, a member of the Royal Household whose duty it is to secure advice from the FA on such neutrality in the wardrobe. Her Royal Highness's handshakes were more lingering and less magisterial than those of her husband's cousin. Nick Pickering, for no apparent reason, wiped his hand across his chest when he had already received the handshake. Keith Houchen stuck to protocol with 'Good afternoon, Ma'am.' Spurs manager David Pleat chatted to Neil Midgley, and took in the surrounding view with awe.

Her Royal Highness returned to the Royal Box where Mr and Mrs Thatcher were seated close, but not too close, to Mr and Mrs Kinnock. The Leader of the Opposition could be seen in close conversation with Derrick Robins, the Life President of Coventry City. Neil Kinnock's sympathies are more Arms Park than Ninian Park but, granted Robins's cricketing pedigree, the common ground could have been Sophia Gardens.

The supporters had given the players a colourful send-off at Highfield Road the previous week, but completion of the League programme came at a cost. It was the cost that a player dreads the week before a Cup Final. Brian Borrows, no slower than Phil Neal had been, was as accomplished a right-back as any in the British game. No one more richly deserved an appearance at Wembley, but 'Bugsy' had limped off with a knee injury in the second half against Southampton that day. As the week wore on, there was growing optimism that 'Bugsy' might yet make it, but the club specialist, John Aldridge, located a small piece of floating bone in the knee that needed a little more than tlc. It must have been some compensation to hear the Coventry supporters, in impressive and heartfelt unison, chanting: 'There's only one Brian Borrows'.

Tottenham, too, had a missing right-back, Danny Thomas. Thomas had a boot in both camps. He had been a product of Coventry's extraordinary youth policy and won two England caps before signing for Tottenham in 1983. On 7 March 1987, Thomas was lying in a hospital bed watching the news bulletin on the television. It included film of the disgraceful challenge by Gavin Maguire of QPR that afternoon that had effectively ended Thomas' career. Three ligaments and two muscles in Thomas' left knee had been ruptured and he required a four-hour operation to rebuild the knee. The main item on the news was the plight of relatives of those missing in the Zeebrugge ferry disaster.

Watching all those relatives put it into perspective. It stopped me feeling sorry for myself. I may not be playing in the final but I know how lucky I am.

Immediately after the Cup Final, Glenn Hoddle presented Thomas with his own losers' medal. The FA acceded to Coventry's request to strike a special medal for Brian Borrows.

Dean Emerson, whose design and destructiveness in midfield had made an immediate impact on his arrival at Coventry in October, was another absentee. His injury in March had left him licking punctured prospects from the loneliness of the gym.

Thankfully, David Phillips was a ready-made replacement for the missing 'Bugsy'. He was an excellent crosser of the ball, who could fall back from midfield allowing Michael Gynn to come in. Gynn's speed was an instrumental factor in the dynamic of the game.

As Richard Gough and Brian Kilcline shook hands before tossing up, Gough presented Kilcline with a pennant. There had been a misunderstanding with the FA secretary, Ted Croker, but Sillett was surely egging the point a little when he commented:

> Killer looked across at me and we were all choked and embarrassed because we did not have a pennant to give Spurs in return. There's no doubt that the incident was on the minds of the players in the first ten minutes and was probably responsible for that early Spurs goal. It could have cost us the Cup.

Greg Downs had run on to the field against Southampton, complete with toupee, to the customary chant of 'Greggie, Greggie, Greggie Downs, got no hair, we don't care'. Downs had fought hard to live down the sobriquet he acquired as 'Dodgy' after his transfer from Norwich. Two minutes into the Cup Final, though, Chris Waddle turned him inside out and crossed to Clive Allen. With a glancing thrust, Allen headed home his forty-eighth goal of the season. 1-0 to Tottenham. Coventry supporters would not have found any solace in the knowledge that it was a long way from being the fastest ever Cup Final goal, Aston Villa having scored after forty seconds of the 1895 Final against West Bromwich Albion.

For Keith Houchen, things looked even worse:

I turned my ankle before the goal; I thought I had done some serious damage. I came back to defend, headed the ball out and landed on the side of my left foot. I thought I had snapped my ligaments or something. As I tried to hobble out, the ball was whipped back in again and Clive Allen scored. I thought: 'Oh God no, I can't believe it, we're losing.' I went off for five or six minutes. They strapped it round the boot first but then I took the boot off and they strapped the sock. Maybe it was the adrenaline that was pumping through me, I got away with it. I had trouble with the ankle for quite a while afterwards but on the day it never impeded me at all.

Strangely, on neither channel did the television coverage pick up on Houchen's absence. Seven minutes after Tottenham's goal, Downs redeemed himself. His chip into the box was flicked on with a backward header by Houchen. Ray Clemence was slow off his line and Dave Bennett turned in one sinuous movement and finished from close range with a left-foot shot. The goal came out of more than the mysteries of instinct. Having headed the ball to him, Houchen could see Bennett widen his eyes to take in Hodge as the Spurs player flew across the penalty area. Consequently, in a flash, Bennett elected to turn the ball inside Hodge rather than risk hitting it straight at him.

A couple of the players had commented that the eyes of the world would be on us, and there was a kind of 'Let's hope we don't lose 8-0' humour about it, so when we went a goal down so early there were one or two wry smiles. When we talked about it afterwards, one or two of the lads admitted thinking, 'We're not going to get battered here, are we?' That's why it was important we got back into the match so quickly.

Houchen feels that Bennett's goal, coming so soon after Tottenham had opened the scoring, was the crucial moment of the game. The Brazil players, watching the match prior to playing England the following Wednesday, were duly impressed. They later expressed their amazement that a player of Bennett's insistent and incisive skill was not in the England team.

Cyrille Regis, bursting with acceleration over the first few yards, deft but supremely powerful, was at the centre of the afternoon. He had the ball in the net after nineteen minutes, only for the 'goal' to be disallowed. Phillips's long throw into the box was headed on by Houchen, but Houchen had nudged Mitchell Thomas in the back. Houchen had already extended Clemence with a cross that had the goalkeeper fingertipping the ball into the air.

Regis, Bennett and Houchen formed a triangle together. Coventry hardly broke the bank or the back page by signing Houchen, but the player's touch and control created space for other forwards around him. All those years of learning at Hartlepool were paying off. And Houchen's dominance and skill in the air were a crucial influence well before the sixty-third minute.

The players had returned to Coventry on the Wednesday afternoon before the Final. In the evening, they gathered at Highfield Road to watch the Youth team beat Charlton Athletic and win the FA Youth Cup. Arsenal in 1971 and Everton in 1984 remain the only other teams ever to complete the FA Cup and FA Youth Cup double. It was a rewarding moment for their coach, Mick Coop, but also for Coop's predecessor, John Sillett. Some of these kids had been brought to the club and nurtured by Sillett before he was shown the door in 1985.

Oggy had left the hotel in Ferndown earlier in the day to be at his wife Carolyn's side for the birth of their second child, Rachel. The newcomer had been eight days overdue when the specialist decided that the birth should be induced at 1p.m. on Saturday. When it was pointed out to the specialist that the patient's husband had a prior engagement that afternoon, he obliged by bringing forward the procedure to Thursday. 'The wife is fine but a bit tired. She's only 5ft 2in and the baby's almost as big as her,' said Oggy.

In a wonderful season, Mrs Ogrizovic's husband could perhaps be forgiven his one or two rushes of blood in the Cup Final. Half-an-hour into the game, he dribbled the ball well out of his area and paddled it straight to Hoddle. Peake blocked Hoddle's effort, but dithered, and Clive Allen was able to get in a shot. Mercifully, it hit the side netting. At the other end, Clemence – to whom Oggy had been understudy at Liverpool for three and a half years – had to parry a shot from Gynn.

Sillett was considering his half-time sermon about the need to get the ball out wide for crosses when City fell behind for a second time. Oggy came for Hoddle's searching free-kick, but changed his mind as the ball swung away from his reach. Gough flicked the ball on to Mabbutt, and it appeared to cannon off Brian Kilcline's right foot before bouncing into the net. The goal was credited to Gary Mabbutt.

The Sky Blues were facing a mountain. At half-time, fans stared across the wastes of north London from the balcony of the stadium, feeling empty, very empty. It was naive to think that this was really going to be Coventry's day, that Coventry City would win the FA Cup… wasn't it?

Some fans may have questioned their faith, but Keith Houchen remained optimistic. He recalls thinking in the dressing room at half-time that Tottenham were there for the taking.

And then, with the game drifting past the hour, it happened. It was the moment when a man's conviction burned itself into a generation of scrapbooks, when Keith Houchen hurled himself across the consciousness of the world, heading a football off a satellite and putting the Pope and the President temporarily into touch.

Oggy's huge kick was headed on by Regis. Houchen instantly controlled the ball and despatched it to Bennett on the right wing. Bennett, given too much space, rounded Mitchell Thomas and cut the cross back. Houchen had turned and run through. Nicky Pickering, who was standing behind, his Geordie lilt infused with urgency, shouted, 'Dive Houchy, dive!' And dive Houchy did. Even for a stadium that had witnessed an Olympic Games and a World Cup, it was one of the truly great sights. It transfixed the very second, 62' 42", like a leap from Greenwich. Time took an extra breath except that the breath had cut through time. What a goal that would have been, you thought, pinching yourself to realise that it wasn't a dream after all.

John Sillett said:

Magnificent goal! In training, he's had more kicks up his backside, Houchy, because he'll lay a good ball off and then stand on his mark. And I keep saying, 'Second movement, turn and get in the box.' I can't believe he did it. Oh, what a moment that was!

It's funny when you watch it now: Oggy gets the ball, rolls it around the box and bounces it. Then there was this great big kick. Cyrille and I used to work at it in training. If Cyrille was going up I got behind him, and if I was going up he would get behind me.

Richard Gough was marking me and having a little tug as I was controlling and passing the ball. Benno was hugging his wing like a proper winger. You try to lose your man by going to the opposite post and I got round to the back post. Then, as you are going, you see the goal – hip hip hooray.

It was just one of those things, so split second. You do all the right things, get in the right position with Cyrille, play the right ball out to Bennett and then try to get in the box, because if Bennett whips it in you might just get on the end of it. I could just as easily have scrambled about trying to poke it in like in the Manchester United game.

I never took my eyes off the ball. I ran looking over my shoulder, watching the ball on the turn, running, running, so, if it came, that was where I went. Obviously, if I hadn't thrown myself, I wouldn't have got on the end of it, which is probably what made Nick scream. There is a picture of Cyrille actually going to head it so it is one of them where you think if someone gets on the end of it it's a goal, and you literally throw yourself.

I couldn't honestly say to you that I was consciously thinking that if the ball comes in I can dive and head it – it's all instinct. I think all football is instinct and the only way I could get on the end of the ball was to throw myself. It all finishes up as perfect timing – the perfect ball, the perfect run – but in a lot of ways it's a fluke. When it is all perfect timing, it is like a dance – it all comes together.

I do remember actually heading it. I knew I was getting it, I knew I was going to get a good head on it, and you do think in the split second, 'Don't head it wide, don't head it over, don't miss-head it.' I like the picture where I am so intent on watching the ball. I am actually watching where I am heading it, and Clemence was right in front of me. I headed right past him, right into the corner. It was past him before he could move, so it was just the perfect header.

When I scored, I got totally disorientated. I hit the ground and bounced back up again. It was the blue end, and all you could see was the colour, and all you could hear was this deafening noise. I wanted to jump up where my mum and dad and family were but I realised as I got to the barriers that I was in the wrong place.

I was literally jumping for joy. I have never seen me do that sort of celebration, just jump and jump. There is a lot of energy expended there – Nick and Micky gave up the chase. If you are really setting off, you think, 'Oh God, I haven't got the energy – where are we going to finish up.' So they went over to congratulate Benno. But I didn't know where I was, it was just massive emotion.

I just felt it was my destiny to get a goal. In the League matches, I had had very few chances and thought I wasn't going to score, but in the Cup it was different. It could just as easily have been a toe-poke but the fact that it was a spectacular goal, a fantastically spectacular goal, made it all the more sweet, especially looking back now all these years later.

I think we were a very resolute side, anyway, but after that it would have taken a hell of a team to beat us that day. It's not anything you say to each other, but you just look at the side when it is set up and kicks off again, and it's 'Come on then'.

I think probably in that moment there was only one team that was going to win. It's like two fantastic boxers and all of a sudden one punch or something changes the whole thing. I think that even before the goal our spirit was very strong.

I think that Sillett never quite got it out of his psyche that I was a lowly player with the knock-backs I had in my career, but a lot of players in our side had had that. When you get knock-backs, they say that you are stronger because of it and I think we were a very strong, very spirited, very difficult side to beat in that respect. It was such a very big occasion and we were not going to give it up to anybody.

The whistle blew. It was 2-2. The relentless pace of the game, and the ground covered by its protagonists, had taken its toll. One of the traditional woes of Wembley was seeing players sprawled in contractions of cramp. On this wearying and humid day in 1987, it was no different, with Ardiles rolling off the pitch in agony. Coventry's players looked the less flogged, although as Patrick Barclay observed in *The Independent*:

> The state of some Coventry legs suggested that Lady Godiva's horse might be needed to carry them through. Houchen was not so much Roy of the Rovers as Limp Along Leslie.

Sillett needed to persuade his players to support their hearts and minds for thirty more minutes:

> I kept saying, 'You're fit. Look at them, look at them, they've gone. Look at their eyes. Look at David Pleat, he looks shattered. He's defeated.' If ever I earned my day's wages, I earned them at that time.

I don't think Tottenham expected the Cup final to pan out like that. I certainly don't think they expected it to go to extra-time. I think they genuinely thought they were going to win – maybe in for a battle – but going to win it comfortably. We were in the ascendancy, and they had to play for another half-an-hour. We were still ready for the fight. I remember beginning to feel very tired myself. It was hard work and really painful by the time we finished. We might be fit but it gets to a point where you get past that level.

Kilcline, still hobbling from an indiscrete challenge on Mabbutt, was replaced by Graham Rodger moments before the end of normal time. In the first half of extra-time, it was Rodger's well-judged pass to McGrath from just inside the Coventry half that led to the winner.

The ceaselessly energetic McGrath, presuming on the area of Bennett's refined skills, purposefully made his way up the wing. The brave Brummie, one of the newcomers to Wembley, had broken his legs and dislocated his shoulders twice over playing for Coventry City. He never promised much of a pass as he shuffled around the Coventry midfield, but on this day he played the game of his life, tailor-made for man-marking the best passer of them all, Glenn Hoddle. McGrath's cross was decent enough but it was deflected by Gary Mabbutt's knee. The ball, in accidental design as if on the beach, took off in a casual arc. It dipped high over Ray Clemence – and into the net. For the first time in the match, Coventry City were ahead.

David Pleat commented later that it was the 'athleticism' of the Coventry midfield that had made the difference. McGrath was 'naïve in the extreme, but he knew what his job was and kept at it superbly'. 'The little impish Gynn' got behind the Tottenham midfield, forcing them to track back. 'In the event we got turned over, but only just.' Pleat was not wishing to appear disingenuous by adding that the number of games Tottenham played that season affected his players' energy, but Coventry had played only three games fewer.

McGrath's performance brought this tribute from John Sillett:

> McGrath was magnificent, he is my man of the match. Not only did he stop Hoddle, he pushed Waddle right-back in the second half to where he was ineffective. Even after all that work, he found the strength in extra-time to get up field and hit over the cross that brought us the winner. What a tremendous player.

Simon Barnes, in *The Times*, caustically observed:

> Mabbutt had done nothing wrong but the match will now be remembered as his own private disaster. At the finish, he sat by himself on the grass, away from his team-mates in ghastly dejection: it's all my fault, he was thinking, all my fault. As well blame the stone for breaking the window.

Mabbutt was in good company – the first person to score an own-goal in an FA Cup Final was Lord Kinnaird. Kinnaird, one of the most influential figures in the early history of the game, performed the feat for Oxford University in 1877, but he did at least have the satisfaction of finishing on the winning Wanderers side, and playing in a record nine Cup Finals. When Lady Alma expressed concern that her husband's whole-hearted style of play might lead to him breaking a leg, Major F.A. Marindin quickly reassured her, 'Yes, but it won't be his own.' Marindin preceded Kinnaird as president of the FA, and between them the two men occupied the post for half a century. It was as Sir Francis, Senior Investigating Officer of Railways at the Board of Trade, that Marindin made several important recommendations about railway safety, in particular in the wake of the disaster at Thirsk in 1892 when a signalman fell asleep through sheer exhaustion.

Tommy Hutchison, in 1981, remains the only player aside from Mabbutt to score for both sides in the Cup Final. It would have been fairer to Mabbutt, and a better reflection of Coventry's superiority, if Gynn and Bennett had made more of two late chances, but it was enough. The whistle went. Coventry had won the Cup.

Harry Barratt, a former Coventry City stalwart, wrote in the *Coventry Evening Telegraph*:

> the last five minutes of extra-time… placed more strain on my system than any other period of tension I have experienced during my life.
>
> I had tears streaming down my face and experienced a feeling of pride and delight at the greatest sporting moment of my existence.
>
> On my return journey, each bridge north of Luton had people waving Sky Blue favours, obviously delighted that Coventry had succeeded.
>
> The greeting at Walsgrave was so moving that delay in reaching home became a pleasure. I arrived home at 8.55p.m. not tired but full of euphoria. A quick meal, into my local, and the rest of the night and early morning was spent in paying tribute to a group of people who had raised Coventry City as a club higher than ever before, and into the history book of professional soccer.
>
> It proves that once again this city can rise to any demands made on it.

Alfred Tennyson, 145 years before, had written:

> I waited for the train at Coventry,
> I hung with grooms and porters on the bridge

To watch the three tall spires; and there I shaped
The city's ancient legend into this…

It was a strange way to win. It was clear-cut, but it was a shame it was an own-goal. I was right behind the ball and, with Clemence where he was, the only way it could go in was where it did go in. I was running in and I thought, 'That's never going in,' but it did. There were other chances where we could have sewn it up and that would have been the end of it.

I always remember a late rally when we were covering our box and everyone was jumping up and whacking it out and you thought, 'Oh shit, don't score here.'

I try to explain to people now that it was such a major trophy at the time because you didn't have all this European football and all this nonsense going on with the Premier League and stuff. It was like the Holy Grail, and we had won it.

Come the Millennium, Manchester United were scratching from that season's FA Cup competition in order to participate in FIFA's specious Club World Championship in Brazil. Members of the government and even the Football Association itself were complicit in this. It was a seminal moment. The cat was finally out of the bag as unalloyed greed held sway over sporting integrity, although you could point out that Manchester United's withdrawal was not without precedent. In 1900, Coventry had pulled out of an FA Cup-tie at Oswestry in order to fulfil a Birmingham League fixture.

This was the 'friendly final', played in a spirit of sportsmanship and ref-ereed with discretion and good humour by Neil Midgley. One moment epitomised it all. Trevor Peake gave Clive Allen a ride on his back as the two of them went for a loose ball. Midgley pulled up the Spurs man for an infringement with Allen airborne on Peake's shoulders. There were grins all round.

Midgley had displayed shrewd psychology when Kilcline upended Mabbutt with one of the few bad tackles of the game. Both physios attended – the limping John Sheridan of Tottenham, and Coventry's George Dalton. As a youngster, Sheridan had lost his footing on the steps of a bus and fractured his hip and his leg in three places. He ruminated with a pipe as he sat on the Tottenham bench. Dalton's career as a foot-baller had been brought to a premature end as a result of a broken leg sustained twenty years before.

Kilcline came off worse than Mabbutt. Half-repaired, he was summoned by the curl of Midgley's finger. The words were fierce, but the seemingly inevitable yellow card remained in the referee's pocket. Houchen respected Midgley, and was delighted years later when he agreed to speak at his benefit dinner. For a few seconds at the Cup Final, a dissenting Houchen was given reason for respect when Midgley thrust out an arm to remind the player where he might find the dressing room.

With the excitement of City's winner, John Poynton committed the faux pas of bringing the Duchess of Kent to her feet. In 1934, Manchester City's goalkeeper Frank Swift had been so overcome by emotion at his side's victory that he fainted after the final whistle, prompting King George V to send a telegram enquiring about his recovery.

In *My Father and Other Working-Class Football Heroes,* Chic Thomson describes to Gary Imlach the aftermath of the 1959 Cup Final in which Imlach's father, Stewart, played for Nottingham Forest:

> A lot of us had teeth missing… four or five of us, including your dad. And we were deciding what to do with 'em because somebody had said, 'You can't meet the Queen without your teeth.' And of course we didn't play in them, we usually left them in the dressing room. Somebody said, 'We'll put them in Charlie's cap.' I said, 'No, what happens if someone belts one in and they're all mashed up, it'll be worse.'
>
> So, in the end Tommy Graham had a big red handkerchief… and we put our teeth in there. At the end of the game Tommy had the hanky out and he was saying, 'Come on, get your teeth.'

By 1987, it had become unthinkable for a professional footballer to become separated from his teeth so young. In any case, Keith Houchen had other things to consider than dentures:

I looked around the stadium because I might never come back again. I'd won this fantastic prize. I looked around and I really wanted to go up and down those steps, a fantastic thing that you might only ever do twice, or once. Even the walk around, I was taking every little bit of it in.

I'm disappointed now that I never got to hold the FA Cup. Everyone holds the Cup at Finals these days, then it was only the first three or four – the rest of us just collected our medals. I would have loved to have got hold of the FA Cup and held it up like Killer did. I look at them these days and it gets passed right along the team. I would have loved to have done that just once, just to have a picture – I've not got a picture of me holding the Cup. After the match, it was my achievement and I had done it and got my medal. I didn't want to be the one hogging it, and I lost out. I should have got the photographers to do it just once but I deliberately didn't and I regret it now. It's a daft regret isn't it? My football career is gone now. It was great when it happened. I'm a different person now, but I do think that I should have got that bloody cup in just one picture!

Houchen extended an arm of consolation to Mabbutt. Only Dave Bennett was behind him as he climbed the thirty-nine steps to the Royal Box. Gingerly, Houchen opened the small case that was put in his hand. It was prize day. For a split second, he was rapt in private concentration. He lifted the medal to his lips. But the gesture was not a flippant one. It was measured, considered, like the man himself.

It was to everyone's disappointment that the rightful ban on English clubs in Europe as a result of the Heysel Stadium tragedy denied 'Coventry, a club whose supporters are among the best behaved in the League', as one national newspaper leader commented, 'its chance of European glory'.

As the winners posed for photographs, their vanquished adversaries walked to the Coventry end and paused in front of the cage. The ripple of huge blue flags was momentarily stilled. The Tottenham players applauded the Coventry supporters, and the Coventry supporters applauded the Tottenham players. It was much more than one of those moments when fans mindlessly applaud a player's 'sportsmanship' in recovering the ball, as if the player would automatically have done the same if his team was 1-0 up rather than 1-0 down. This was mutual and sympathetic acknowledgement of what the Tottenham team had contributed to Coventry City's special day. And, as David Pleat observed:

> Everyone will remember the result, but I think it was the spirit of the '87 Final which hopefully will linger on.

Fans felt drained as they came away from the ground, as they had after the semi-final. They needed time to draw breath, time to believe that it really had been Brian Kilcline holding the Cup. There was many a tale to tell.

A Tenner and a Box of Kippers

John Malcolm wrote:

Ten of us travelled up from Brighton after an all-night party. We actually had a picture on the front page of the local paper of the house all decked out in sky blue banners.

We arrived at the TGWU hotel, next door to the FA headquarters at Lancaster Gate, where we tried to get the manager to open the bar at 7.45a.m. He was a cousin of one of the lads and a Cov lad himself, but he had to refuse us.

We all had tickets for the Spurs end (after having to get them from down south) but we exchanged them with Spurs fans who had City tickets. This was through the closed connecting door of a tube train with a window that only went down eight inches.

After the game we all went for food, and a middle-aged gent in the company of a very pretty young lady sent us over three bottles of 'bubbly'. He proudly stated that he was an Arsenal fan, and well done to the City – it had made his day.

As dawn broke, with my feet out of one window of the car and my head out of the other, I woke up thinking I was back in Brighton, but I was in Cov, so I stayed the rest of the week to celebrate.

Michael Williams remembers:

Having moved into a new job at Barclays, I had no choice but to go to San Francisco in the week of the Final. The problem was that the meeting ran right up to just before the return flight and I couldn't change it. So you can imagine my mind was more on making the plane and then crossing my fingers it wouldn't be delayed. I can remember nothing about the meeting but I made the plane in time, and thank goodness there were no delays.

I had suit cases, brief cases and piles of paper with me – and of course a sky blue scarf carefully placed in my hand luggage. Fortunately, I was travelling with a colleague (a Spurs fan, believe it or not) who was 'volunteered' to take both my luggage and his back to my home in Hertfordshire – pulling rank does have its advantages.

So, in a business suit and attired with a sky blue scarf, I hailed a cab at Heathrow and arrived at Wembley in style.

I then had to track down another bank colleague who was stewarding and had managed to get me a ticket. Easier said than done in the huge crowd, but I managed it.

The game, of course, was a dream. My one-third bottle of BA champagne was suitably quaffed at full-time and even shared by at least one other fan.

My final challenge was to find my father-in-law who had offered me a lift home. I had no idea where he was sitting but fate was on our side as I bumped into him on the steps down to Wembley Way.

It typified the day. None of this should have worked and we were crazy to think it would – a bit like the match really!

For the Coventry players, the return to the dressing room was like leaving the beach at the end of a glorious childhood day, one they knew would continue to break over them for the rest of their lives. They returned to the same cracks and marks on the walls, the same squeaks and bangs in the corridor. But such servants to sensation, tiny portents of trepidation three hours before, had been smothered by the size and elation of the experience these young men had just shared.

'Cyrille Regis sat in the corner of the Wembley dressing room, his bulging ebony muscles shimmering. He looked for all the world like a Greek statue,' wrote Steve Curry in *The Sun*. Regis said:

> It's about comradeship and spirit between a group of people. It's something that has brought a confidence this year that almost borders on arrogance. We went to Bournemouth this week to get that spirit right. We had a few drinks together, we laughed with each other, we argued among ourselves. We built ourselves up and knocked ourselves down. But we got very close to one another.

Houchen carefully placed his winners' medal to one side as he packed his soiled kit into a transparent plastic bag.

All this isn't supposed to happen to a ragamuffin like me. I'm the guy who plays at Halifax and Rochdale, not Wembley.

Dave Bennett used the scarf a fan had festooned him with to polish the lid of the Cup, and Oggy admired the names of previous winners around the base. 'I'm Mr Nobody,' Lloyd McGrath kept telling reporters, up went a discordant chant of 'There's only one Brian Borrows', and Houchen neatly packed away the flag a fan had draped round his shoulders on the way up to the Royal Box.

David Miller summed things up in *The Times* on 18 May 1987:

Clive Allen's headed goal after two minutes of Saturday's FA Cup Final had all the authoritative finality of a wheel-clamp. It was as though Coventry had no right to have parked themselves upon Wembley's lovely pitch… Although Waddle was sending them in more false directions than a Le Carré double-agent, they grimly clung to the ledge, at times by fingertips, before gaining a platform from which Bennett, Regis, Houchen and others would lead them to an historic summit… Hoddle, in what is said to be his last appearance for Tottenham, for much of the match was a lonely, broken-down motorist tramping the hard shoulder. Great artists are not required to have physical bravery, but they should have inner fire. Hoddle had none… The embarrassment inflicted upon Downs by Waddle was enough to have had him asking for emigration papers yet, by the finish, this former Norwich full-back had grown in presence and composure… Houchen, a repertory centre forward from the League's anonymous fringes of Hartlepool, York and Scunthorpe, finally reaching the West End, made a greater impact on a Cup Final than any little-known player since Trebilcock, an Everton reserve, sank Sheffield Wednesday 21 years ago…

'The Thunderer' relayed Miller's descriptions of the 'lyrical little Bennett' and of Regis 'as balanced as an Aintree steeplechaser'. Meanwhile, Bill McFarlane in *The Sunday Post* confined his poetic instincts to, 'the gangly striker made his ground to head home the cross', with Houchen one of four Coventry players whose performances he merited with only two stars out of five.

Football Monthly gave Houchen eight out of ten on the basis of the following: Accurate passes – 30; Bad passes – 2; Tackles, etc – 5; Dispossessed – 7; Goal attempts – 6 (1 header scored, 1 header saved, 2 shots saved, 1 header wide, 1 shot blocked); Fouls – 2.

The television commentators revelled in it all. 'Are you watching, Jimmy Greaves?' chanted the Coventry supporters, Greaves having forecast defeat for the Sky Blues at almost every hurdle. Brian Moore, on ITV, observed about Spurs, 'They'll always remember this day as something they'll want to forget.' In his autobiography, Moore described it as the 'most exciting and open' of all FA Cup Finals, 'I shall long remember Keith Houchen's flying header for Coventry, by my reckoning one of Wembley's finest-ever Cup Final goals'.

Moore related a minor storm over Tottenham's shirts:

'Tell me, Mr Moore,' said young Tom, as we drove round Trafalgar Square. 'Why did some Spurs players have advertising on their shirts and some didn't?' It's a wonder I didn't drive into the fountain! I had no answer. It was the first mention of it, and I went cold. It cost me a night's sleep.

I tossed and turned imagining the inquests. 'Mooro, what a cock-up… what were you thinking of? You didn't even mention that the Tottenham players had snubbed their sponsors.' I could also imagine the cutting words of those oh-so-smart television critics, particularly as I was convinced that Motty would have swept up the whole business with his customary efficiency for the BBC. I rang John early that Sunday morning – he hadn't even got out of bed – and feared the worst.

'No, I didn't spot it either,' he said to my huge relief.

According to Brian Johnston, writing about commentator friends in his book *Chatterboxes*, such private diffidence and modesty was wholly characteristic of Brian Moore. Johnston, probably in a spirit of 'There but by the grace of God go I', cited the occasion when Moore announced, 'The referee is now looking at his whistle, and will blow his watch at any moment'.

The final whistle had been blown a long time when the dirt and sweat of the players, the pencil stubs and camera flashes, were sucked into the huge hole at the bottom of the tunnel.

The usher brought champagne and whatever you wanted but all I remember was the bedlam and the massive scrum in the dressing room – the lads, reporters, photographers, were all in there. They had me in a corner for quite a while. I was getting it a little bit in my mind that I was taking up too much of the attention, and what did the lads think – it did cross my mind a couple of times. It worried me a bit because I was the sort of person people wanted to know about and write about, especially if I kept doing it. So imagine, this was the Final and it had happened again, and so I was thinking, 'Go and see some of the other lads.'

Eventually, we got showered and changed and were herded into the lifts to go to the studios at the top. That took a long, long time.

I can remember looking down through a plate glass window, turning away from everyone, and Wembley was deserted, empty, just paper blowing across the pitch. We'd just been out there and won the FA Cup – then it was finished.

We did a lot of interviews. We actually missed the wives, missed all the families, never got to see them at Wembley at all.

There was a big players' bar. The families had tickets and they went in, and waited and waited and waited until they couldn't wait any longer. Mobile 'phones didn't exist. We were still stuck in the TV studio. By the time we came out, Wembley was locking up; it was time to go. So we literally had to get onto the bus, and drive all the way back to Rugby where we had a hotel for the reception.

It must have been devastating for Bugsy. He was a proper football player, and in training he was the best. I tried picking his brains a few years later, 'Between you and me, it must break your heart when you think back. You were supposed to be there.' He has this Scouse way of talking, and he said, ''Ouchy, honest to God, I get just as much looking back at all you lot winning; it doesn't bother me.'

He is absolutely adamant about it. We went to the hospital to see him the next morning and took the Cup to show him. He came with us on the bus – Sillett insisted.

The coach was rocking along the M1. We started singing, '2-1 down, 3-2 up, Coventry won the FA Cup.' It seemed like five minutes from getting on it at Wembley and getting to Rugby. We kind of crept into the town – they had obviously kept it very private.

When we arrived back in Coventry from Old Trafford and Stoke, some people came out of their houses and waved. After the quarter-final, there were hundreds, after the semi, thousands. It got to the stage where I would go home to my estate, and my neighbours would have big signs up saying 'Well done'. People I had never spoken to were hanging out of their windows. I think it captured the whole town, grabbed a hold of everybody.

The first we saw of the wives and stuff was as we pulled into the driveway. It was a country hotel, a great big old-fashioned building with big steps and columns. All the staff of the hotel and all our families were dancing on the steps as we pulled in and got off the bus.

Keith recalls Yvonne's first words, 'I'm so proud of you,' but Yvonne suggests that Keith's alcoholic intake may by then have served to dim their vividness.

I remember the banquet that was laid on for us. It was fit for a king. It was all set out with salmon and champagne, lobster and all expensive foods. I imagine that it was paid for by the club, win, draw or lose. We went up and changed into more casual stuff and lay on the bed trying to take it all in because we knew once we went down it was all going to be drinking and back-slapping. Yvonne and I stayed in the room for a bit, and she talked about the day.

My mum and dad were there. He used to love new technology and we were one of the very first ones to get a video. He had his video camera with him that night – all the directors drunk, the local policemen who were guarding the hotel coming in and drinking out of the Cup and dancing round the room with us, you can imagine. You know, about five or six years later, my mum accidentally taped over it. They always regretted that. My dad's dead now, he died a couple of years ago. I missed him even when they went to live in Paphos. He still means so much to me.

Trevor and I were singing Elton John, My Song, word perfect about three o'clock in the morning. We then went up to the bar and asked for another bottle of champagne and there was none left. We had drunk all the champagne, all the lager.

Yvonne's sister and my mum and dad went back to the house after the party to look after things. My best bottle of brandy was gone when I got home – my dad had invited the taxi driver in to celebrate.

We were up bright and early the next morning, we didn't get much time to reflect. We jumped in a taxi and rushed home because Ross was a tiny baby at the time. Then it was onto the open-top bus. From the final whistle going to parading the Cup was a whirlwind. It was a bit off the wall, really, and you didn't know whether you were coming or going.

There were two other guests at the Brownsover Hall Hotel that night – a dustman and his bride. Ron and Fiona Adams, whose matrimony had been longer in the offing than the football club's excuse for a knees-up, had declined the hotel management's offer to cancel their bridal suite booking. With characteristic zest, *The Sun* reported that 'despite the late night, and buckets of bubbly with the Sky Blues, Ron DID score.'

> Fiona tried to make out she'd got a headache because of the champagne. But I reminded her it was still our honeymoon and we got down to doing what people do on their honeymoon. It was lovely. Up the Sky Blues.

Tom Brown fell into a local stream, and up went the shout, 'Brown's over!' The Hall itself was a baronial pile which had at one time been haunted by the antics of the One Handed Boughton, an Elizabethan squire who had lost one of his hands in an accident. Boughton marauded the locality from above a ghostly coach. Maybe the wildness of his horses was down to the lack of an adequate surgical appliance with which to facilitate simultaneous control of the reins and the whip.

Elsewhere in Brownsover, one of Coventry City's vice-presidents, Tony Mann, had told his wife that he would name their house after the scorer of what he expected to be the Sky Blues' winning goal, little anticipating that this could present a dilemma. In the event, rather than call it *Mabbutt Manor* or *Own Goal Hall*, he settled for *Houchen House*.

One of the Coventry directors, Ted Stocker, had extra reason to rejoice. In October, he had placed £1,000 at 50/1 on Coventry winning the Cup. To put the value of his winnings into perspective, the total receipts from the Cup Final – a record at that – were only £1,286,737.50.

The Coventry players enjoyed the night, but they paid for it the next day. John Sillett said:

> We spent six hours on the bus which had no toilet. That was tough after a night of celebration.

Coventry had won valiantly with a performance of fitness, skill and – above all – indomitable spirit. John Sillett was an exceptional motivator who sent his players out feeling like giants, and fostered a rare friendship and camaraderie between his players.

The *Coventry Evening Telegraph* commented:

> It would be difficult to overestimate the effect of this football match on the spirits of our city... Its footballers have now given proof to those workers whose skills were written off that seemingly impossible dreams are attainable. There is fresh hope in the air today.

Rod Chaytor, in the *Daily Mirror* on 18 May 1987, amplified the point:

> Almost overnight the good times of the Fifties and Sixties vanished. The giant factories went silent and thousands of jobs were wiped out.
>
> Great names such as Alfred Herbert and Morris engines disappeared. GEC cut back its workforce from 10,000 to 5,000. The foundry industry was flattened. Standard Triumph closed its car factory. Triumph motor cycles shut down. Massey Ferguson cut its payroll from 5,000 to just 1,000. And all over

the city the back street workshops, which had provided the nuts and bolts for the big manufacturers, went bust.

Coventry, symbol of British wartime grit, was down and almost out.

The city's union leaders battled to save what jobs they could. Bill Lapworth, regional transport union official, said, 'People didn't know what hit them.'

Coventry was in the grip of the recession and it was difficult to see a way out. In many ways it still is.

But the spirit of the people has always been there beneath the surface. It just needed something like this FA Cup victory to bring it out.

Simon Barnes, in *The Times,* offered a hard-nosed alternative:

> It might easily have been Big Oggy's match: the man who went mad and threw the FA Cup away. Had the ball made slightly different contact with Mabbutt's knee at the last, or had Allen shot straight after Ogrizovic's famous dribble, it would all have been remembered quite differently. But memories will always be edited and histories will always be written to suit the victors. That is what losing means.

Keith went outside the hotel for some air. For a few moments, he stood on the steps. Silence had settled, with the occasional treetop twitter the only certainty of yet another day.

I think it was one of those one-off events and we were in a position to make it happen. That's what makes it so special, so magical that you can do that, but you can make it happen only the once. You watch top players and some of them do it the whole time – playing at Wembley, in cup finals, for England, in this and that. That group of lads didn't, it was something actually unfolding before us as we did it. I don't think I could get that same feeling again if I was a regular for England, or in cup finals – not after every match. It just comes along.

We all thought we could go on from that, strengthen the squad a bit, bring in one or two different players, but not replicate the magic of that season.

When it was all over and it was dark, you wondered where it had all come from. 'What was that all about?' And you knew you were never going to repeat it, not in a million years.

One Coventry supporter, Barry Nicholls, has particular reason for recollection:

A Tenner and a Box of Kippers

If Keith had not scored that memorable goal to help City to win, then I don't know in what sort of emotional state I might have finished up. I will always be grateful to him and all the rest of the City players and management for that spectacular day.

I was living in Sheffield at the time. My father, who still lived in Coventry, had been diagnosed with lung cancer and was becoming increasingly ill. In the weeks prior to the Final I was constantly travelling to first Walsgrave Hospital and then Gulson Road Hospital where he was virtually in a coma.

On the day of the Final I set my video to start when the football coverage began, which was about eleven o'clock, and had eight hours playing time.

I took my sister and my mother from her home in Coventry to the Gulson Road Hospital and we began to watch the match in the day room with other patients and nurses.

Periodically we would check on my father in his room. Obviously everyone was extremely excited during the game. During a particularly exciting part my mother and sister came into the day room in tears saying that my father had just whispered 'Goodbye'. This was the first thing he had said in a long time, and the last. You might imagine the emotions I was going through: Coventry's first Cup Final appearance in 104 years and I had missed my father's goodbye.

After the game the city went wild and I had to drive my mother and sister back to Holbrooks. We were elated that City had won and devastated about my father. On Lockhurst Lane I had to follow a naked man who was running along the road in front of us waving a flag. I thought that maybe I was losing my mind at this point.

When I arrived back at Sheffield later, I checked the video and found that I had recorded everything up to two minutes past three, but there had been a power failure and, of course, the match had not been recorded.

My father died later that night.

8

Coventry to Edinburgh

Keith Houchen's FA Cup goals and his pivotal position in the Coventry attack should have guaranteed him a place in the team. However, John Sillett had other ideas and went out to spend the stockingful of notes the FA Cup had provided.

With George Curtis's elevation to managing director, Sillett had become team manager in his own right. Caricatures of Falstaff or Pickwick played too predictably on Sillett's ruddy and rotund appearance, and on an overt ease and effusiveness, all of it carved in the accent of the Rufus Stone. However, the image may have concealed something more vulnerable. Sillett's father, Charlie, had played at the rear of Southampton's Second Division side of the 1930s, and his uncle Alf was on Charlton's books. Charlie was in his late twenties before he established himself, but was a regular for almost four seasons before being transferred to Guildford City in 1938. When Charlie was killed in the War in 1945, he left two young boys to develop a filial rivalry.

At Chelsea, John occasionally vied with his elder brother Peter for manager Ted Drake's favour. Peter was more successful, to the point of winning a Championship medal in 1955 and three England caps. John made one appearance for an experimental Football League team against the League of Ireland in 1960. He emerged from under the shadow of his brother to become an important component of Coventry's vibrant Third Division side of the early 1960s. In 1966, with Jimmy Hill away on holiday, assistant manager Alan Dicks transferred him to Plymouth. 'I learned later that J.H. was not too pleased,' Sillett later claimed.

As his playing career receded, Sillett took to coaching and management. He learnt through experience how to goad and to galvanise. He developed an instinctive persona, a seemingly natural facility at communication. Never an intuitive player himself, it helped that he had needed to give more thought than most to his own game. His experience beyond the touchline was confined to Bristol City and Hereford United (he was manager of Hereford's 1976 Third Division Championship side), as well as a couple of spells in the small print at Coventry. John Sillett had never quite struck the big time. In that sense, he shared something in common with Keith Houchen.

The unveiling of Chelsea's David Speedie, Coventry's record £780,000 signing, was a media event, 'For too long this club has shopped at Woolworth's, from now on we'll be shopping at Harrods,' was Sillett's brassy comment.

Speedie had scored 3 goals in 22 League appearances for Chelsea during the 1986/87 season and never as many as his partner, Kerry Dixon. Houchen had scored 2 goals in 20 League appearances for Coventry, and Sillett was determined to replace him, despite his 5 goals in the FA Cup. Sillett could be seen shrugging his shoulders in astonishment when Houchen scored in the Cup Final. Whether Speedie's talent was sufficient to compensate for his cussedness remained to be seen, and whether it was sensible to break up the triangle in which Houchen was the apex for the success of Regis and Bennett was questionable.

Sillett, a trifle star-struck perhaps, underestimated the effect of his new signing on the balance of the team and the delicate chemistry so elusively achieved. Accommodating Speedie didn't just mean ditching Houchen, it meant forcing Regis back into the rigid and less effective target-man role he had successfully persuaded Sillett to abandon only months before.

It's something I feel very bitter about. John Sillett will never know how much that hurt. I scored the goals that helped the club make a million pounds and they spent it replacing me. John was a bit like Frank Clark with me and we were never that comfortable together.

I know about the highs and lows in football – if you're on a real high you're closing your eyes cringing, waiting for the low – but I didn't deserve that. I always used to say to Mark Lawrence that if one of these big clubs gave me a chance, just one chance, then I would show them what I could do. I never thought in a million years that we would go and win the FA Cup in the way we did. Then it all came to a shuddering halt.

After the end of the Speedie press conference, Sillett came across Houchen in the canteen. It looked as if Houchen was moping but he was just finishing up after two of the others had left the table. 'Don't worry, I'll still play you in the Charity Shield,' was Sillett's condescending aside. It was the most wounding moment of Keith Houchen's career.

Shortly after the Cup Final, Houchen had negotiated an improved contract with Sillett. A few weeks afterwards, when Houchen asked him what had happened to it, Sillett was forced to admit that it had completely escaped his mind. On a wider scale, there was discontentment throughout the squad about the level of bonus payments for the 1987/88 season.

These were the days before footballers had agents to look after their interests. On one occasion, Houchen was amazed to see a huge picture of himself on a charity poster – nobody had even bothered to ask his permission. Memories are also short. In years to come, in response to a one-off request, the Coventry secretary Graham Hover baulked at providing him with a ticket to a Coventry game at Middlesbrough unless Houchen paid for it in advance with a credit card.

Fame facilitated certain privileges. Keith had expressed his admiration for Mrs Thatcher. It brought forth an invitation from Sir Basil Feldman to attend a 'Family Rally' that he was organising at the Wembley Conference Centre. The event was going to be compèred by Bob Monkhouse and Jimmy Tarbuck, with forty or fifty major sports and showbiz personalities appearing on the platform. The climax would be a major speech by the prime minister, and all those on the platform would then be invited to join her for tea at around 3.00p.m.

For all his enthusiasm for Mrs Thatcher, Keith elected instead to go water skiing. Keith had joint ownership of a motor-boat on Lake Windermere, which led to his team-mates occasionally addressing him as 'Captain Pugwash'.

The Coventry City entourage returned to Dorset before the start of the season. The Dormy Hotel, near Bournemouth, had become like a second home, and the hotel staff were thrilled to bits to have played their part. It was reassuring to recall the special days spent there during the Cup run, but Keith Houchen also reflected on how transitory experience can be. In Cup Final week, an interviewer had asked him about instant fame. 'I wouldn't want to be as famous as Glenn Hoddle,' came Keith's reply. During the summer, Hoddle took his fame to a new home

in Monaco, whilst Houchen had already been made aware of how frag-
ile fame could become.

The team sallied forth to dispense some local largesse. It was a short
trip to Poole Stadium for the friendly against Poole Town, and the sheen
of media interest continued to glow with *Football Focus* carrying Cyrille
Regis's goal.

Only eleven weeks had elapsed since the Cup Final. Tens of thousands
of Coventry supporters returned to Wembley to watch the Sky Blues
play League Champions Everton. The first FA Charity Shield match had
been played in 1908. Among the beneficiaries of the 1912 game were
families of the victims of the Titanic disaster. In 1974, the event moved to
Wembley where, aside from raising greater sums for charity, it became a
fanfare – overblown at that – for the hyperbole of the months ahead. In
the Borough of Brent, chanting fans and replica shirts in August seem as
incongruous as cricket at Christmas.

*I felt nothing but flat, and I thought, 'This isn't the same, it's not right.' I was
back at Wembley, back walking into the sunshine with all the crowds. But the
magic wasn't there. It was just a different day, a completely different thing.*

In 1987, the first day of August was particularly hot and sunny. However,
the game itself went off like a damp squib, with players feeling their way
out of tans and back into fitness. The 88,000 crowd saw Everton win
with a goal from Wayne Clarke. Brian Borrows gained some consolation
for missing the Cup Final by coming on as a second-half substitute for
Michael Gynn. Cyrille Regis missed the match through injury, which
opened the door for David Speedie.

*The disappointment of Sillett bringing in Speedie was a massive, massive knock-
back at the time. I remember Graeme Sharp bending over me at the Charity
Shield and saying, 'Get up, or you won't be fucking playing next week.' That
really stunned me. I had worked too hard to get there.*

In the way of things, Houchen and Speedie soon became great friends
despite Speedie having been bought to take his place.

City's opening League game was against, of all sides, Tottenham. Years
before, the managers of the two clubs had had dinner together at a fish
restaurant. Sillett professed himself an aficionado, and said, 'I'll get you

some good fish.' At the Cup Final, as they walked out side by side, David Pleat jogged his memory, 'I haven't had that fish yet.' When the Spurs team disembarked at Highfield Road, Pleat was presented at reception with a carrier bag. The contents were wrapped in more than just newspaper, but it soon became apparent what was within. 'I think I owe you this,' said Sillett. David Speedie immediately endeared himself to the aficionados on the terraces with more than a piece of fish, scoring a terrific goal in a 2-1 victory for Coventry. Thirteen minutes from time, he was replaced by Houchen. There was a rapturous ovation for both players.

On the back pages of the national papers that day, it was all about me. I had gone missing, done a runner!

Yvonne would never let anyone come near me on a Friday. I used to go to bed in the afternoon, and if anyone wanted to speak to me Yvonne used to say I was out. They had got wind of the fact that I wasn't going to play in the first game of the season, that I was only on the bench. I had been dropped, and Yvonne was saying, 'He's not here, blah, blah, blah.' The next morning, they were saying I was so upset that I had gone into hiding, which wasn't the case at all.

An 11-match run without a win, including defeat by Luton in a League Cup-tie played at Leicester owing to Luton's ban on away fans, saw Coventry plummet to seventeenth in the table just after the turn of the year. There was no miracle multiplication of goals. The Sky Blues scored 22 in the first 22 League matches, 4 of them from the spot, and failed to find the net on 8 occasions.

Houchen had made 11 starts in the League, scoring the only goal of the game against Watford, and with a fine late header in a win at Loftus Road. He was ill for a lot of the season, and had disappeared from the side by the time Coventry mounted their defence of the FA Cup with a 2-0 home victory over Torquay. On account of drainage problems, the Coventry pitch was so bare of grass that it resembled a Caribbean batting strip. In the next round the Sky Blues met Watford at Highfield Road. They could have played all day without getting the ball past Tony Coton in the Watford goal and surrendered the trophy to a second-half goal by Dorchester-born Trevor Senior.

Coventry went from 3 October to 13 February without a League victory at Highfield Road, but 12 points from their last 6 away games enabled the Sky Blues to finish as high as tenth. Lloyd McGrath and

Dave Bennett sustained broken legs in February and March respectively, but Brian Borrows and Dean Emerson were restored to full fitness. Young David Smith was beginning to make an impact on the left wing, as Sillett sought success by trying to work the ball increasingly via the flanks, and Steve Sedgley was now established in midfield. Speedie scored only six League goals.

In 1985, partly as a consequence of the ban on English clubs in Europe, the FA had introduced the Full Members' Cup for First and Second Division clubs. Some clubs shunned it but it was bestowed – to use cricketing parlance – with first-class status. Simod, a sportswear company, became its sponsors in 1987 before the computer company Zenith Data Systems took over in 1992.

There was a joke about the Simod Cup to the effect that the difference between the competition and the ears of *Star Trek*'s Mr Spock was that Spock's ears had a point to them. It's a joke that amplifies the frustration about a season in which the Simod Cup had become Coventry's only aspiration and possible compensation. Having beaten Wimbledon and Ipswich at home, the Sky Blues were one step away from another trip to Wembley. Reading and Elm Park symbolised a world Coventry City had long since left behind. On this drenched evening the last balloons from the previous May were finally burst. It was nearly twenty-to-eleven. when Reading scored the winner in a penalty shoot-out in which a Coventry player – Phillips, not Bennett as suggested – had reportedly opted out.

Houchen was not there. He had been in hospital for a week:

I had this really bad flu and cough. I just kept playing and playing, and coughing and coughing. I literally collapsed one day at the Connexion. When they took me over and gave me X-rays, they found that I had this massive infection on my lungs which had been there for quite a time, and I had been playing and training with it for weeks.

When team-mates asked me how I was feeling, I kept replying, 'A bit wishy-washy,' and to this day David Speedie still addresses me as 'Wishy'.

The doctors diagnosed a bad bout of pneumonia, and Houchen was convalescing on doctor's orders. Coventry paid for their player to spend a fortnight recuperating in Tenerife. Houchen came back into the side at the beginning of April, sliding home Coventry's second goal in a win at Wimbledon only to be substituted in the next match against Charlton after almost scoring an own-goal.

The season ended with another unexpected turn of events. Houchen had stayed on at Bramall Lane for a few drinks after playing against Sheffield United in the last reserve game. On account of a family commitment in Middlesbrough, he had been given special dispensation not to go on the team coach that day. He finished his beer, collected his bag, and paused for a piss. The sound of automatic flushing seemed to regulate the night, and would no doubt stretch through the summer. Houchen made his way out to the car. He was contented, he had scored, and the season was almost done. The floodlights were long since extinguished, the only illumination coming from the reception area where other late-goers momentarily mingled like mannequins behind the frontage.

He muttered a mutual Yorkshire 'Good night', felt the unexpected-ness of rain, and re-arranged the stillness within his car. The brick walls beyond were the boundaries to which Wilfred Rhodes had bowled nearly a century before.

It was about 3.00a.m. Keith was driving quite fast, with the confidence of an athlete, when he lost control of his new XR3i Escort on a back road near Bubbenhall and rolled the car over. The car finished on its side in a hedge, invading brambles and thorns. Keith clambered out. He tried to get the car back on its wheels. It was a forlorn hope.

It was only a year after the Cup Final, and Houchen knew this wouldn't look good. There he was in the middle of nowhere with the only option to run the three miles home. Bramall Lane seemed a long way back into the night.

When Houchen got home, he knocked up Dave Phillips. Phillips clambered into his casuals, and the two men drove back to the scene. Between them, they still couldn't move the vehicle. But they drove to the next village to enlist the help of Oggy. Oggy looked dishevelled in the moonlight, his crooked nose bristling as both the car and house alarms went off, waking the whole household as well as next-door neighbours.

Oggy came with them and helped get the car back on its feet. Houchen drove it home very gingerly and parked it in the drive.

On the following morning, the unlucky motorist bumped into John Sillett on the way into training. Houch's face and hands were covered with marks. Sillett scrutinised the stigmata but appeared to swallow

Houchen's explanation that they had been caused by recovering his kids' ball from the brambles.

On 14 August 1988, Houchen, along with Trevor Peake, was selected by Graham Taylor to represent a Football League XI against Scunthorpe United at the opening of Glanford Park, Scunthorpe United's new home. Taylor, Tony Jacklin also it seems, had attended the junior school just down the road.

Houchen scored once in a 6-1 win. The event did not go entirely to plan. Princess Alexandra, having performed the opening rites, was awaiting the National Anthem with the players when the public address system failed. Scunthorpe's Labour councillors were not bothered as they had foresworn to attend the opening out of protest at the guest appearance of Kevin Keegan. Keegan had coaching links with South Africa.

The second season was written off really, being dropped and then getting ill. I can't remember how the third season went. I remember playing one time in the third season and I think I scored, against Aston Villa, and the Coventry crowd started singing 'Houchy's back, Houchy's back.' I took umbrage to myself that it wasn't my fault that Sillett had left me out of the side and one thing and another. Didn't we beat Villa for the first time in fifty years?

Coventry's Boxing Day win over Aston Villa in 1988 was indeed their first over the old enemy since 6 February 1937. In a 2-1 win at Highfield Road, it was goals by Regis and Houchen that clinched the game. Beating the Villa is as lopsidedly significant for Coventrians as Scotland's victory against England in 1314 remains for many Scots. You suspect that it is not quite such a big deal for the opposition.

Houchen's memory sells him short. He came into the side at Highbury at the end of October and survived until the end of the year, also scoring the equaliser at White Hart Lane three days before the Villa game. David Speedie, in the most sustained vein of goalscoring he produced for the club, then scored six times to give the Sky Blues three League victories on the trot.

Understandably, but only momentarily, Houchen's memory also deletes a particular FA Cup tie.

For Coventry City, the draw for the third round of the Cup can be a bit like a visit to the Reptile House at London Zoo. There they are, the most venomous snakes lined up in a row: cobras, mambas, rattlesnakes,

taipans. On each window you can read a CV of their deadly achieve-
ments. Among them is a humbler but more common killer called the
saw-scaled viper. Saw-scaled vipers are plentiful in certain parts of the
world. Tread on one of these camouflaged, nondescript creatures when
you are a long way from help and its venom will most surely kill.

The twenty, apparently nondescript teams – some of them non-League
– that make their way from the undistinguished ranks of hundreds of others to join the First and Second Division sides in the third round are the
camouflaged threats. On a West Country slope in 1949, Sunderland trod
on Yeovil Town, with mortal consequences. In Herefordshire in 1972,
Ronnie Radford spat like a cobra at Newcastle. In 1986, Altrincham
from cosy Cheshire won at Birmingham.

In 1989 Coventry City visited the gin-and-jaguar belt of Surrey to
play Sutton United. Back in 1897, in their original guise as Singer's
FC, the club had courted its first humiliation in the FA Cup with a
defeat by a village team called Wrockwardine Wood. When Singer's
first made their bow in the competition in 1892, against Burton Swifts,
the tie had to be played at eight o'clock on a Wednesday morning on
account of their opponents' other commitments. By 1925, and now
ensconced in the Third Division, Coventry were beaten by Midland
League Worksop, many of whose players had been on the morning
shift down the local pit.

Gander Green Lane sounds picturesque and innocent enough, like
somewhere you might find the Fat Controller residing. The football
ground is not an oasis amidst smoky stacks but a field nestling between
homes pitted with bird baths and stained glass. At one time it was the
Adult School Sports Ground. Sutton United belonged to the heyday
of the Isthmian League and the FA Amateur Cup. Now they were a
semi-pro outfit, holding their own – but not much more – in the GM
Vauxhall Conference. Average attendances that season, up by a quarter
to 857, were poor even by the standards of the Conference. Meanwhile,
it was less than twenty months since Sutton's visitors had won the
Cup. Aside from David Speedie and David Smith, they were the same
Coventry players.

There was a bumper crowd of 8,000. The Sky Blues were quick to
create a hail of chances. This would be a formality. But a year before
on this ground, Sutton had held promotion-chasing Middlesbrough to
a draw. It soon became clear that, despite all the usual pre-match guff

about not underestimating the opposition, Coventry were struggling to turn superior ability to tangible effect.

Three minutes before the interval, Sutton scored. Ogrizovic failed to deal with a corner to the near post and the flick-on was headed in by the unmarked Tony Rains. However, the mood remained blasé at half-time. When David Phillips was put through by Steve Sedgley for an equaliser seven minutes after the break, there were few – even Sutton diehards – who could have believed that the pumping of adrenaline and fitter legs would not now see Coventry home. But six minutes later there was more atrocious marking on the edge of the box and Matthew Hanlon volleyed Sutton into the lead. Unease turned to discomfort, discomfort gradually to panic. Regis missed a sitter and was replaced by Houchen. Hard as Houchen tried, this was not a day for Roy of the Rovers – certainly not in a Coventry shirt. Sutton dug in and, with a little luck, fought off everything that an increasingly desperate Coventry could throw at them. The final whistle went. Sutton United had won a richly deserved and famous victory. They were applauded from all around the ground.

Such a terrible and almost unprecedented result needs to be put in perspective. Six-and-a-half weeks later, Coventry beat the eventual champions, Arsenal, to go third in the League. The season fell away, although the Sky Blues were never out of the top eight. There were some deeply satisfying results to compensate for that one dreadful day. The double was done over fourth-placed Norwich City and, among others, Manchester United.

As always after such a result, the papers the next day were full of stories of the butcher, the baker and the candlestick maker. The two goalscorers received the accolade of an appearance on *The Wogan Show*. It was a triumph for Barrie Williams, the popular Sutton manager. Williams was fond of quoting Shakespeare, Kipling and the Venerable Bede in his programme notes. On this occasion, 'Our Visitors' slunk away with their tails between their legs, pursued by the brickbats of their own supporters. It had indeed been a shocking defeat but, in the context of the whole season, not that shocking. Coventry City went on to finish seventh in the League. Only once in their thirty-four consecutive seasons in the top flight did they finish higher. Sutton, meanwhile, were stung 8-0 at Norwich in the fourth round.

Keith Houchen had fulfilled a dream beyond dreams at Coventry but his career was in danger of sliding away in frustration:

I do feel unfulfilled, unfulfilled that I didn't play at that level long enough, and I should probably have scored a lot more goals. But I became a different player. I went from an out-and-out goalscorer to someone who linked in with everyone else. You can't link in with everybody else and score dozens and dozens of goals. It doesn't work like that because you wouldn't be making the right runs.

Sometimes you have to come short and hold the ball up. I honestly think that I didn't get noticed for that at Coventry. I was going out for a meal in a village near Middlesbrough after we won the Cup and I bumped into George Smith, my old coach, and he said he was a bit disappointed watching all the coverage that I didn't get the credit I deserved.

Cyrille had scored 12 goals in the League, but nobody else more than a handful. I could understand Sillett feeling that we needed to score more, but we needed a goal poacher. Instead, they bought Speedie. I don't think Cyrille was comfortable going back to playing as a target man. He felt easier when he could have little bursts and go past people and get a shot. Then, if he had someone beside him that could carry on chasing balls into the area we could get it back. It might come to me and I could lay it inside, and all of a sudden there was Cyrille – boosh!

Cyrille was a really great player. He would pick up the ball on the half-way line, beat five men, and the commentator would go purple in the face and the machine nearly blow up, and the ball would fly in or go over the bar, but then it was like you had stuck a pin in him. He would shuffle slowly back into life. We daren't put it down in the corner for him, but I had enough puff to play from end to end. I would run into that corner, get back, run across, play it long again, run behind the full-back, hold it up and come back in again. He was told not to go any wider than the eighteen-yard box, 'This is your little bit here, we don't want you tired.' He was the strongest and quickest player but when he got tired it was like popping a balloon. It didn't matter. He was probably the most powerful and explosive centre forward over the first few yards that England ever had. I was the one who lost out on goals but I think it was a better way. We could have had that for two or three years. It didn't make sense to break it up.

At one stage, Sillett wasn't happy with any of us, and said he was going to get someone else. Speedie used to say what he thought and didn't hold back at this. In the end, Sillett brought Gary Bannister back, and played all four of us in one combination or another. I played the odd game here and the odd game there, but it was a huge disappointment. I think that changed me as a person, right to the end of my career.

Speedo could do anything. He was an all-round player, an out-and-out front-man who would probably play in the hole nowadays. I had seen him score goals where I didn't see them coming, like turning and chipping the 'keeper. The other thing was that he was a really good header of the ball. But that was where I felt I got pushed out. I felt that I was one of the best headers of a ball in Britain at the time, but all the set-pieces were worked around Cyrille and Speedo. Never in my three years at the club was there a set-piece worked around me heading the ball, although, sometimes, it made sense when Speedo could catch teams by surprise with a header of his own.

But that was one of the gripes. Why never set things up around me? I jumped on the plane, went to Hibs, trained with them once, and spent an hour working on a set-piece where everybody cleared a big space for me. In the match, I ran round the back and there's the ball, bang, right into the top corner. I remember saying after the match, 'Why didn't Sillett ever use me for that kind of a set-piece?'

Sillett decided to replace Houchen after the Cup success, pointing to his goalscoring record, but this was founded on a run of 22 appearances in which Houchen scored 7 goals. Whatever the wisdom of signing David Speedie, it made little difference to the goals-for column. In 1987/88 Coventry scored 46 League goals compared to 50 in the Cup Final season. In 1988/89 it was 47.

Speedie scored thirty-one goals in 122 League games for Coventry. Seven months after Houchen left, Sillett spent a club record fee of £800,000 on Kevin Drinkell of Rangers. Drinkell scored 5 goals in 41 appearances for Coventry, and spent an increasing, and remunerative, amount of time in the reserves.

The Cup Final side was dismantling, with Pickering, Bennett and Houchen gone by the end of March. Houchen, who had been sent off playing for the reserves, took over the injured Regis's shirt for the Southampton game at the Dell on 27 March 1989. It was his last appearance. The fulfilment and frustration of his career at Coventry City was over. Two days later, he was transferred to Hibernian for £300,000 or, as it turned out, £325,000.

I went to see the chairman, and George and Sill. I said, 'You paid only sixty grand for me and now you're selling me for three hundred. The club have made millions out of the Cup run. I have helped win you a major trophy, but it's hardly made me anything. I've never had big wages. Give me twenty or twenty-five thousand – I think I'm owed it. I should get something. They sort of went, 'I'm not sure we can do that.' In the end, they said, 'Alright, that's fine,' and we agreed on about twenty-five thousand. I think that Coventry and Hibs worked it out between them and I ended up getting an enhanced signing-on fee of £65,000.

When Houchen went to London to play for Orient, he was in innocent awe of the city. The journey to Edinburgh was convoluted and equally unexpected.

It got to Christmas and I had reached the stage where I was fighting back. 'I think I should leave,' I snapped at Sillett. QPR were taking an interest. Trevor Francis rang me at home. I told him I was desperate to move but that I had an aversion to living in London after my Orient experience. We arranged to meet at the hotel just up the M1 at Luton. But the secretary came instead and drove me to Loftus Road. I remember we sat in the office. There was a lot of small talk – it was when Brian Clough was cuffing that supporter, and we watched it on the TV. Trevor Francis was interested, being a Clough protégé.

I said, 'I would love to come here, but I can't live in London.' Francis was one of those who seemed a bit weak to me. He had this twenty-four-year-old chairman with lots of money. He was talking to him on the 'phone, and Francis was acting like an interpreter:

'We've checked that it's going to be four thousand a year for a season ticket for him to commute, and we've agreed seven hundred a week.'

'He doesn't want you to travel. Will you take eight hundred and live in London'

'No, he wants a season ticket.'

'You can have nine hundred, but live in London.'

This was mega money – you can imagine: this was 1989.

'Let me give you one thousand a week plus appearance money, but he wants you to live in London.'

'No, I'll take nine-fifty a week and a season ticket. I would never miss a day's training. He doesn't have to worry about me, he can check my background, blah, blah, blah.'

Straight away, I am thinking this is a bit of a weak little man here. If I was him, I would say, 'This is the deal,' and then present it to the chairman. So it was a bit like I didn't like it. On first impressions, I didn't like him, but it was something like a fifty thousand pound signing-on fee. It was mega money to me, to anyone at that level. They had a game to play, and he was going to 'phone me to confirm it. We would have done it.

I was waiting for the call one evening that week, and all the Coventry lads were going out to get drunk in Coventry – it was the Superbowl. Phillo was waiting for me:

'Come on, he'll ring another time.'

'No, I'm not the sort of person to do that.'

Later in the evening, Francis did 'phone. He was so evasive that I put the 'phone down in the end. I told Phillo that the deal was off.

'Don't be stupid. He's just bid 350 grand.'

The next morning, I went in to see Sillett and asked whether he had heard from Francis.

'No, but it's a good move and all.'

'I think you should 'phone him. I don't think he had the bottle to tell me last night, but I could tell from his voice that it's off.'

Francis had bottled it. Low and behold, he rang up and called me a mercenary. Maybe that was an excuse. Thinking back, if I had been in his position I wouldn't have been too keen on signing a player who wasn't prepared to move to London, but it's the one place in Britain where I couldn't settle. It hadn't all been doom and gloom at Orient, but I think it was the wrong time for me to be in London – perhaps I was too young.

I was absolutely devastated, because then I wanted to go, and the deadline was almost over. Terry Dolan rang me from Bradford. They were up and coming, money was going in, and it was going to be a good little club. They had sold 'Sticks' Ormondroyd, so they were looking for a big centre forward.

'I'll ring you again tomorrow. Do you want to come up?'

'Yes.'

I was sitting there waiting for his call and flicking through Teletext – I was supposed to be playing squash – when I saw 'TERRY DOLAN IS SACKED'. That was it, the deadline had passed.

A lot of managers show an interest – Howard Wilkinson had been keen at Sheffield Wednesday, but until it actually happens it doesn't mean anything. Graham Taylor always fancied me, but never took a chance.

Villa bought Ormondroyd from Bradford City for a lot of money. 'Sticks' was a good player and deserved his chance (he's someone I like and meet a lot in the press box at Bradford) but I do think that would have been a good move for me, and Villa.

I was totally fed up at being at Coventry by now. I went in to see Sillett and said, 'I am getting really bitter about things here.' I never wanted to be bitter at Coventry because it was too magical for that.

I was at home watching the telly a few nights later when I got a call out of the blue – from Alex Miller.

'Would you come and play in Scotland?'

It was a proper Scottish voice, but I was thinking, 'Is this Phillo, or one of the other lads?'

'Och, aye. I would love to come to Scotland. Hibs, is it? Och, aye, I'm a Catholic.'

But it was genuine. Their deadline was a week later. I was the clown in the dressing room up there. I threw some of my best lines in but I never made his face crack. I really couldn't make him laugh.

He flew down to meet me, and again, they were offering fantastic money, something like six hundred a week, and a hundred pound appearance money. I agreed getting on for fifty thousand for the signing-on fee and the bonuses were four to five hundred for a win, five times what I got at Coventry.

A Brummie recognised me in the toilets at Birmingham Airport and asked where I was going. I told him I was going up to Edinburgh to sign for Hibs.

'You deserve a grand a week and a ten year contract at Coventry even if you never play a single game,' he said.

'How bloody right you are,' I thought.

I was going into it blind, but I accepted as much because of the football as anything else. I was interested that it was going to be a different kind of game. The Sky money was coming, and Souness was starting a bit of a revolution at Rangers with all those international players. In Scotland, we were also playing in Europe at a time when English clubs were banned.

When he arrived in Edinburgh, Houchen was surprised to turn on the television in his room at the Hilton and find that he was a headline item on the News.

There was me at the airport. I hoped I could live up to the expectations. I used to moan about the lack of publicity I got a lot of the time at Coventry but now I was a focal point in Scotland.

Despite a few well-known Sassenachs at Rangers, it was unusual to find English players in Scottish football. Houchen flew up on the Friday. He hardly had a chance to meet his new team-mates. The only one he knew was Gareth Evans who had been a youngster at Coventry.

When Charlotte Brontë visited Edinburgh from her home in

Yorkshire, she described the city as a 'Lyric, brief, bright, clear and vital as a flash of lightning'. Certainly, there was little of the lyrical about the Edinburgh derby between Heart of Midlothian and Hibernian, a Yorkshireman's induction with Scottish football. Hibs *v.* Hearts is about as nasty as Celtic *v.* Rangers. Indeed, in 2005, sensibility was as unrefined as ever, with Hearts fans interrupting the minute's silence for the dead Pope with persistent cheering.

They picked me up at the airport, and drove me around Edinburgh, saying, 'This is very famous… this is Princes Street.' I'm thinking, 'This is very nice, but I don't know anything about it.' It was a lovely hotel, you could see the top of Arthur's Seat from it.

'We play Hearts tomorrow. It's a local derby – you'll love it.'

We pulled up at this dilapidated old ground. The changing rooms at Easter Road were like at Hartlepool, but bigger.

Wearing the distinctive light green hoops, Houchen ran out into a steamy bar of maroon-clad villains. This was Tynecastle Park, the enemy ranch in a cowboy thriller, with the smell of fermenting barley wafting over it from the nearby distillery. The fans were well-rehearsed, with their hatred off to a tee.

It was a lovely, really hot, sunny day, right at the end of the season. There was this seething mass of Scotsmen, and it scared the fucking living daylights out of me to be honest. It was the hardest match I've played in, in my life. It was nothing like anything I'd ever been used to before. It was spitting at each other, punching each other, and stamping on each other.

But I was loving it; it was completely different: 'Give us the ball!' – and I was playing a little bit.

At that time, I was as good a header of the ball as anyone in the game, whether it was flicking it on, heading for goal, laying headers off, whatever.

There were twenty minutes gone. We set it up, they all moved. I ran at Craig Levein, headed it right over the top of him, and it flew into the top corner. It was a fantastic goal.

Houchen felt he had intruded. No-one jumped on his back, no-one offered him a hug or even a pat on the cheek. The players broke away to every corner of the ground, rattling their arms at the crowd like sabres.

The goalscorer was left on his own, just the bloke who happened to have thrown the switch.

It really kicked off after that. I needed an iron lung. It was one long run, at 1,000 mph, with both teams flying. It was like two dogs having a fight. Then they equalised and I realised how poor our defence was.

God, what an eye-opener the game was for me. Some time later Craig Levein and I were doing a promotion for Nike in a sports shop in Princes Street. He was telling me that he and his other centre half had been saying that although I was a big lad they should be able to block me off without falling foul of the ref, but that I just went straight through them for my goal and they didn't know what hit them. I played against Craig on the Saturday after the promotion and I couldn't believe it when he started punching me in the back at the beginning of the match. They got a free kick and I thought I would stand and block Craig off. He went through me like a fucking rhinoceros, and I finished up with my nose in the dirt. When I got the chance, I made sure I gave him an elbow right in the chops.

A week after that first game against Hearts, we played Aberdeen at home. Easter Road was packed to the rafters. It was a really old-fashioned ground with a real football atmosphere. I scored another great goal – it dropped for a right-foot volley and flew into the bottom corner.

But then, a fortnight later, we went and played at Hamilton – you know, one of those teams you hear on the pools coupon on the telly. It was like a non-League ground, with only 2,000 or 3,000 there. The changing rooms were the size of this chair and just really horrible. So, you got the real extremes when you were in Scotland.

Shortly after his transfer, a letter arrived at the Houchens' Bubbenhall home in Coventry:

Dear Keith,

I would like to take this opportunity to wish you all the luck in the world with Hibernian. I hope you have a long and successful stay with them.

As far as we are concerned at Coventry City you are now a great part of the Club's history.

I would personally like to thank you for all your efforts and for the happy moments we had as a team.

Your Wembley goal still excites me when I see it on television. It is now an important part of the Club's history and deservedly so. Let's hope you get many goals for Hibs.

We have had times I hope you will remember for the rest of your life. I certainly will. Keith – thank you for those times and for all you have done for Coventry City. You will always be welcome at the Club.

If at any time you need me, just pick up a 'phone and I will do my best to help.

Love to the family, and I look forward to our next meeting.

Yours sincerely,

John Sillett

At Easter Road, Houchen received a letter from a Mrs Richardson:

I would like to just say 'Welcome' to Hibs and Scotland. I hope you will be very happy here – it is a nice city and there is a good quality of life up here still… and there is a golf course round every corner it would seem, if you are interested!

I am a 'young' lady of 72 who loves football since my dad took me to see my first league game here when I was 10 years old. I don't support any particular team, though I have a soft spot for Hibs – I just love the game watching all the different skills and styles of the players.

My husband and I go often to Easter Road, Tynecastle and Meadowbank and are grateful to be fit and healthy to be able to do so.

No doubt you have had many glorious moments in your football career and I am sure you will have many more with Hibs. It will be super to go down to Easter Road to see you play. My very best wishes to you and yours for the future.

Mr Cook from Cirencester was 'certain you will give as much pleasure to the followers of Hibs as you have always given to the fans of Coventry City,' and Mr Wagg wrote from Milton Keynes:

As a long-standing supporter of Coventry City I was very sorry to see your transfer to Hibernian take place. I speak for many Coventry supporters when I say how much we appreciate all you have done for our club and the piece in history you helped to create in 1987. You have the reputation of a true club professional who always gave 100% when called upon. No supporter can ask for more!

I was at Derby County on Saturday, the disappointed travelling supporters however were quick to praise your achievement on scoring on your home debut for Hibs. I hope the move opens up new avenues for you to reach new heights by means of silverware for Hibs and entry into Europe.

Good luck and thanks a million. You will always have a lot of friends back here in the Midlands.

Both the Hearts and the Aberdeen games resulted in 2-1 defeats, but even if Houchen felt momentarily nonplussed by his isolation at Tynecastle, his goals in the two matches immediately endeared him to the Hibs supporters.

In 1950 Houchen's new home at Easter Road had bulged to a crowd of 65,860 for a game against Hearts. The approach to the ground is through a canyon of characteristic Edinburgh tenements and shops. Close by are a church and the buildings of Leith Academy. On the northern side of the ground stands the city's Eastern Cemetery.

The growth of Hibernian was central to the development of Scottish football. Whilst the rawer edges of life were one step removed from football at Eton, in Scotland they were more pertinent. In *Drink, Religion and Scottish Football 1873-1900,* John Weir describes how 'the Church grew to accept that as the game was there to stay, it should take the sensible attitude to use football as a means to win over young men, rather than to regard the game as a competitor for young minds'. This was not so readily accepted by those whose faith was on the other foot. The Revd John McNeill, at the Assembly of the Free Church in 1892, spoke of the 'wiles of the serpent who was busy wriggling into the country a terrible sin in the shape of "fitba", which had already devoured many.' The Revd G.A. Smith, a Free Kirk minister, believed that professionalism in football would be 'satanic', and the Revd Cumming of the First Free Church, Forfar, shouted at his congregation for putting money into Forfar Athletic and not into his collection plate.

Hibernian, in 1875, was the first prominent all-Catholic club to be formed in Scotland. The constitutional requirement that its players must be practising Catholics was dropped on the club's recrudescence in 1893, although the original rules may have been enforced as much to keep out nominal or lapsed Catholics as to bar Protestants.

As to drink, there did not need to be a distillery to tickle the nostrils of temptation at Easter Road, as there was at Tynecastle. Willie Groves,

Keith Houchen's predecessor at centre forward when Hibs defeated Preston North End to win the 'Association Football Championship of the World' in 1887, first succumbed to the influence while working at Mitchell's Brewery in England.

Groves also had English blood. One of his eighteenth-century forebears from London had been seconded to Edinburgh to help solve a series of crimes which culminated in the arrest of the notorious Deacon William Brodie.

Brodie was a respected Edinburgh town councillor who, by night, was an enthusiastic burglar. According to the *Annual Register* he had 'a too great propensity to that destructive, though too predominant passion, gaming'. His undoing was an armed raid on His Majesty's Excise Office in Canongate. Brodie fled to the continent and was apprehended in Rotterdam. He was extradited and stood trial with an accomplice, George Smith.

> Mr Brodie's behaviour during the whole trial was perfectly collected. He was respectful to the court; and, when anything ludicrous occurred in the evidence, smiled, as if he had been an indifferent spectator. His demeanour, on receiving the dreadful sentence, was equally cool and determined. He was carried back to the prison in a chair. Smith was much affected. Mr Brodie was dressed in a blue coat, fancy vest, sattin [*sic*] breeches, and white silk stockings; a cocked hat; his hair full dressed and powdered. Smith was rather meanly dressed.

Execution was set for 1 October 1788 at the Tolbooth. Brodie was a skilful cabinet maker, part of whose work involved making and repairing security locks and mechanisms. He proudly boasted to the crowd that he had recently redesigned the gibbet from which he was about to be hanged, and that it was the most efficient of its kind in existence. One story goes that he bribed his hangman to provide him with a kind of harness from which he expected expeditiously to be released after the drop. However, it seems likely that his own workmanship was more worthy of confidence than the executioner's susceptibility to any kind of bribe.

Exactly a century later, young Willie Groves signed for Celtic. Celtic – a club dominated from the start by publicans – induced Groves with a capital sum of £500, far in excess even of the illegal bonuses he was receiving from Hibs. Groves later applied – unsuccessfully – for a license for a public house when he was still not quite twenty-one. Fame and fortune eventually washed 'Darling Willie' down and he died destitute at the age of thirty-eight.

Groves was a team-mate of James Cowan, Scotland's celebrated centre half, in Aston Villa's English League Championship-winning side of 1894. When England won 3-1 at Parkhead in 1898, newspaper reports described the crowd's reaction to Cowan's 'strange play'. 'Whit are ye playing at Jamie?' was a cry taken up all around the ground. Cowan, it was said, failed with his tackles again and again, and then began taking off in a series of eccentric dribbles.

> A hasty conference of selection committee members had been held a few minutes before the game was due to take place, and opinion as to whether Cowan should be allowed on to the park tended towards the negative. Only the influence of the Chairman swayed the decision.

Later, correspondents were despatched to interview Cowan's mother in Dumbartonshire, and Cowan himself claimed that a head cold had been a malign influence. However, a writer in *Scottish Sport* commented that if Cowan was indeed suffering from a cold, then it must have come on all of a sudden. On the night before the match, he had spotted the player in fine spirits in Glasgow's Central Hotel. Never again was Cowan privileged with an invitation to represent his country.

The men in black were also not above temptation. Referees had already been fighting a losing battle for public esteem when a Scottish Cup-tie in 1886 had to be re-played because the ref was officially inebriated. According to his two colleagues, he had 'tasted' at two public houses on the way to the match. He was 'in a beastly state of intoxication,' could not say why he disallowed a goal, and admitted that he remembered little about the game. He even had trouble with the final score.

When Houchen joined Hibs, the club was suffering from the disastrous upshot of emulating Tottenham's flotation on the Stock Exchange. The share price dropped as dramatically as the debts shot up, and Hibs were turned into a lame duck PLC. By the following summer, a takeover bid was tabled by Wallace Mercer – of all people, the chairman of Hearts. Mercer tried to sell the idea of merging the two clubs under one new roof as a means of mounting a more effective challenge to Celtic and Rangers. With protest rallies at Easter Road and the Usher Hall, and the sympathetic efforts of enough businessmen to buy up the 75% shareholding required to repulse the predator, the people of Edinburgh won the day.

Houchen's third game for Hibernian was at Hampden Park. Along with Murrayfield, Hampden is the spiritual home of Scottish sporting pride and endeavour, at that time a tired giant of a stadium which had played in the heyday of unrestricted terracing to bigger crowds than Wembley. It was the semi-finals of the Scottish Cup, and Celtic the opponents. Hibs followers had been gratified to avoid Rangers in the draw, despite being denied the prospect of some sectarian fisticuffs.

Unfortunately, the hoops of Celtic plundered a three goal half-time lead and, but for a goal from Steve Archibald, Hibs were never really in it. For Houchen, one of the attractions of joining Hibs had been the possibility of winning a Scottish Cup-winners' medal to add to his English one:

If I look back on my career I had some awful games. I was bloody awful at some time or another at every club I played for. But I always performed in the big matches. This was the only big match I can remember where I didn't really perform, but we were beat after twenty minutes and the game was gone, you knew it was gone.

I got the blame for one of the goals, but it was not my fault. If I was picking up at the back, it was rarely that anyone got away from me, throughout my career. As the corner swung in, big Mick McCarthy was supposed to be picked up by our centre-back, Rae, but I could see that Rae had got under the ball and that he was going to miss it with McCarthy coming in behind. I left my man to try and get to McCarthy. If you look at the ball, I'm right on McCarthy's shoulder as he heads it in to the top corner. I got a lot of stick after that. The commentator was Ian St John — it was live on Scottish TV, and he blamed me for missing my man. I had cost Hibs the semi-final when it wasn't even my man in the first place. That made it hard for me again until the start of the next season.

The Englishman had soon discovered the tribal unpleasantness of the Scottish game, with players spitting in each others' faces and provoking opponents into raising their elbows.

The lack of protection from referees was also a novelty. On his debut, as he lay upended by one bloodcurdling challenge that would have had the offending Hearts player frogmarched out of an English ground before his feet could touch the bath, the ref leered at him with a laconic aside, 'Welcome to Scottish football, Mister Houchen.'

Home defeat by Dundee United three games from the end of the season did not matter on a day when Hibs were ensured of qualification for Europe. Hibs finished fifth in the League.

Houchen's first visit to Parkhead in the penultimate match was an eye-opener:

Celtic were the first team that really beat it out of me. 'You cheeky bastards,' I thought.

For the first six months in Scotland they literally kicked the hell out of me. The standard of refereeing was awful. People came through you, almost killing you, and they waved play on. It was crazy.

I was a big lad and I stood out, and refs were tying me up.

On 15 April 1989 came the Hillsborough disaster, which appalled the nation and affected the consciousness of a whole generation. At the time, Mrs Thatcher's government had been evading the wider social reasons for the unconnected problem of hooliganism by seeking to impose a fatuous identity card scheme on people entering football grounds. Lord Justice Taylor intimated in his report into the disaster that identity cards were at best a waste of time and at worst could compound further accidents. The government dropped its proposal overnight, leaving Sports Minister Colin Moynihan – an Olympic medal winning cox – without a paddle in pursuit of his mistress's bidding.

Two years before, Hillsborough had represented sporting aspiration and achievement to Keith Houchen. Now, its gymnasium was full of corpses.

The opening of the 1989/90 League season could not have been more challenging for Hibernian. Defeat by the only goal at runners-up Aberdeen was followed by a 2-1 victory against champions Rangers at Easter Road, with Houchen scoring the first goal. Hibs supporters took the Englishman to their hearts. 'Houchy, Houchy, Houchy,' they cried genuflecting with their arms outstretched.

I was twenty-eight, as fit as I was ever going to be, and I knew the game inside out. Everything was played towards me. It was really good, and I enjoyed it.

Losing then at Tynecastle to the old enemy was a major disappointment, but there were consecutive home wins against Dundee United and St Mirren.

Houchen's performance against the Saints led one reporter to gush:

> On the basis that there is nothing more pleasing to the eye than the sight of a good old-fashioned striker, it's no wonder Hibs fans adore Keith Houchen.
>
> The Englishman likes nothing more than going in where it really hurts.
>
> Keith certainly had the green and white brigade in raptures with this latest barnstorming display.
>
> A couple of goals, numerous near things, and two legfuls of bruises ensured Hibs keep their 100% Premier League home record.

Sandwiched between these two games was the first leg of the UEFA Cup tie with Videoton-Waltham. These were heady days for Scottish football as English clubs, shorn of European competition after the Heysel ban, looked on covetously.

When the European Cup was launched from the platform of the French daily sports paper *L'Equipe* in 1955, Hibernian accepted an invitation to represent Scotland. Whereas the English thought it beneath their noses to participate, Hibs paved the way with a 4-0 victory in the Rhineland against the German champions Rot-Weiss Essen, and went on to reach the semi-finals. Hibs enjoyed some memorable European nights down the years, with which a record 7-0 win in their 100th Scottish League game with Hearts – being on the day Britain entered the EEC – deserves honorary inclusion.

Whereas Videoton had been finalists in the UEFA Cup in 1985, it was Hibernian's first European campaign since 1978. Graham Mitchell's looping header was the only difference between the two teams after the first leg.

A large and noisy support followed the side to Szekesfehervar, a coach ride west of Budapest. Szekesfehervar, a sort of glorified Scunthorpe with a population of just over 100,000 and poured over by the aluminium and metal industries, had been known since Roman times and was the ancient Hungarian capital. The trip was memorable:

There were about 1,000 Hibees and we were led out by a piper. It even stirred my blood.

After nine minutes of the match, Mitchell took off on a run down the left and rode a heavy challenge on the edge of the penalty area before lifting over a perfect cross. Houchen rose majestically at the far post and headed home the opening goal.

The Hungarian tackling was bull-blooded. Three of their players got booked and, in the second half, Tamas Petres was red-carded for pole-axeing Neil Cooper off the ball.

When Houchen struck the post with a header from an Alan Sneddon free kick, Gareth Evans rammed home the rebound to make it 2-0. With half-an-hour to go, Videoton were a beaten side, and the tempo slackened. However, Hibs had not yet finished. With eleven minutes to go, Brian Hamilton struck the bar from thirty yards out. John Collins, with a rasping volley, finished off with aplomb.

The 4-0 aggregate victory was thoroughly deserved, and for Keith Houchen – at the peak of his powers and patently the best player on view – it was a triumph. Houchen recalls it as the best performance of his career. For the Hibees, it was a win to rank alongside legendary victories against Barcelona and Napoli.

Back at Easter Road, Hibs were brought down to earth. After an early Dunfermline goal, Houchen took the ball on his chest and hammered a volley for an impressive equaliser. He then set up Collins before the Pars pulled it back to 2-2. Hibs would have topped the League had they won at Celtic the following Wednesday, but they lost 3-1. Houchen hit the bar, was booked and admits he was nearly sent off. One of that day's Scottish editions quoted Tony Fitzpatrick, the St Mirren manager:

> It's a criminal league, just murderous. It takes a special kind of beast to make it in this set-up. It's just one battle after another.

Houchen scored the first in a 3-2 home win against Motherwell as Hibs prepared for the second round of the UEFA Cup. A frustrating evening against RFC Liege finished 0-0. Hibs went out a fortnight later in Belgium to a freak goal in extra-time from de Sart. At a time when English clubs were banned, British interest in Europe was therefore over by the end of October. Hibs' elimination was a particular disappointment to Houchen, Coventry having missed out on Europe after winning the FA Cup.

Hibernian's season continued steadily but undemonstratively. A draw at Parkhead, followed by consecutive wins against Dunfermline, St Mirren, Aberdeen and Rangers, pushed the team up to fifth by the end of March. The win at Ibrox was the highlight of Hibs's domestic season – Rangers had led the table from mid-December. In a match in which Brian Hamilton broke his leg, Houchen scored the second-half goal to add to his winner at St Mirren. For Rangers, it was the jockey's whip before cantering away from Aberdeen and Hearts at the end. Houchen scored an equaliser against Dundee, with John Collins – on his final home appearance – missing a last-minute penalty. With a few minutes to go in the final match at Dunfermline, Hibs were still playing for fourth place and a European spot. It was not to be. Hibs, who scored just nine away goals all season, and only one of them before the Boxing Day win at Pittodrie, nevertheless won 4 and drew 5 of their 18 sorties. Houchen finished clear of Collins as top scorer with eight League goals.

Houchen had mixed feelings. He was playing better than at any time during his career, and the family were happy both in their new home and in their Scottish surroundings. The Houchens had bought a house in North Berwick on the hump of the East Lothian coastline overlooking the Firth of Forth. Golf courses and sandy beaches proliferated beneath the steep conical hill that overlooks the town.

In 1590 witches were said to have attempted the sinking of King James VI's boat as he sailed up the Forth on the way back from Norway with his new wife, Anne of Denmark. A live cat was thrown into the waters, to whose paws were tied lumps of flesh from the body of a hanged man. The King, thirteen years away from assuming the English throne, presided over torturous interrogations. A schoolteacher, a midwife, and Euphemia, the daughter of Lord Cliftonhall, were all executed.

North Berwick was at the end of the branch line into Waverley and less than thirty minutes into work by car. The Houchens bought a plot of land and rented nearby.

We watched the house slowly getting built. It was beautiful, brand new. It was the start of a new adventure. We had more money than we could spend, the kids were lovely little toddlers, and I was playing for Hibs in the peak of condition.

The game was rough and the referees irksome, but the Yorkshireman had been 'absolutely phenomenal' in that first year at Hibs, and was looking forward to his second full season. Hibs kicked off with a Skol Cup-tie against Meadowbank Thistle, originally scheduled to be played at Meadowbank Stadium close to Easter Road on 21 August 1990.

Queen's Park Football Club may rattle around in Hampden Park, but akin to the gallery of the Stuart kings at Holyrood it is their very own legacy. In contrast, at Meadowbank Stadium – built for the Ninth Commonwealth Games in 1970 – the field is isolated within its running ring, a piecemeal plot for leaps and jumps and separate sandcastles, never a fitting focus for football.

The Hibs game, however, had been re-scheduled – to take place at Raith Rovers. It was one of those days when it was difficult to summon up more than a routine enthusiasm. Houchen assembled with the others at Easter Road. It felt like a dreary, if fitfully very picturesque drive across the Forth to Kirckaldy, and a bit like making a journey to see your sick auntie.

A Sassenach ignoramus on *Grandstand* had once suggested that 'they'll be dancing in the streets of Raith tonight,' after a rare Raith success had intruded onto the teleprinter. The club was founded in the same year, 1883, as Coventry City, and took its name from the Laird of Raith and Novar who leased a ground in Kirckaldy to them. The economist Adam Smith came from Kirckaldy and, a couple of centuries later, Gordon Brown. The town, where employment used to be lined in linoleum, has a main street that goes on for ever.

Stark's Park, on a grey evening with the whisper of autumn in the wind, can be a little dispiriting, but this was where Jim Baxter – fresh from Fordel Colliery – opened his petals to embrace one of Scotland's greatest and saddest legends. Baxter went on to toy with England's World Cup-winners at Wembley in 1967, having taunted the squeaky-voiced Alan Ball during the pre-match kick-in with the suggestion that his father was *The Clitheroe Kid*.

It was only after extra-time and an only goal, scored by Houchen, that Hibernian could turn for home. Exactly a week later, Hibs were repeating the journey, this time to play Raith in the third round. A second-half winner from Raith's McGeachie was not the worst of it.

I used to play at Raith when we went on tour with Hartlepool. It was depressing, decrepit, run down. If I thought some of the grounds I played at in England were bad, suddenly I was seeing grounds that should have been condemned. I hated it, I hated every minute of it.

It was just horrible and we were poor, really poor. It went into extra-time. Alex Miller singled me out at the end. He stood on the pitch, having a go at the team and me in particular. I can't remember why – 'Not good enough… Who the hell do you think you are…blah,blah,blah.' It was bad, but everybody else was bad.

It was the last kick of the game. It was a left-wing cross and I headed it into the top corner – we were through.

I sat in the dressing room, and said, 'This is the most godforsaken, depressing place I have ever been. If I ever come back here it will be too soon.'

Then, when they made the draw, we had only got Raith Rovers away in the next round! We were abysmal. I came from Hartlepool when it was falling down but this place was just too depressing for me. We were awful, I missed a few chances, and we lost.

As we trooped off the pitch, the Hibs supporters ran to the tunnel and were leaning over, spitting, throwing their scarves, giving right stick. So when I came in behind, I said, 'Oh, for fuck's sake, why don't you fuck off,' and I stuck a finger up at them. It's not as if you're losing on purpose, is it?

All hell let loose, and the police came to the dressing room. They took me to the ref's room, and he said he would be reporting it. It was touch and go whether I was going to be arrested. They couldn't get the bus away because all the Hibs supporters were waiting for me, so they had to give me an escort – Hibs fans were following the bus up the motorway.

From then on, you can imagine, I played very few matches. When they did play me, I got, 'Houchy, Houchy, time to get out, fucking English,' clapping hands. Much as they had liked me as a player, I was English, and if you've lived in Scotland you understand what that means. We played Chelsea at Easter Road in a friendly just before I left. They were shouting, 'If you hate the fucking English, clap your hands' for most of the match. You think, 'Why do I want to be here?' As I was trying to warm up, it was just real vile stuff coming down at me, even from the Family End.

It turned really nasty. I played one or two games and did OK, but I think Miller was a bit scared to play me.

It was a pity. We loved it in Scotland, absolutely loved it. It was probably the one place I played where I would go back and settle if I had to. The kids were becoming quite Scottish too. Ross was just learning to talk and Cara was in primary school.

Aberdeen was the only place we went where we had to stay overnight, and we always seemed to get them at Christmas. We stayed at the Skidoo Hotel, and I remember phoning home. When Yvonne put the kids on, they sounded like proper little Scots – I've got them on tape. Cara had picked up a Midlands accent when we were in Coventry, and they seemed to pick up the accent wherever we went.

Houchen's professional life became a misery as he was subjected to increasing abuse. He regretted his gesture from the very second he made it, but he had lost the pilgrims' faith, and no longer did they bow to him from the terraces in supplication.

I ended up having a wasted season because the crowd turned against me big-time. When you are really popular, if they turn against you there is no in-between. They either love you or hate you. They made it very uncomfortable for me.

The League season got off to a poor start in 1990/91, with one point and not a single goal in the opening four games. Houchen opened and closed his account for the term at Tynecastle on 24 November. The season was a disaster for the club from start to finish and, at the end of it, Hibs and St Mirren were only spared relegation on account of the Premier Division being expanded. Hibs averaged less than a goal a game, and in only 3 out of their 36 fixtures did they manage to find the net more than once. It was certainly not a season for the manager to fall out with his key striker. After such a depressing winter, only 3,500 supporters bothered to turn out for the last home game. Many a time in the last ten minutes of a match did Houchen find himself running through a carpet of scarves, hurled onto the field by disgruntled customers.

They were very quick to turn. There was a mate of mine called Joe Tortolano, a left-back, funny little Scottish/Italian. The crowd used to slaughter him, booed when his name was announced, and crucified him all game. The home crowd could make it very difficult for you as a footballer, and knock your confidence. There were one or two others. If we lost, they would be swearing and spitting and giving it all this.

The Raith Rovers experience had been a bit like becoming aware of a fishbone in the throat, when you would have preferred the kipper filleted in the first place.

It was all beginning to tie in together. We had been on a pre-season tour in England. We played Burnley, Watford and others, and we were very good – we beat them all. I played well against Watford – I was outstanding that day. I got a call back home in Scotland from David Speedie of all people, hinting that Colin Lee was desperate to sign me. Speedo and Lee had been team-mates at Chelsea.

There is all this thing about tapping that goes on with players, and always has gone on, 'Do you want to come here, or don't you?' Lee had offered Hibs

£350,000 to take me to Watford and was keen to give me this and that, and mega-bucks to go with it. But Hibs never told me, and wouldn't let me negotiate. I think that when there's that kind of money involved you would expect to be told, even if they were turning it down.

I was past thirty, and in those days players didn't make it far into their thirties. I was thinking, 'Do I really want to finish my career up here?' I had a huge reputation in the lower leagues in England, but higher level people described me as a journeyman player and the only thing I had done was score a goal in the Cup Final for Coventry. I hated that.

I was thinking, 'Oh God, I could have a couple of years back in the Premier League,' and so I asked Hibs about it. They denied it, but I knew they were lying, not treating me properly.

Speedie said that the only way to get out of there was to rock the boat. Rocking the boat means being a bit belligerent, being difficult to get on with, a bit like Bellamy, although I could never be like Bellamy.

Houchen made what turned out to be his last appearance for Hibernian in a fourth round Scottish Cup-tie at St Johnstone, having scored at Clyde in the previous round. The Perth club had a player called Turner, whom Houchen still refers to with contempt. Houchen, used to playing most of his football at the less aesthetic end of the English game, had already been dumbfounded by the crudity of the said Turner in a previous encounter.

I had got sent off against St Johnstone in a League match at Easter Road. I was having a poor game – sometimes you do, your touch isn't there, the ball's bouncing off you, and the crowd begin to get at you like anybody would.

Then, this bloody lad Turner – little horrible sod – who I couldn't stand, was there in my face, just niggling at me all the time.

Sledging was laced with spittle: 'I thought you were supposed to be a good player. You're useless' – all of it delivered in a weasel-like Scottish accent. Then came the peckering of toecaps at Houchen's heels.

He was irritating me. I said, 'You better watch it, sunshine, or you're going to be lying on your back looking at the sky anytime now.'

He started to pinch my sides to provoke me into raising my elbows. I duly obliged, I caught him right in the face. We were in a group of players but the linesman was looking straight at me. I was looking at the dressing room.

If Kirkaldy was the turning point for Houchen's career in Scotland, Perth was the scene of its denouement. Scotland's first King James had been stabbed to death in the city while attempting to escape down a privy. This time, it was the loathsome Turner at work again.

I should have had a penalty. I went round the 'keeper and he brought me down – it was a blatant penalty. I got up and was in possession again when Turner brushed round me. He was trampling all over me, all over my heels. The ref did nothing – I remember him just grinning at me – that's what sent me over the edge.

Something snapped. I ran after Turner – twenty or thirty yards – and kicked him, and that was the end of it. I thought, 'Oh shit!' I was angry that he had got to me like that, because I could have waited, but I reacted at the time.

From the preciseness of Houchen's gestures, you suspect that the effect of his assault on Turner really was like a Catherine Wheel.

The assailant recalls the frustration of watching the rest of the game on the dressing room telly and seeing one of the opposition players run half the length of the pitch to score a last-minute winner. The reaction of manager Miller was public and predictable, 'He cost us the game. He was a disgrace.'

There was a conspicuous absentee from the players' lounge after the match. The St Johnstone layer was anxious maybe that a particular opponent might not wholeheartedly enter into the 'all pals over a beer' spirit of the occasion.

Miller fined Houchen two weeks' wages. Houchen admitted at the time, 'It was silly. I lost my head. But the retaliation just sums up how everything has got to me.' He pointed out that, rash as his action was, it wasn't his fault that Hibs had lost, and he talked of his frustration at Scottish football:

Within weeks of moving to Hibs, I knew deep down it was not for me. I love where I live and I love the Scottish people. But I'm not enjoying their football and if you don't do that, you have problems.

Houchen had not anticipated the problems with Scottish referees. In ten years in the English game, he had been booked only five times, but during his short stay in Scotland he had been shown fifteen yellow cards and been sent off twice. Scottish refs allowed defenders to get away with murder, but were quick to wag their cards at any wisp of a reaction.

Houchen admitted:

It's getting to the point that if anyone does or says anything to me I just blow up. I'm doing things I can't believe now and my situation at Hibs has affected me so much that I am taking my feelings home with me and being miserable around the house.

What esteem Houchen may have felt for his manager had gradually dissipated. Alex Miller was probably too frightened ever to pick him again but the player knew that he had reached the end of his time in Edinburgh. In August, Houchen was transfer-listed.

I never liked his attitude to people. His man-management was really poor, and he would not speak to people particularly nicely. His training was boring, I mean really boring. He was a clone of Andy Roxburgh. It was very robotic, 'X runs to Y, Y to...' and so on. One day, I said, 'I've got no fucking 'A' levels, I'm only a footballer.'

Miller said:

> If Keith wants to leave, we won't stand in his way. We're willing to speak to any club interested in him. He's been told that. Others have got hammered in the past, and Keith's red and yellow cards haven't been for tackling. His previous misdemeanours were taken into account.

I was kind of stymied with Alex Miller – we never got on after that Cup-tie. He'd pick arguments with me and look for trouble where there wasn't any trouble. Then I would start to pick arguments with him and it began to get a bit nasty. It was tough for me because I had a real problem with referees, and with the anti-English things the crowd used to sing. I would react all the time, and throw punches at players who called me an English twat, and who spat at me.

They were always singing about hating the English in Scotland. Celtic, in particular, was a really nasty place for that with horrible stuff about the British Army. When I was playing, I was thinking they shouldn't be allowed to sing things like that.

Miller put me in the reserves and I was scoring two or three goals a game. I was playing fantastic football, back to how I was playing when I first went. But he wouldn't pick me. He would say that 'So-and-so wants you on loan,' but I didn't want to go anywhere on loan. If someone wanted to buy me, they could buy me but I wasn't going anywhere to prove myself because I think I had already done that as a player. Miller pulled me aside before a game at Dundee United and told me that Colin Todd at Middlesbrough had offered £300,000 but that his chairman wanted to see me play first. I heard no more, and presumed he hadn't been impressed.

One day, Miller told me that Port Vale wanted me to go down and play in a friendly against West Brom. They were a good side, played proper football. The air was good.

Scottish football had been a shock to the system.

You have to be really fit to play in this league the game is so physical. There are two or three English style clubs but most aren't all that skilful. The whole emphasis in Scotland isn't on winning, it's on not losing. I don't like reading about Scottish football and I don't particularly enjoy watching it either.

With only ten teams in the Premier League, sides played each other four times a season – more if they met in the cups. And things got remembered. Houchen thought, 'That's it, I'm coming home'.

9

Burslem

The golden angel used to dwarf the town of Burslem. High up on the hill, it soared above the town hall in days of civic significance, and it glitters in the sun to this day.

It was to Burslem that the sinuous figure of Keith Houchen stretched in yet another unexpected career move. Those who perceive football exclusively through the designer appeal of Manchester United and its ilk may find Port Vale an irrelevance, and certainly a mystery. Promptings of Talbot and Ebbw suggest a limb of South Wales. The club is actually at the heart of the Potteries, and takes its name from a number of landmarks in the Longport area which are called Port Vale.

Both Port Vale and Stoke City were already well into middle age when the *Evening Sentinel* reported of a dinner at the Grand Hotel in Hanley in 1930:

> A new page in North Staffordshire football history was made when, for the first time, players of both clubs sat down together.

Only rarely did Port Vale emerge from under the shadow of their local rivals, but the club is imbued with a fierce sense of identity, personified by Roy Sproson who made 837 first-team appearances for it. In 1954, Port Vale came as close as any Third Division side to the FA Cup Final. Supporters maintain to this day that the team was hard done by in their semi-final, Ronnie Allen – an ex-Vale player – scoring from the spot when an Albion player allegedly took a dive. A debatable offside decision also still sticks in the craw. The Valiants finished that same season eleven points clear at the top of the Third Division, conceding only 21 goals in 46 matches.

Burslem was the mother of the 'five towns' (there are actually six) and is connected to Stoke in one long sprawl. The crossroads, between Newcastle-under-Lyme and Leek, with Congleton to the North, meets as if on a bun. The road recedes in a 'Grand Mile' to the South, slung like a hammock with Cobridge. The local accent – flat but with a curl – is to match, the hilly perspective almost Roman. Arnold Bennett and Royal Doulton jostle in the shorthand of outsiders' knowledge.

In his novel *The Old Wives' Tale,* the cosmopolitan Bennett spreads his backdrop, describing preparations for a Paris execution:

> 'You,' cried a drunken English voice from an upper floor – it was the middle-aged Englishman translating what the executioner had said – 'you, you will take the head.' Then a rough laugh, and the repeating voice of the Englishman's girl, still pursuing her studies in English: 'You will take ze'head. Yess, sair.' And another laugh.

It was a bit different from the monkey in Napoleonic Hartlepool. The 'monkey' of Burslem folklore is a witch, 'Molly' Leigh. Molly was attended by a black bird – apparently the spirit of a schoolmaster whose gown shrivelled into flight. A nineteenth-century descendant of Burslem's most famous son, Josiah Wedgwood, described the extreme measures adopted by the local parson to exorcise the creature:

> Once it is said the parson shot at the weird bird, and he became so affected that he never durst be sober for three weeks after, but was forced continually to drink the stiffest brewed ale he could get as a remedy against the black spells of Molly. And full well did the tap of the old 'Turk's Head' do its duty on the occasion, and assist the reverend gentleman in his affliction, supplying him with the strongest brewed that could be found. Strange diseases require strange remedies, so let not the sceptic be too eager with his laugh, to mock at the parson's humble way of meeting his trouble.

Scrape away common commerce at Burslem's ground-level, and irregular windows reveal themselves to the raised eye. Tiled roofs are drawn down firmly like Sunday hats, trees sprout incongruously from some of the chimney pots.

Enter the George Hotel, the site of the fictional Dragon Hotel, and the only information available on the reception desk is a leaflet: *Your complete personal service for Funeral gatherings.* Order the local oatcakes and you are rewarded with succulent pancakes of a sort, rather than the austere tartan biscuits you might expect.

The Bull's Head was probably the focus for bull baiting. In 1814, the local rag reported:

> We lament to be informed that nearly a dozen persons at Burslem have been much injured by an infuriated bull (brought forward by barbarous custom to be tormented for the amusement of the populace), two or three of them so seriously that their lives are despaired of. An inhabitant of Burslem had his thigh lacerated several inches deep; a man from Chesterton, two ribs broken and his head cut in a dreadful manner – a person in Longport, so much hurt, that their recovery is doubtful.

Bugs Gutter and other Bennett evocations breathe through the very brickwork of Burslem. Beyond the fiction, the statue of Sir Henry Doulton, son of the company founder, is still standing but the business has been bought by Wedgewood, the factory closed. For a time, much of Royal Doulton was being manufactured in Djakarta.

Remnants from the Potteries perch on our mantelpieces as sugar bowls and saucers. What happened to all the dippers, mouldrunners and wedgers who created them? Modern science is more synthetic, flint dust and lead poisoning long since transcended.

In springtime, as you make your way to the football ground, you walk over carpets of pink blossom in Burslem Park. When he inaugurated the park in 1893 Lord Dartmouth commended its potential:

> There were several classes of people who would be benefited by the park. In the first place there were the little children who would come and play there and obtain health and strength to enable them to compete in the struggle of life. Then the young men and maidens would come in the sweet summer time and make arrangements for their future life. Then the old men and women, whose day's work was over and whose faces were turned to the setting sun, would come to see their children and grandchildren playing around them…

It was whilst playing in Burslem Park that the football club adopted the name Burslem Port Vale, and turned professional. In July 1885, it was probably the first football club to become a limited company.

> The Bursley Football Club had recently swollen into a genuine rival of the ancient supremacy of the celebrated Knype Club. It had transformed itself into a limited company, and rented a ground up the Moorthorne Road, and built a grand stand. The Bursley F.C. had 'tied' with the Knype F.C. on the Knype ground – a prodigious achievement, an achievement which occupied a column of the *Athletic News* one Monday morning! But were the tradesmen civically proud of this glory? No! They said that 'this football' drew people out of the town on Saturday afternoons, to the complete abolition of shopping. They said also that people thought of nothing but 'this football'; and, nearly in the same breath, that only roughs and good-for-nothings could possibly be interested in such a barbarous game. And they spoke of gate money, gambling, and professionalism, and the end of all true sport in England. In brief, something new had come to the front and was submitting to the ordeal of the curse.

This is from *The Old Wives' Tale* which was published in 1908. A year before, Burslem Port Vale's financial difficulties had prompted its resignation from the Football League for the second time since the club's election to the new Second Division in 1892. In *The Card*, Bennett's next novel, 'the Bursley club had come to the end of its resources. The great football public had practically deserted it.' Bennett also describes how both Knype and Bursley employed trainers 'who, before an important match, took the teams off to a hydropathic establishment far, far distant from any public house.'

In 1886, Port Vale had moved to Cobridge. After mining subsidence nearly caused one player to disappear down a hole during a match, they were tempted in 1913 to retrench in Hanley. The youth of Staffordshire were devoured in the trenches of Flanders, but athleticism reasserted itself and in the first season after the Great War the club made an unexpected return to the League, when they took over the fixtures of Leeds City who were thrown out after eight matches for 'irregular practices'.

The Hanley public remained loyal throughout the 1920s with attendances at the Old Recreation Ground averaging just over 10,000, but cinemas were beginning to compete for people's pockets. The Regent opened in Hanley in 1929, boasting a twenty-two piece orchestra as well as a Wurlitzer, and soon resounding to Al Jolson in *The Singing Fool*. Their rivals, the Essoldo, were still charging only 9d in the late 1950s for the pensioners' matinee, but closed in 1962 after a final double bill of *Naked as Nature Intended* and *Call Girl Business*.

On a rather different note, the Potteries spawned the composer Havergal Brian. Born in Ricardo Street, Dresden, Brian wrote thirty-two symphonies – three times as many as Mahler and some of even bigger dimensions. The *Gothic Symphony* reached the Royal Albert Hall and Third Programme ears in 1966, and the scoring for another included sixteen horns, two pianos and an organ. Brian's first wife, whom he married in 1899, bore him five children, and the composer sired a further five children after his second marriage in 1933. He retired to Shoreham, where he died in 1972 at the age of ninety-six.

It was only in 1950 that Port Vale Football Club moved back to Burslem. Although the stadium could not fulfil its promise to be the 'Wembley of the North', it had a spaciousness unexpected in the claustrophobia of the post-war years. It has played to 50,000 people and there is no danger of anyone being clattered into the advertising hoardings from the wide arch of its pitch.

Port Vale appointed Stanley Matthews as manager shortly after he hung his boots up at Stoke City at the age of fifty. Matthews believed in blooding young talent and in 1966 put out a team against Bradford City with an average age of barely eighteen. Matthews's tenure reached an unhappy conclusion in 1968 when the club was fined and forced to apply for re-election because of breaches of regulations concerning payments to schoolboys and illegal bonuses to players. In his autobiography, Matthews described the tip of the iceberg:

This boy wasn't naughty but he did have habits that were considered by many to be, for want of a better expression, unsociable. The landlady complained to me on several occasions about this lad's peculiar idiosyncrasies, in the end saying that she could no longer provide a roof for the boy. The boy came from a poor background and his family were in no position to send him money, so the club provided the lad with a nominal weekly sum to cover his living expenses. The boy's headmaster found out about this and immediately complained.

Disenchantment at the lower end of League football was not always the exclusive preserve of Hartlepool supporters. After Port Vale's home defeat by Hereford on 20 August 1979, the *Evening Sentinel* published the following letter:

> Just about the only point worth remembering about Port Vale's match with Hereford on Monday evening was the fact that the attendance figure, 2744, is a perfect cube, 14 x 14 x 14.

The sands were already beginning to quicken for the Port Vale team when Keith Houchen signed for the club on 9 August 1991. Darren Beckford and Robbie Earle, who between them had scored 32 of Vale's goals the previous season, had been sold for a total of £1.7 million. Houchen was one of the replacements. He submitted himself to his new supporters in the opening game. The fee was only £100,000, but Hibs had been happy to unload their English difficulty. The other new signing in the forward line was Martin Foyle from Oxford. He scored twice to give Vale a 2-1 win over his former employers. When Houchen opened his account with a brace of goals at Molineux, gloom had not yet descended on the Valiants.

The newcomer with the big reputation felt that he had to earn the trust and respect of the locals:

I could tell when I first played for them that the crowd were a bit reticent about me. I could sense them thinking, 'Big time Charlie, is he going to bother, is he here for more than just the pay?' But they took to me, and really loved me down there. And, as at Hibs, they did the 'Houchy, Houchy, Houchy' thing.

If he could sort out his accommodation – the Houchens spent the first year in a rented farmhouse near Leek – he would be happy. The family eventually gave up the search in the locality and fixed on the children's future by moving to North Yorkshire. This was going to be a real home, somewhere on which to build, which would be more than just a bolt-hole before the next change of job. Having made the move, Houchen normally commuted to work, but sometimes he stayed over and had a boisterous time in digs as Peter Swan's lodger. Swan had signed for Vale at the same time as Houchen.

October and November fell away with an occasional victory and even a 2-2 draw at Anfield in the Rumbelows Cup, but 17 games without a win then pitched the team towards relegation and a bottom-of-the-table finish. For Houchen, it was like being greeted by the leer of a familiar face, but for much of the season he was only a fitful component of the team. Having sought to sign the player on so many occasions, manager John Rudge began to reject him. A substitute appearance in the last game was an afterthought to a season in which he played in only 21 league matches. However, only Foyle scored substantially more than Houchen's four goals.

Small things can affect the relationship between a manager and his player. What starts in a tickle of laughter can end up in a growl. This was the case with Houchen and Rudge. When Houchen was at Hibs, some of the players had gone along to the Playhouse to see the comedian Russ Abbott. When the group spilled out onto Leith Street, they all commented on the close resemblance of Abbott to Houchen. This stuck. When presented with a ball to sign, Houchen got into the habit of adding 'Russ Abbott', having always signed his own name.

On one occasion, the Port Vale players signed a programme to be presented to a hospice. One of the residents was thrilled to discover the signature of the comedian. Rudge got to hear of this and tore Houchen off a strip in the dressing room. He wouldn't be doing with any explanation, 'Don't piss down my back and say it's raining.'

This was prior to a team talk about Saturday's opponents. The names of the opposition players were chalked up on the blackboard from one to eleven ready for Rudge's assessment. However, one of the Vale players, early into the dressing room, had taken the duster to the name of the no.2 and replaced it with ABBOTT. Rudge, having delivered his raging homily about Houchen's attitude to those less fortunate than himself, duly turned to the board to address the weaknesses of the opposition right-back. Chaos ensued. Thereafter, it is fair to say that Houchen never quite recovered his store with the club's executive.

Rudge was born just down the road, in Wolverhampton. When taken by surprise, his favourite invocation was 'Fuck my tin hat!' His team talks were laced with indigenous wisdom and wise saws, knotted by a cousin of the Revd Spooner, 'You're as dead as a sheet and as flat as a dodo.' Advice such as 'Stick to him like sheet to a shit,' was especially confusing for a young Dutch player, Robin van der Laan, who enquired, 'What is this sheet to a shit?'

Silversmiths and trophy makers are kept busy in the summer months manifesting mementos for many a meaningless pre-season football tournament. Houchen contributed a goal to a 5-0 win against De Graafschap in Deventer and, despite losing on penalties to Go Ahead Eagles in Doetinchem, Port Vale had done enough to have their name inscribed as winners of the TNT Tournament and provide Keith with a new medal.

In the middle of another sojourn at Peter Swan's, Houchen went through a further motoring crisis:

From Thirsk, I used to have to leave home at 5.45a.m. when it was still dark.

One morning it was snowing, so I was driving very slowly, but up near Boroughbridge the car started to slide. I remember thinking, 'Here we go again.' The car fell sideways into a large ditch and a big tree came through the windscreen. It took me a while to get out and to stagger onto the road. I frightened the life out of a couple of ladies going to work, but they kindly gave me a lift home. As it was the club's car in the ditch, I was able to drive my own car back to get my stuff out.

It was surrounded by police, fire engines and an ambulance. The indicator had been set off and a local farmer reported a crashed car on fire. With my clothes hanging in the back, it looked like an occupant.

The incident ran for a while as John Rudge was having his little spat with me. The club gave me a knackered old Mondeo with a broken gear box when my contract stipulated that I should have the use of a new car. Once, the gear box fell out of the Mondeo on the M62, but I managed to coax it in fourth gear all the way to Stoke. I had to involve Brendan Batson at the PFA before the matter was resolved.

The introduction of the Premier League resulted in the irritating realignment of the remaining three divisions as First, Second and Third, with the effect that Port Vale found themselves relegated from the Second Division to the Second Division.

Houchen scored 6 goals in 28 League appearances in the 1992/93 season but missed out on two more appearances at Wembley on account of a body that was increasingly in need of repair and the simmeringly unsatisfactory relationship with his boss. The Valiants had finished third, but lost 3-0 to West Brom in the play-off final, with Peter Swan being sent off. The team found solace against Stockport, winning 2-1 in the Autoglass Trophy Final.

Rudge took me off against Bradford when I had been playing really well, and I stood up in the dressing room and had a right go at him. I told him we wouldn't have lost if he had left me on. He liked to play with two small forwards. Bernie Slaven had been injured and was on the bench that night. It was one each, and I had set up the goal. It needed another striker to come on and play with me. But he actually took me off, and brought on Bernie to play with Nicky Cross. I mean, it was a crazy, crazy decision. I wasn't one for throwing my shirt at people or anything like that, but I did go and sit in the dressing room. I could hear from the sound of the crowd what was happening. We ended up losing the match – I could hear them losing it. I knew they had lost when they came in.

After that, he used to drag me to every away match and then not even put me on the bench. He could be quite petty, and I was an experienced player who warranted a little bit more respect. It got very silly, and I fell out with him at half-time during the Autoglass Final.

A supporter asked me to get the lads' signatures. I said, 'You are joking, aren't you? It's half-time, I won't be able to do something like that.'

'Oh please,' he begged me, 'it would mean so much to me.'

So I walked into the dressing room with Rudge doing his team-talk. I'm a proper professional if nothing else, so I waited for him to finish, and just stood by the door and asked one or two of the players to sign the programme. Rudge just went off at me, 'What do you think you are doing? This is the Final. It may not mean anything to you.'

He was bobbing about. One of the lads came through from the bathroom and said, 'What's going on?'

When I gave the programme back to the bloke, he was really thrilled. It was such a big day for the Port Vale fans.

Again, things fizzled out to nothing at Port Vale. Rudge gave me away – for nothing, literally nothing. I still had three good seasons left in me, as I proved at Hartlepool. I should have done something when we were not speaking and he was just dragging me around. I should have knocked on the door and said, 'This is stupid.'

On the following day, there was an open-top bus parade around the town. Bernie Slaven had permission to get back home to Middlesbrough – he had only recently signed for Port Vale. I was supposed to be on the bus even though I hadn't played any part. I had been away for a week and was going back to Middlesbrough so that I could be with Yvonne, so Bernie gave me a lift. I crouched down on the back seat so I couldn't be seen as we drove through the crowds.

A few days later, I got a letter from Rudge to say they were giving me a free transfer.

Houchen had not even been on the bench but, as with the Charity Shield, the occasion hardly had the frisson of the real thing. He was tired of making long journeys and not being required to change into his football kit at the end of them.

For Keith Houchen, the mementos of his time at Vale Park were humble but occasionally humbling. Kevin Monks, who had been one of the organisers of the Keith Houchen fan club during the player's Coventry days, wrote:

> We saw Keith turn out for Port Vale Reserves against Coventry at Highfield Road. This brought Keith up against City 'keeper Steve Ogrizovic. Keith gave me a lift home that night and told me that he'd had a bet with Oggy that he would score. Late in the second half, Keith attacked down the right flank and promptly slammed the ball low into the net. The whole Main Stand jumped up to celebrate this goal. It was the only time I have ever seen Coventry supporters cheering an opposition winning goal.

10

Second Hartlepool

It was a bit like coming home, but only a bit. This was where it had all started fifteen years before when his mum had taken him over to the Victoria Ground that first time.

He drove round the roundabout. The rickety ground reared up in front of him, the wooden fence waving like a broken concertina, the North Sea still but grey in the distance.

The old wooden stand that was there when I was a kid had been knocked down because of the Bradford fire. They just had two portakabins and loads of waste ground. It was pretty bleak.

What was he doing coming back to Hartlepool? 'Let's turn round,' he half-joked to his team-mate as the ground came into view. But this was where his ambitions had taken shape, when Wembley was not yet on the wing, the five years at Coventry and Hibs a dream away.

He was thirty-three, but outwardly fit. Port Vale had given him a 'free', and there was plenty of interest. There were prospects in Switzerland and Scotland and he had even been negotiating with the Cypriot champions, Omonia. Omonia were about to embark on their European Cup campaign and were offering plenty of inducements to fill the gap between sun and sand. Why Hartlepool, a broken-down outfit that had not moved on in all that time, in a town with its back to the sea? 'They came, they asked,' was the answer. Poor health had seen off the other summer opportunities. Hartlepool United were also enjoying a rare sabbatical in the Third Division with promotion three years before.

A goalscorer was Hartlepool's chief requirement. Earlier in the year, the team had gone 1,227 minutes, the equivalent of kick-off time until Sunday lunch, without scoring. It beat Coventry's record for impotence into a cocked hat – one that had stood since 1919.

When the doors swung open at the hospital, the footballer was propped up in his pyjamas. At the end of the previous season, he had had a double hernia operation in Liverpool. In undergoing the operation he caught a serious infection which saw him in and out of hospital all summer and for which, with the PFA's help, he successfully sued the surgeon. He was even more ill than he had been with pneumonia at Coventry.

Manager Viv Busby greeted him. It was 1 August 1993. Busby had been Denis Smith's assistant when Houchen signed for York, and had found his way to Hartlepool via Sunderland and a year on the dole.

There was a gentleman with an attaché case whom Houchen didn't recognise. He was Garry Gibson, new as chairman since Houchen's day.

Gibson's touch did not always inspire the trust of those around him. In 1988, company information specialists Jordans, in association with the accountants Peat Marwick McLintock, issued a financial report on all ninety-two Football League clubs. They reported that Hartlepool United had not filed any company accounts for five years. While Gibson was happy to solicit sympathy for himself through a regular column in *The Northern Echo,* he made sure to place a press embargo on the players when they were not getting paid.

Houchen never did find out from Vince Barker, the chairman from his day, what it was he should never 'forget'. Barker had left the club in 1985 under a cloud. Ed Law describes what happened when Barker, still a director, sought to oust John Smart as chairman:

> Barker alleged that the club owed him £82,000 and was given leave by the High Court to apply for a winding-up order which, had it been successful, would have seen the end of Hartlepool United. In the event the matter was resolved without recourse to any High Court judgement and Barker ended his association with the club… Sadly, Vince Barker, the man who had invested his own capital to save the club only a few seasons before, was no longer welcome at the Victoria Ground.

There were flowers but no grapes for Houchen, a view from the window but not for very far; time was eating at his legs, the future almost spent. Surrounded by senile and juvenile in varying states of decay, hospital is not a propitious pitch for transfer talks, but the attaché case opened and Hartlepool United wanted their son home. They knew what they were getting, and the invalid was commissioned on a basic wage – stratospheric for Hartlepool – of £600 a week. The two parties sat in the canteen of the South Cleveland Hospital in Middlesbrough and scribbled their signatures on a piece of paper.

The ageing athlete might get to do some coaching. He had no particular desire to become a manager but it kept the door ajar for when he ran out of puff and his legs finally collapsed.

It was not York or Edinburgh. The surroundings make a difference, even if going to work is playing football. If it's not your town, a besieged backdrop of docks and council houses is not going to be as congenial as the Minster or the Castle.

Certain football grounds have a feisty smell, a feel that can be oppressive to those whose workplaces they become. For Keith Houchen, memories of the Victoria Ground were through the nose, as of a school or a hospital. It was a ramshackle spot with those wooden shacks as offices. Drop your change and it disappeared through the floorboards for ever.

There was that real dour, working class, swimming-against-the-tide sort of thing.

However, this was the place where one young man had been given his chance, where the schoolboy who had been excited by seeing his name in the papers in Middlesbrough embraced a wider audience. This was the turf on which he had scored many a memorable goal, in days before cameras came to grab every moment as if it was a diving header at Wembley.

Yes, it was putting something back into the game, but it was also about putting something back into himself. The nomadic existence was coming to an end. It was back on familiar territory, a chance to sow long-term roots for the sake of all the family, to plan a home for longer than the next whim of the transfer market. It was also only a forty minute drive from home.

I didn't need to go back – it nearly broke me. But I always had it in my mind to finish off my career at Hartlepool.

There were a lot of old pros who were at the club but they took the piss out of it – I wanted to give something back. And I did; I was top scorer for two seasons.

He adored the people in Burslem, stuttering place as it was, and the Potteries generally, but things had not developed as well with John Rudge as he had hoped.

At Port Vale, as at Hibs, the manager ended up taking me the wrong way, and instead of just dealing with things in a proper managerial way he became really petty, which was a shame, because I wouldn't change my first year at either club.

He loved Vale Park – a big ground – and the atmosphere generated by the supporters, but he had not found a home in the area. The round trip from Yorkshire was hundreds of miles long.

While the Burslem of Bennett had become embossed on tourist arrows, Hartlepool's haemorrhaging had yet to be entirely stemmed.

I couldn't begin to explain to people how poor and down-trodden and dull and difficult Hartlepool was in the late seventies and early eighties, as a town and as a football club.

You'd go in and it was freezing cold. There was a little wooden walkway into the dressing-room. The wind would blow through it, the bath was minute. Sometimes we trained on a field at an ambulance depot inside a housing estate. More often, you'd have to get your kit on, jump in the cars and drive up to the power station with all these pylons over your head and the freezing cold coming off the sea. It was a hard way to make a living and the players were not always getting paid, with the wages bouncing.

The pylons dwarfed the beach at Seaton Carew. Training was once abandoned when a lady was spotted struggling with a seal. 'It had become separated from its mother and made its way up to the sand dunes where it was quite distressed,' said the RSPCA Inspector. Seal pups have teeth like adult dogs and can be quite aggressive if frightened. The track-suited assistants bore the three-week-old pup a mile to its transport.

Hartlepool's footballers cranked their season into life with successive home wins over Stockport and Blackpool, and after seven games the team was comfortably placed in mid-table. Only momentarily, on Brian

Clough's foundations, had Hartlepool hitherto stuck its head out of the bottom division.

Six defeats followed. In the last of them, the side did at least score, with a goal by Lenny Johnrose, but it was not enough to keep Viv Busby in a job. It was Busby, at York, who had helped extend Houchen's horizons to the novel pleasure of playing in a winning team.

John MacPhail took Busby's place the next day. MacPhail had started his career at Dundee. When Hartlepool signed him in 1990, he had already made 433 League appearances for Sheffield United, York, Bristol City and Sunderland. Now, he was in his fourth season at the heart of the 'Pool defence. At nearly thirty-eight, he was reaching the end of a distinguished playing career and was the natural choice as manager.

Houchen made his comeback. He had been getting fit after all his illness, and was stretching himself in the Reserves. On 2 October 1993, he ran out at Turf Moor for his first League game for Hartlepool since 20 March 1982 – eleven-and-a-half years before. He had been top scorer in each of his last four seasons at the club. The hero was back, but it was six games before he scored, with the first goal in a 2-1 home win over Barnet. A six-match losing streak had been spiked by a draw at Cardiff.

A depressing Cup defeat at non-League Macclesfield set the tone for a slide into the relegation zone. Houchen was sent off on 27 December as 'Pool crashed 4-1 at home to Huddersfield. The gloom was briefly punctuated by a 2-0 home win over Rotherham on New Year's Day – both goals coming from Houchen – but it was nearly thirteen weeks before the next win. Then, in a season which saw no team in the division score fewer times, Hartlepool struck 7 of their 41 goals within the space of five days. Houchen scored the last in a 3-0 victory over Cardiff, and then hit two against Burnley who were eventually promoted. This 4-1 win was the biggest of the season. Houchy completed a great week at the Victoria Ground by scoring the only goal of the game against Swansea. However, after a good draw at Huddersfield, it all collapsed. There was a seven-goal stuffing at Rotherham, and 'Pool bowed out with an 8-1 home defeat by Plymouth. Houchen scored in a win over Bristol Rovers but relegation was long since confirmed. Only Barnet finished lower, with Hartlepool seventeen points behind fifth-from-bottom Blackpool. Despite the thrashings, the principal problem was still the lack of goals.

So, after three seasons, the 'Pool were back on the more familiar fields of the old Fourth Division. And for Houchen, it was a return to the regular struggles that had characterised the early years of his career before signing for York.

The arrows were no sharper at the beginning of the 1994/95 season, and Chris Lynch's winner against Darlington was Hartlepool's only goal in their first six League games; all the more surprising that they pumped five past Bury in the Coca-Cola Cup.

On 9 September, the inevitable happened with John MacPhail being sacked. MacPhail's assistant Alan Hay – both men were friends of Houchen – was also dismissed.

Billy Horner stepped briefly into the breach, long enough to appoint Houchen as player-coach. There were plenty of applicants for the post of manager, some of them with reasonable track records. The appointment of David McCreery came as a surprise to many, particularly those on the playing staff who had experienced him before.

The former Newcastle and Northern Ireland midfielder originally joined Hartlepool at the start of the 1991/92 season as a player. He had a brief spell as assistant-manager to Alan Murray, before being appointed manager of Carlisle in September 1992. Carlisle's brash new owner was Michael Knighton, a former director at McCreery's first club Manchester United. Knighton brought publicity and big ideas to the Cumbrian club but his manager didn't deliver the results and lasted only a season.

John MacPhail reflected in *The Observer,* on 28 September 2003, on his time as Hartlepool boss:

> I was absolutely devastated when Hartlepool sacked me as their manager. Although they retained me as a player, that did not last long. For some reason David McCreery refused to play me. Having to turn out for the reserves against awful teams was demoralising and, because of the circumstances of my sacking, I sued the club for unfair dismissal. I never had my day in court because, acting on solicitors' advice, I settled, with a condition being that I had to sign a confidentiality agreement not to speak against the club.
>
> Although I had no real idea what the job entailed, I was certainly not about to turn it down. I had learnt from the various managers I played for and I felt I could do a good job. You are constantly looking at players, thinking about money, deciding how much you can pay a new signing and debating tactics. It consumes your whole life.

Why did my one attempt at management not work out? Basically because the players were not always being paid by the then chairman [Garry Gibson]. How can players be totally committed if they are not sure of their wages? And how was I expected to carry out my job successfully with the players in that position? I can recall countless occasions when the lads met to decide if they were going to play on the Saturday. I would have to ask the chairman if they were going to receive their money. Sometimes the answer was yes, at others the money was just not there.

We never found out where the money was going. All I do know is this situation made my job virtually impossible. There was no way of bringing in new players and some of the players were earning as little as seventy pounds a week which even then was nothing. I tried to bring David Moyes in from Preston as my number two – we had played together at Bristol City – but that fell through because we could pay him only £400 a week, half of what he was earning at Preston.

This is basically why results went against me and, although I wanted to carry on, a new chairman bought the club and I was out. I'd been a player for twenty-three years, made more than 700 appearances, but there I was, thirty-nine and with no education or any other skills to build a life away from football.

Not that I walked away from the game right then. I sat by the 'phone, but it never rang. Once you get pushed off football's magic roundabout, it's very hard to get back on. Unless, of course, you know a few people and go crawling to them. But I'm not one of those.

That period of my life was difficult. For six months, I woke up feeling I was going loopy. It was very difficult, after all the time I had spent in the game, to be left with nothing. Of course, it affected my family as well.

I started up a kitchen furniture business, but that lasted just a year. Fortunately, I had a friend who worked in a car showroom and I was lucky enough, as I have an interest in cars, to start working there as a salesman.

I don't regret my time as Hartlepool's manager. Even when we were getting beaten, it was a great job. I would love to get back into the game, but I know deep down it will probably never happen.

MacPhail left the club as a player in March 1995. At thirty-nine, his body was beginning to creak, and his relationship with McCreery had become increasingly uneasy.

Houchen's relationship with McCreery was also uneasy. It was clear from the start that McCreery did not intend to team up with him as coach. The new manager had invited the former Hearts boss Sandy Clark to 'Pool for a few days in an 'advisory role'. It was all very sly. Houchen returned from a coaching course under Don Howe in Sheffield to find Clark ensconced in the office. Houchen changed into his track suit, and Clark gave him a lift up to the training ground with one of the players. In the car, the player turned to Clark and said, 'What are we going to do today?' as if it was Clark's decision. Houchen, sniffing a rat, bided his time, but not for long.

At the end of the session, Clark addressed the players. It was 'Dirty Dozen' stuff:

> You lot are the lowest of the low. You can't get any further down than this shitty little club.

That was too much. Houchen rose to his feet. 'Whoa!' Who did Clark think he was, talking to the players in such a manner? This was Hartlepool United and people should be proud to play for the club and to make something of it, not to knock it down.

Clark's crude psychology was blown out that day at the power station. McCreery had been at the training session and, back in the office, Houchen grabbed him and verbally let rip.

Houchen was getting changed before the game the next day when Sandy Clark walked into the dressing room.

'Can I have a word with you outside?' said Houchen. The two men went into the passage.

'I am the coach at this club and I don't want you anywhere near the players. Do you understand?' Sandy Clark was never seen again.

When things came to a head over McCreery's attempt to bring in Clark, Hornsey and the club's chief executive Stuart Bagnall called Houchen and McCreery into the office. Houchen was unexpectedly forthright.

I think everyone got a bit frightened that it was all going to fall apart. 'We have just got something going here, calm down Keith, relax a bit,' I remember Bagnall saying to me. I don't know whether they thought they could push me out and I would take the hint and go back to just playing, but I really went berserk about it. Maybe it put it in their minds for me to take over, that I was a strong character.

Hartlepool had eventually begun to find their sights in the 1994/95 season. Houchen netted in a 2-0 win against Gillingham and was on the score-sheet again in consecutive matches against Preston and Walsall. In the next round of the Coca-Cola Cup against Arsenal, 'Pool lost 2-0 at Highbury having lost the first leg 5-0. The few bob the club made from the tie could afford the treasurer a rare glint of a smile. In the FA Cup, a 6-0 thrashing at Port Vale was particularly galling for the Valiants' former centre forward.

A week later, the 3-0 defeat at Doncaster plunged 'Pool to the bottom of the League. But then came a change of wind. Victories against Rochdale and at Darlington were followed by a 3-1 home win over Bury. Bury were flying, second in the table and beaten only twice, but a hat-trick by Houchen dramatically shot them down. A third of the way into the game, a pass from Nicky Southall split the Bury defence. Houchen, looking a shade off-side, sprinted onto the ball and swept it around the Bury 'keeper before honing in on the target. 'I don't get the chance to do that very often,' the striker purred, relishing his run on the 'keeper. He then pounced on Scott Sloan's parried shot to put 'Pool ahead and added his third with a header from a cross by Paul Daughtry.

Unfortunately for the goalscorer, his goals were not the only memorable aspect of the game. Houchen – 'most politely described as "talkative" during matches', as one paper put it – had already been booked in the first half for dissent when referee Kevin Lynch dismissed him late on for using foul and abusive language. Houchen said at the time:

I would never swear at a ref. All I said to him was 'get away'. I will fight it if that is what he is saying. There was a breakdown in communication between us early in the game. It was all pretty silly. I'm just frustrated. I used to be able to get on with referees – there are still some good ones around – but things have changed. For every high there is a low. I had three highs and one big low. I would love to complain but I have never seen one of those decisions overturned. It is frustrating if I get a ban now and miss important games.

Houchen was being admonished by Lynch for time-wasting while lying on the ground receiving treatment for a knee injury. The damage to his ligaments kept him out of the team for the next six matches and was the lingering injury that eventually finished his career. Mr Lynch is now a refereeing assessor.

He lied about the reason for sending me off.

On Boxing Day, Carlisle crushed their Christmas hosts 5-1. Hartlepool's season never recovered. Houchen did notch a brace in a home win against Doncaster, but a month later his life took a new turn.

On 20 April 1995, David McCreery resigned after being informed that his contract would not be renewed in the summer. On the previous Saturday, 'Pool had gone to Brunton Park for the return with League leaders Carlisle. 'Pool won with a goal from Houchen. A disappointed McCreery trudged away from his office at the Victoria Ground with his possessions in a bin liner.

Despite the unexpected victory, the club was in the lurch. Harold Hornsey might never have appointed McCreery had he thought that he could interest Houchen in the job, but Houchen had appeared reticent. This time, Hornsey made sure to sound Houchen out in advance. Billy Horner had felt all along that his protégé was up to it.

Hartlepool needed Houchen, but 'poisoned chalice' is too accurate a job description for it to be a cliché. Managers came and went at the club like janitors in the night, Houchen being the twenty-third appointment in thirty-eight years. Of the ten previous managers, only Billy Horner had lasted longer than two years; John Duncan and Michael Docherty didn't even make one, still less did Busby, MacPhail or McCreery. Duncan accepted a better offer from Chesterfield and Tommy Docherty's son was sacked after only 1 win in 23 matches. Bobby Moncur, who saw 'Pool into the fourth round of the Cup after his appointment in October 1988, only survived until the following November.

Houchen was the fifth person to take charge at Hartlepool in the four years since Cyril Knowles stepped down. Knowles (the eponymous 'Nice one, Cyril') had suffered a brain tumour and died six months later.

Why take the job? There were various reasons: a little bit extra in the pocket with his playing days coming to an end, an ambitious chairman, and to a professional like Houchen the challenge – and belief – that he could make all the difference.

Houchen's undoing in the job was in daring to have the conviction that he really could make all the difference. In reality, you could no more argue with fate than with a ref.

I have gone through my whole career saying I would never stay in football once my career was over. Being manager never crossed my mind when I came back eighteen months ago, but I have always had a real feeling for the club. The worse we have done, the more I have wanted us to get better. We were down the bottom of the division last year and have been down the bottom this year but the fans have kept coming because we are their team.

I would never have said it was the hardest job in football. A lot of people, and a lot of players, have this image of Hartlepool as a bad place to come to. But I have always been really fond of the club, it is a family club with a good atmosphere. If anything, the stadium has let it down in the past. I remember starting here at seventeen when the chairman Vince Barker showed me plans for the stadium that were out of this world. But sixteen years later the ground has got worse if anything. But now we have a chairman who does not just say things, he gets things done.

I am very proud to have been appointed manager but I will be even more proud if this club can really take off with me still a part of it. I remember how Port Vale used to be down in the dumps but they have gone from crowds of 1,500 to about 6,000 to 7,000 and a decent position in the First Division. We can get there too, but we need to get the foundations right first. I would like to be here four or five years down the road when that 'dour Hartlepool' stigma has been taken away.

I do think we need three or four new faces but it is important to get consistency. I won't do anything too drastic because we have some good players here, the nucleus of a good side.

Thus Houchen set out his store to Sean Atkins in the *Hartlepool Mail*. At the same time, the outgoing manager was bitter, and ill-disposed to any token of good wishes to his successor:

It is annoying because I thought I could have done something. You look at what I have done and we have got 29 points which is good under the circumstances. When I came here I knew it was going to be hard but it was way beyond my expectations. I was not able to bring in my own people and I inherited a lot of things like the situation with John MacPhail. You think things are going to change but they don't, and people expect miracles. It has been draining. I don't mind hard work if you are going to see something at the end of it, but I have been up against a brick wall.

A new broom should come in and sweep the place clean. I think this club is like a closed shop and I felt like an outsider from the start. I know that I haven't played as much as I wanted to but it comes down to staff, and I need to see what is going on which you can't do when you are playing.

Terry Cochrane, a former Northern Ireland international and a friend of McCreery, went on local radio to accuse Houchen of having sought to undermine his pal's position.

I don't like pundits on TV or radio. It's just jobs for the boys. They pop up and say something they know nothing about, and get paid for it. And basically that was what Cochrane was doing on one of the local radio stations.

Some years later, Houchen was amused to hear from a mutual contact that Cochrane was now expressing himself a little more ingratiatingly.

McCreery said that he felt shut out by the 'old boy network' at the Victoria Ground. In truth, as Houchen says, he was 'a weak little man' who did not enjoy much respect. He was criticised for not playing himself often enough and it seemed that his constant use of five-a-sides in training was less to sharpen up the players than to avoid actually having to coach them.

He was a little cheat, didn't train properly, didn't play. When the chips were down he went missing. He was fully qualified, took all his badges up at Lilleshall when it was a lot harder, but he couldn't put things into practice. He talked himself into that job, but I think when he got there he didn't like the idea of working with me. His problem was I was his best player; I was getting all the headlines; I was scoring all the goals. So he had to work with me.

Houchen was happy to appoint from within. He couldn't have asked for a better shoulder to lean on than Billy Horner's. Horner was steeped in football in the North-East. Born in Cassop, Co. Durham, he made over 400 League appearances as a wing-half for Middlesbrough and Darlington. Having succeeded Ken Hale in 1976, he had two spells as manager of Hartlepool – for a total of more than nine years. With the exception of Fred Westgarth after the war, Horner's tenure was the longest in the club's history, making it, in monarchical terms, almost Victorian in span. As player-manager at Darlington, he was one of the few to take over at Hartlepool with previous managerial experience. Hartlepool had to seek re-election in his first two seasons but finished ninth in 1980/81.

His best season in charge was when they finished seventh in 1985/86. Horner, who had brought Houchen to the club as a seventeen-year-old, said:

> I would never have thought he would go into management, but he is the kind of player who takes in what managers tell him, and he can use it now. You don't get to have the kind of career he has had, and go to Wembley, without learning a lot. I first noticed he had something when John MacPhail and Alan Hay asked him to take charge of the warm-ups.

Horner's official position was as youth team coach. Another recruit to the coaching staff was Brian Honour, who had made well over 300 appearances for 'Pool before injury forced his retirement earlier in the season. Houchen completed his North-Eastern 'gang of four' with Mick Tait who moved into Houchen's old shoes as player-coach. Tait, a midfielder with 740 League games already under his belt, had made friends with Houchen since becoming his team-mate at the Vic. His career looked like a spider's web in an AA book: Oxford, Carlisle, Hull, Portsmouth, Reading, Darlington and Hartlepool. 'Rather than taking it all on my shoulders, decisions will be made by the four of us with our physio Gary Henderson having more involvement on the fitness side,' added Houchen.

Harold Hornsey was enthusiastic about his new appointment:

> I always thought Keith had management potential, but when the job came up before I felt he needed more time. I think Keith is going to surprise a lot of people. He loves Hartlepool United and he's willing to give the same commitment as me to the club. It's not going to be easy – like David he will have no money to spend – but Keith's convinced he can do it and I'm sure he can. He's very impressive. He's got the respect of the players, he's positive and most of all he wants Hartlepool to succeed. I can't see any fan doubting the wisdom of my selection.

Brian Clough wrote of the challenges that he and Peter Taylor faced at Hartlepools:

> We learned how to ship-out the deadwood and bring in better players. We learned how to lift a team from bottom in October to the safety of eighteenth place by the end of the season. We learned where to place buckets to catch

the rain that leaked through the holes in the roof. We learned how to sign a youngster [John McGovern] from grammar school whose headmaster wanted him to go to university rather than to Hartlepools United, which wasn't an unreasonable point of view, I suppose.

There were three games left of the 1994/95 season. For the first time since the mid-1960s, the average attendance had dropped below 2,000. There was no party to greet the new manager, despite the team's salesmanship at Carlisle the previous week. And Hereford, who had no more to write home about than 'Pool, were hardly going to bring coach-loads. In the event, a miserable crowd of 1,596 witnessed 'Pool's best win of the season, with loan players Steve Holmes and Damian Henderson scoring a brace apiece in the second half to give Houchy a 4-0 start. It virtually assured the club of avoiding bottom place and relegation to the Vauxhall Conference. A good beginning.

The following week, Houchen was sitting at the front of the coach for the first time as the team departed to play promotion-chasing Preston. He recalled how, as a young player, he used to slouch on the back seat, lager in hand, thanking his lucky stars that he didn't have to shoulder the burden of the poor bugger at the front. On the return journey, a 3-0 defeat served to reinforce the memory.

Deprived of the prospect of watching their heroes through the summer, there was a crowd of 3,049, the second highest of the season, for the visit of Mansfield on the last Saturday of term. Mansfield were already into the play-offs. A 3-2 win, with a hat-trick by eighteen-year-old Stephen Halliday, enabled 'Pool to finish fifth from bottom. The Houchens could look forward to their summer holiday.

Whilst the Houchens were on that holiday, dramatic changes were taking place at the dilapidated Victoria Ground. Harold Hornsey took over as chairman in 1994, and had made much of his fortune from property and the DIY trade. The club couldn't develop unless it spruced up the hapless theatre that was its home.

The ground was laid out by West Hartlepool Rugby Club in 1886. In 1908, the newly formed Hartlepools United took over, and divided the ground into two separate parts, with the southern half later becoming a greyhound stadium. For a time, United shared with West Hartlepool Football Club who had won the FA Amateur Cup in 1905, but West Hartlepool FC disbanded in 1910. During the same year, the Queen's skating rink was opened adjacent to the ground. The local economy, based on shipyards and steelworks, was thriving.

The shipyards and steelworks were presumably the targets on the night of 27 November 1916 when, for the second time, German Zeppelins flew over from Nordholz on a bombing raid. Apart from thirteen people injured, the main casualties were a woman who died of shock and Hartlepools United's wooden stand. The stand was flattened by two bombs jettisoned after one of the Zeppelins was intercepted. Lieutenant I. Pyott, who was based with the squadron at Seaton Carew, shot the Zeppelin down, and it fell into the sea in a ball of fire less than a mile off the Headland. On 11 January 1917, the burial took place at Seaton Carew of two of the crew whose bodies had been washed ashore. Three more bodies were subsequently buried with them. Another Zeppelin had been pursued and brought down at dawn over the Norfolk coast. A further raid in 1918 was more serious, killing eight civilians and injuring twenty-two others.

The beleaguered Victoria Ground presented some unusual attractions during the Great War. On 7 July 1917 there was a Military Girls Sports Day, including three and four-legged races, hobble skirt races, tug-of-war and, no doubt, strange variants of egg-and-spoon. The takings were divided equally between The Crippled Children's Guild and The West Hartlepool Indignent Sick Society. Seven weeks later, a football match took place between Browns Girls and a male team representing the 347 Works Company of the Durham Light Infantry. In order to ensure a more evenly balanced contest, the gentlemen had their hands bound behind their backs. Two goals by a lady called Snowball helped secure the Girls a 5–5 draw. What is not clear is whether the opposition goalkeeper had also been deprived of the use of his arms. Such a consideration brings to mind the armless person plaintively surveying a toilet roll in the cartoon by Siné.

A £2,500 compensation claim, subsequently submitted by Hartlepools United to the German government, was rebuffed. In the Second World War the German bombs just missed the ground.

In 1919 the club played three games at a ground at Foggy Furze, where a temporary wooden stand was built. The stand was re-erected a few weeks later at the Victoria Ground. After Hartlepools joined the League in 1921 it was still in use, and remained so for many years while the council deliberated on a scheme to widen Clarence Road, behind the stand. In *Football Grounds of Britain,* Simon Inglis describes how the plans gathered dust, as did the increasingly ramshackle stand, which apparently became a 'favourite haunt for canoodling couples from the skating rink'.

Inglis continues:

In fact, the first major changes at the ground did not occur until a young Brian Clough became manager in 1965. Clough would later recall how part of his duties involved regular repairs to the rickety Main Stand and, on one occasion, humping 150 sheets of corrugated iron across the pitch in order to re-roof one of the end terrace roofs (which were in essence hardly more than elongated bus shelters).

It was during Clough's period that floodlights were belatedly installed. Then, after having helped earn promotion to the Third Division in 1968, up went the new steel-framed, £40,000 Mill House Stand with cantilevered roof. United planned to move their offices and players' facilities into the voids under this stand, but by then Clough had moved on and, with pennies almost as scarce as golden sovereigns, in 1971 the club had no alternative but to sell the ground to the council for £10,000.

This could have signalled the start of a new era of co-operation and joint planning. But like the Clarence Road scheme, nothing ever happened. Instead, the Queen's Rink was demolished (as were all the town's cinemas and, in 1977, the last steelworks), while behind the Mill House Stand the council built one of the first of a new generation of leisure centres, incorporating a pool with waterslides, squash courts, all-weather pitch and indoor bowls club.

Meanwhile, over the flaking fences of the Victoria Ground a deep gloom prevailed. In 1980 the chairman was so frustrated at being rebuffed in his attempts to buy back the ground that he threatened to move United to Scarborough. Five years later the continued lack of investment told when, following the Bradford fire, the 620 seat 'temporary' stand was finally taken down after sixty-six years. It was so unstable by then that the stifling cubby-hole rooms and creaking corridors underneath seemed welded together by thick blue paint, damp carpets and formica panelling, while there were times when high winds forced games to be postponed lest the stand just blew away.

As a result of new laws relating to wooden structures in the wake of the Bradford fire in 1985, the stand was unusable and it was demolished. Aided by a £60,000 City challenge grant to tidy up the environs, plus £490,000 from the Football Trust and £25,000 from the local council, United were finally able to plug the Clarence Road gap with the construction of a £650,000 stand. Opened in July 1995, it was named after former manager Cyril Knowles who had died in 1991. (This at least made up for the fact that when Hartlepool had played a testimonial for Knowles's family, the cheque had bounced.) Also in 1995 the Town End was re-proofed and roofed, thus providing decent cover on all four sides of the ground for the first time in the club's history.

The cheque for Knowles's widow had in fact bounced not once, but three times. Things had changed by the time Graham Taylor, the former England manager, came to visit Victoria Park (the Victoria Ground had become Victoria Park in August 1995). Taylor commented on how things had developed since the days when he took Lincoln and Watford sides to Hartlepool:

> The whole town has changed so much and even the approach to the ground is very impressive. I have been looking around the ground and there should be some praise given to the people responsible for this…There is a lot of emphasis on the Premier League but I believe clubs like Hartlepool should be given due recognition. There has got to be a place for the Hartlepools in football.

Hartlepool's rookie manager reflected:

> *Sometimes to be a manager in the fullest sense you have got to serve an apprenticeship, and Hartlepool is like Lincoln in that respect. At this level you learn the nuts and bolts of management and it is not easy, it is never easy.*

Houchen's first full season in charge was just over a fortnight away. The player-manager took his players to Scotland for a friendly at Ayr United. The referee's report stated that K. Houchen – no.9 – was cautioned in the eighty-third minute for showing dissent by word or action.

The following day the team travelled from the Firth of Clyde to Methil, overlooking the Firth of Forth, to play East Fife. K. Houchen – no.9 – was cautioned in the eighty-first minute for showing dissent by word or action.

The League season opened on 12 August 1995 with a 2-0 defeat at Chester. On this occasion the ref went into more detail. He reported that in the seventy-sixth minute the Chester 'keeper had finger-tipped the ball over the bar for a corner. K. Houchen had raced towards him shouting for a penalty. The ref had again indicated for a corner. At this, the player had allegedly shouted, 'You want to take a serious look at yourself.' K. Houchen was immediately booked for dissent.

A week later at the Vic, Hartlepool played out a goalless draw with Exeter. Then, at Spotland, Rochdale dealt 'Pool a four-goal thrashing. Frazer G. Stretton was on hand to administer a caution to Houchen 'for a late reckless challenge on his opponent'. There was victory against Northampton, defeat at Doncaster and – thanks to a goal from the manager – a share of the spoils with Darlington. The team was already perched perilously in twenty-second place.

A Tuesday night trip to Hartlepool doesn't readily recommend itself if you're a Torquay United player. 'Pool duly took a half-time lead through Houchen only for Torquay to pull back to 2-2. In the forty-second minute, Mr Riley penalised Houchen for offside. Houchen gestured towards the linesman that he was not in full accord with his decision and shouted 'rubbish'. Having already warned Houchen, Mr Riley now administered an official caution for dissent.

The reward for knocking Scarborough out of the Coca-Cola Cup on penalties was, for the second year running, a tie with Arsenal. The first leg was played at the Victoria Park. Did Dennis Bergkamp, formerly of Ajax and Internazionale, know where Hartlepool was? An extra 3,000 people turned up in the hope that he would be given reason not to forget, but two goals from Tony Adams and one from Ian Wright ensured that the second leg would be a formality. At the Vic, the referee was again less than grateful for the benefit of Houchen's views. In the seventieth minute Houchen made strong, persistent objections over a decision. Having spoken earlier to the player about his conduct, the referee reached for the yellow card. The booking took Houchen to over twenty-one penalty points and an automatic two-match suspension.

Over 27,000 people turned out to watch Arsenal complete an 8-0 aggregate victory at Highbury. Bergkamp scored two and Wright three.

A fortnight later, 8-0 reared its head again, but this time in a single match when Hartlepool lost their Auto Windscreens Shield game at Crewe. Houchen, who did not play, was sufficiently vexed by his team's performance to call the players in for extra training. As the naughty kids buckled down, it was their turn to be vexed when suddenly there was a big explosion from the nuclear power station. This was followed by a firework display and enormous belchings of smoke.

'Shouldn't we stop, gaffer?' bleated one of the miscreants.

'Not until we've finished the training session,' came the bald reply. Twenty minutes later, as they ran for their cars, the players found half of Cleveland's fire services blocking their exit. They didn't lose 8-0 again in a hurry.

The season continued to engender little excitement. In October, having sold midfielder Nicky Southall to Grimsby for £40,000 Houchen persuaded the chairman to spend the money on a new centre forward. Joe Allon had scored freely during a previous spell at the Vic. His 28 League goals in 1990/91 equalled Hartlepool's club record for a season and earned a £250,000 transfer to Chelsea. Houchen had first met and got to like Allon when they were together at Port Vale. Allon did score nine times on his return, indeed more frequently that season than Houchen. However, the manager felt let down. Experience is no substitute for hunger.

Sometimes pros are finished, and mentally Joe just didn't fancy it anymore. It put pressure on me because I was having to play him to justify the fee, but then the fans are asking 'Why are you playing him?' when he's not doing it. If he had done what I bought him to do, we could have been comfortably up there.

Allon and his manager were both in trouble on 28 October 1995 when they were sent off in the home game against Gillingham, with Gillingham also losing Tony Butler.

Houchen scored twice in a 3-0 victory at Mansfield, in time to get home and play Santa to the children, and in the next match at Bury celebrated the first day of 1996 by opening the scoring in another 3-0 win. It was his 150th goal in the Football League. He was not to know that it would also be his last.

Momentarily, mid-table seemed a realistic aspiration, but by February penalty points were again overflowing. After the Rochdale game, the ref complained that the player-manager for Hartlepool generally bemoaned most of the decisions made against players from his team. The ref eventually warned him regarding his attitude to the game. In the eighty-fifth minute, he stopped play and duly cautioned Houchen for a loud outburst of verbal dissent, to the effect, 'That's crap man, you're just a joke, and you cost people their living.'

At Plainmoor, the ref warned, and subsequently advised Houchen as to his comments on decisions given in the game. In the eighty-third minute, Houchen commented again regarding a previous incident. In adopting such a phrase as 'disgraceful decision ref,' Houchen's objective was clear and he was cautioned for dissent.

This yellow card at Torquay on 17 February brought the dissenter's points tally to thirty-three, the next benchmark for a ban. The statutory letter from the chief executive of the Football Association duly followed. Suspension would commence on the fourteenth day following the date of his last offence and endure until such time as his club's recognised senior team had completed two matches in approved competitions. During Houchen's absence, home fixtures against Hereford and Mansfield yielded only a point – and just one goal.

At home to Doncaster on 20 February, Houchen was cautioned in the seventh minute for a late reckless challenge on his opponent. Another letter from the chief executive of the FA arrived, concerning matters arising from the game. Not for the first time, referee Frazer G. Stretton had taken exception. Houchen felt moved to reply:

> I write with reference to your recent letter outlining the charges against me, arising from our match against Doncaster Rovers on 20.02.96. I do not dispute that I was extremely upset and angry after this game, and did approach the officials. Whether I actually said what I am alleged to have said, I think is open to dispute.
>
> I feel very strongly that there has been a steady decline over the past few seasons in the relationship between referees, managers and players. It has become a them and us situation. There is very little rapport between officials and players, though obviously there are exceptions, and red and yellow cards seem to be given at every opportunity rather than as a last resort.
>
> I realise that in the lower divisions we are working with a number of recently qualified referees and that they are feeling their way into football to a certain extent, but there needs to be a lot more common sense and flexibility towards players.
>
> I am in constant touch with Trevor Simpson, my local referee co-ordinator regarding the problems that keep arising in this area, but feel that with no right of appeal against decisions the dice are loaded very much against players and clubs.

Regarding the incident for which I am being charged I would ask you to take into account the fact that we had 3 players sent off in the previous 2 games which were very, very harsh decisions both on the players concerned and on the club, bearing in mind that because of financial restraints put upon us we have a small playing squad of only 17, including myself and my assistant Mick Tait.

Though I have been in management a relatively short time, nine months, I have been involved in professional football since 1977 and basically devoted my whole life to it, and feel that both my experience and opinion should be taken into account. My staff and myself work very hard to turn Hartlepool United into a successful football club, rather than languishing in the bottom region of the Football League.

After the recent spate of sending offs, which have cost us valuable points, we as a club are feeling very hard done by. On the night in question, major decisions went against us (video of which is enclosed) i.e. a blatant penalty which we were not awarded together with a disgraceful one awarded against us, after yet another of my players had been sent off for swearing after the penalty decision.

My reactions after the game in question, whilst not being justified, I think are understandable given the lack of appreciation and the pressure that managing a club like Hartlepool entails.

In finishing I would also like to state that I find it very disturbing that referees are actually writing reports that conflict with or on occasion bear no resemblance to the actual events that took place.

I am willing to attend a hearing to discuss this further if you wish.

A very late tackle, and jumping at an opponent in a dangerous manner, were other things that referees felt constrained to put pen to paper about. By 20 April, Mr Houchen had again upset Mr Riley, who cautioned him for the second time that season. In the sixty-ninth minute, Riley signalled loudly as Houchen fouled an opponent. As the game stopped, Houchen responded to the decision by kicking the ball some ten yards away in an obvious show of dissent. Riley duly suspended the restart of the game and cautioned Houchen. Forty-five points – and further suspension.

On the field, forty-nine points were enough to enable Hartlepool to finish no worse than the season before, ahead of Leyton Orient, Cardiff and Scarborough, and Torquay who were adrift at the bottom.

It had been a frustrating first year in charge. When Houchen had been in harness for only a few months, the local paper ran a series of critical letters calling for his resignation, and conducted a telephone poll on whether or not the manager and his assistant should call it a day. Football fans are quick to point the finger, their fantasies fevered with magic wands. Nonetheless, the result of the poll was an overwhelming 'No'. Houchen wrote an open letter to the fans:

> Do the people who supported me when I took the job expect me to run away when it gets difficult? Mick and I aren't in it for the money and the perks, and we want to get across the point that we are doing this job because our hearts are in it. If we went, Hartlepool United could not afford to bring an experienced manager in. And if they did, he couldn't be as committed as we are.

Houchen also wrote to the sports editor of the *Hartlepool Mail,* Roy Kelly. In reply, Mr Kelly suggested meeting for lunch in order to discuss the relationship between the paper and the club. 'For the record, myself and the *Mail* are not anti-Keith Houchen,' he wrote. Houchen's response was laced with sarcasm:

> I write with reference to your recent letter and thank you for understanding my annoyance over the poll you recently conducted. I hope you also realise how you undermined my position when I released players in the summer with the subsequent petitions to reinstate them.
>
> Thank you also for the front page story, which was blown up out of all proportion regarding players having a night out locally. After working very very hard during the day, are they not entitled to wind down?
>
> Thank you also for the criticism directed at my team selection in your match reports, and making every game sound so terrible and dull, no matter what the result.
>
> Regarding your invitation to lunch, I find I must decline as my staff and myself are working very hard to make this club the *success* the town deserves. It would be nice if this could be done with the support of the local newspaper but sometimes I am not so sure.

Houchen had released several players in order to cut costs. One of them, in particular, he had in mind in his letter:

There was this left-back, Anthony Skedd – tiny little thing, bonehead, skinhead, earrings, tattoos, couldn't talk without swearing, couldn't play. I thought I'd do as George Smith and others had done with me, and take the player for an afternoon, try to teach him how to cross a ball. He was dead fit, could run for ever, and he'd always get down the wing, but couldn't cross a ball to save his life. Some players you can go through things with over and over and they don't develop, never change. I used to spend hours and hours and hours but he couldn't play, he was patently not good enough to play. He never got another League club, not even a non-League club – he went local. But the fans loved him because he was a skinhead. And that's Hartlepool, you see. I released him and the fans were getting petitions up. I'd get letters addressed to Adolf Houchen.

The *Mail* led with a hard-luck story and a front-page photo of the player surrounded by his grieving family.

These were not the only kinds of problem Houchen had to contend with. One morning, he and his chairman were in the office together when Sunderland manager Peter Reid rang. Houchen had suggested that their mighty neighbours were poaching Hartlepool's players. 'I think it stinks,' said Houchen in the local paper. Reid announced himself in his guttural scouse. The torrent of 'fooking' that followed was so gross and sustained that Houchen held the receiver up to the ear of his astonished chairman.

There was a further exchange with Reid when Sunderland tried to sign Stephen Halliday:

He could have been a really top player. It was borderline whether he was or wasn't. He was starting to score goals and was another one I'd spend hours with. He was a bit like Huckerby, probably better on the ball. He was that good that he would be half-a-dozen times through on the 'keeper. But he could miss half-a-dozen times. I would work just putting him one-on-one with me, hitting it straight, lifting it over, aiming to the bottom, because, if he could do it, he would be a thirty-goal-a-season man.

The player trained with Sunderland for a fortnight before the beginning of the 1996/97 season. Sunderland then offered £50,000 for him, way beneath Hartlepool's valuation, and Hartlepool refused. Halliday was nearing the end of his contract but the full impact of the Bosman ruling was yet to take effect. His agent Jonathan Barnett had 'phoned from the

Cloud Cuckoo Land of London to negotiate a new contract. 'This is Hartlepool, not Liverpool,' snorted Houchen.

I wouldn't deal with him in the end. I'm not going to speak to this bloke in London who doesn't know anything about football. I don't see what we and the players can't see and sort out in a club like Hartlepool.

With Sunderland and Hartlepool not agreeing a fee, a Football League tribunal had to set the figure. Customarily, each side pleads separately and then together in front of a panel. Judgement follows on the spot.

Houchen's new bunch of free transfers had been 'rubbish' on their trip to Scotland so there was plenty to prime the manager's belligerence on his solitary drive down to Blackpool. He met up with his chairman in the morning as the respective representatives trooped into the headquarters of the Football League in Lytham St Annes.

Houchen had no doubt of the validity of Hartlepool's case and knew that Reid was not articulate enough to make a persuasive one for Sunderland. The two entourages, Halliday in the red-and-white one, sat in an ante-room. The verdict didn't take long; Sunderland could eventually have to fork out a total of £375,000. That was a fortune to Hartlepool but certainly not to Sunderland. 'I suppose I'll have to shake Reid's hand,' Houchen thought, as he went out onto the steps licking his lips at the prospect of such bounty.

'I'm not doing it,' Reid said.

'What do you mean "you're not doing it"?'

'I'm not doing it. I'm not taking him. It's too much.'

At that, Reid and his cohorts dived into their cars and sped away, abandoning the bemused twenty-year-old to his broken dream. Stephen Halliday was born in Sunderland – it had been his childhood ambition to play for the club. But now he was being driven home by the manager of Hartlepool. An ebullient footballer, and the person within, was punctured. It would need more than, 'There are bigger clubs than Sunderland' to pump him up. By the time he was twenty-two, Halliday – injury prone and disaffected – was playing his last match in the Football League. And this was a player, Houchen had forecast, whose dream could one day be worth three million.

A player's responsibility normally ends with the last loving application of the comb in the dressing room mirror; at this point the manager's is only just beginning and, as in the Halliday instance, can be much more onerous.

Houchen had a budget of £260,000 a year which had also to provide for the manager, his assistant and the secretary. After the manager had opened talks with a player, the chairman would sit in on the final negotiations. If Houchen was lucky, Harold Hornsey might find an extra few bob, but things were always tight.

You had players on £100 a week, people like Steve Howard from Tow Law who went on to do really well at Luton. It was amazing how we made it stretch.

The tightness was such that the club could not even afford to pay for lunch on match-days. Unbeknown to the players, Houchen himself would sometimes fork out for them, at the same time keeping his fingers crossed that they would eschew the foie-gras.

One of the lessons of having a foot on either side of the touchline is that you can no longer remain one of the lads. Houchen got into the habit of changing into his kit in the office. But at least the players become your team-mates when you run out together. By contrast, the isolation of the ref is only relieved by a couple of men running up and down with flags.

Houchen's sensitivity prompted an understandable coyness about his pay. This and a sense of propriety led him to object to players being able to read each others' payslips when they were all laid out on a big table.

When he first returned to the Victoria Ground under the chairmanship of Garry Gibson, players had to queue up at the end of the game until the takings had been recovered from all the turnstiles. Houchen used to wait until last, but the weight of £600 or more – if the secretary was down to the small change – could be burdensome after a game, so one weekend he arranged to leave it in the safe. 'You bloody didn't,' said Yvonne, 'you'll never get it.' It was Houchen who served as the players' PFA rep when there was talk of strike action over unpaid wages. Matters had improved since his first spell at the club when players would leg it to the bank on the corner to cash their cheques on pay day, knowing that the slowest would be the rubberiest. There were some weeks when all of the cheques bounced, and kept bouncing for several weeks.

Another dubious privilege of being manager is to stand closer to the crowd. More than in the big stadiums, the whole cast are aware of the audience's comments. You get to recognise 'the usual scum', the shaven-headed morons whose aggressiveness finds its voice in the spittle of abuse. Once when Houchen was standing by the touchline, a man threw a full can of lager at him. It missed by an inch. The crowd then parted like a curtain as Houchen gave chase. He carves out the path to the turnstiles with his hand, recalling every turn. The yob got away. Eric Cantona, infamously, was provoked into a two-footed attack on a fan when playing for Manchester United at Selhurst Park. Understandably, Houchen has some sympathy with him.

Hartlepool kicked off in August 1996 with victory at Colchester and a home win against Fulham. For the first time in almost thirty-nine years, the club was top of the league. Houchen celebrated by having a drink with Fulham's new manager, Micky Adams.

'Pool were still in third place when Carlisle, in fourth, came to visit. Mark Cooper scored early on but Carlisle snatched victory with two goals in the last few minutes. Houchen was less than happy with referee Eddie Wolstenholme:

It was very, very cruel. I can't blame the players at all. We defended magnificently. I ask my players to track men and defend which is exactly what Steve Howard did, and the referee was conned into giving a foul. I went to see him afterwards and he just said 'let's have a look at the video'. But it's too late then, the points have gone. I just feel totally robbed by the officials.

The crucial moment came in the next game: Houch's legs, oozing cortisone, finally gave out. He was thirty-six, and against Wigan Athletic on 14 September 1996 he played his final Football League match. He had scored 92 goals in 279 League appearances for the club. How he would have loved to have beaten Ken Johnson's all-time Hartlepool record (98 goals in 384 League matches). Johnson, in turn, had beaten Johnny Wigham, a Jarrow schoolteacher, who scored 95 goals in 264 League games for Hartlepools during the eight seasons following his signing in 1931.

Houchen also scored twice in the League Cup but never in the competition to which his name had brought such a frisson. The decision to hang up his boots came less than a week after undergoing surgery on the knee that had been giving him trouble for almost two years. It was also announced on the day that Mick Tait, four years senior to Houchen, became the club's oldest ever player.

It really punched me in the stomach when I read the specialist's report. But it's the sensible thing to do. I've been in a lot of pain since well before last Christmas so it hasn't really come as a shock. I've noticed this season that people are hitting me and hurting me like they never used to. I think Old Father Time is saying 'No more'. But I've had nineteen brilliant years. I'll settle for that. I've got some fantastic memories and done everything that I wanted to do in the game. I never desperately wanted to play for England or anything like that. I just wanted to play at the highest level, play in a cup final and get into Europe. It was difficult on Saturday. It was the first time in my adult life that I knew I couldn't get out there and play. I get very uptight when I'm just managing, but I've got to get used to that now.

The *Mail* observed, 'Houchen's retirement brings greater urgency to the ongoing search for a striker'; there was no replacement. The difficulty for Houchen of knowing that he was no longer a professional footballer was tempered by a 2-0 victory over Chester that took 'Pool to seventh in the table.

It was a very poor game. That's as badly as we've played all season, but Chester were three times worse.

It would take more than such a magnificent defensive display to maintain their position. Fans dream of success but the professional could see exactly what was going to happen.

Referee Graham Laws booked six Hartlepool players.

He was the worst referee I have ever come across in all my years in the game... I felt sorry for both teams.

In the *Hartlepool Mail,* on 2 October 1996, the *From the Goalmouth* columnist weighed in:

Just when you thought you could relax they come back to haunt you. What? Clueless referees that's what!

Last season Pool had every variety of poor referee visited upon them – the out of touch, the biased, the card-waving robot, the downright poor – every variety in fact, except those who awarded penalties to us.

This season had been somewhat better, most referees have been virtually invisible – exactly how I like them. I pay to watch a football game between two sides, not to watch how wonderful the ref thinks he is.

Then we had Mr G. Laws for the Chester game. He had one of those bad hair days when he started off by booking Sean McAuley for kicking the ball away in frustration – but of course failing to be consistent enough to book a Chester player for doing the same thing later in the game. Refs like this are so predictable it's not true.

Having set the precedent, they go downhill, booking everyone in sight for every petty offence they see and often end up sending players off when there hasn't been a bad foul all day.

...

Just about every foul or offence is bookable in the eyes of some refs. 'I was just carrying out orders – the assessor is watching me,' you can almost hear them say.

...

Accountability seems to be one of the buzz words in business today. Managers and players are accountable to the club chairman and ultimately to the fans.

Who are referees accountable to? In theory to the FA, but when was the last time the FA did anything but back a referee no matter how laughable, crass or plain stupid a decision he made?

Why not make referees appear at the post-match press conferences to explain their decisions? If they're so convinced about their decisions they should be able to explain them to us – and I think we have a right to know.

Trial by television I hear you say – too bloody right. You never know, they might be right once or twice, and we might be wrong.

On the Tuesday after the Chester game, 'Pool lost 2-1 at Doncaster.

It's a man's game...People are just trying to win the ball and referees are pulling cards out for fun.

Houchen took his team to Cambridge where they lost by the only goal. What looked like a perfectly good Hartlepool goal was disallowed for off-side and two plausible penalty appeals were turned down. Houchen was spoken to by referee Alan Bates for comments he made from the dug-out after a Hartlepool 'goal' was disallowed, and went to see the official after the game for an explanation of the decisions.

There's a bit of blatant cheating going on. It's as if the officials have had a meeting and said 'Hartlepool are in the top ten, we'll have to do something about that.' I went in to ask the referee about the first penalty and he had the temerity to tell me it was a block tackle that ricocheted out. The linesman who gave off-side for the goal was twenty yards behind play all afternoon, and right at the end of the game when Michael Barron was pushed off the ball, he said he saw no offence. All I want from the officials is our fair share.

Houchen's concerns about the men in black had certainly not mellowed with his departure from the field of battle. On 8 October, Hartlepool's chief executive, Stuart Bagnall, wrote to the secretary of the Football League:

My manager, Keith Houchen, wishes to bring to your attention his concerns about the overall standard of refereeing in the 3rd Division. Whilst he agrees that it is essential for younger refereeing blood to be brought into the fold, this is sometimes at the expense of experience and consistency and, in the modern game, mistakes can sometimes mean a great deal more than the three points on offer for either team.

He is concerned that current refereeing practice appears to work against the production of a flowing game of football. All dialogue is forbidden and, instead of the referee and players working in conjunction, his only role seems to be as a penaliser.

This club has made an extreme effort this season to 'clean up its act' in respect of discipline on the field of play. However Keith still feels that in some matches it has appeared that we have had to play against, not only the opposition, but the match official's opinions of the team based on previous season's disciplinary records.

On 12 October, Darlington were the visitors; local derby day and – with so many Darlo supporters in the crowd – twenty per cent on the gate. Local pride was at stake. Darlington's 2-1 victory was 'Pool's third defeat on the bounce. 'HOUCHEN FURY', trumpeted the *Mail*.

The referee reported that during a stoppage in the game Mr Houchen, the Hartlepool United manager, encroached onto the field of play to voice his opinion, directing foul and abusive language at him. As the ref was dealing with other players Houchen repeatedly harangued the referee in a loud manner, or so it was asserted in the report, 'You blew the whistle, you cost us a goal you fucking twat.' When the assistant referee asked

Mr Houchen to leave the field he was told by him, 'Oh, fuck off you.' Mr Houchen was asked to leave his position as he was being reported for using foul and abusive language in the eighty-first minute of the game.

Houchen was impressed by the ability of all three officials to recall verbatim the precise detail of his alleged repartee. He wrote to the chief executive of the FA:

> In reply to your letter dated 16th October 1996, I would be more than happy to attend a personal hearing to explain the circumstances of my alleged misconduct.
>
> I would also take the opportunity to express my concerns again regarding the very serious problem which exists within football.
>
> Considering that I have been involved in professional football as a player, coach and manager for 20 years I feel justified in feeling both grievance and anger at the current incompetence and ineptitude of the match officials currently plying their trade in the football world.
>
> Angry about the fact that I am in such a high pressure job, ten hours a day teaching, cajoling and encouraging my players, who are desperately trying to get the right results to enable me to sleep at night, at least for another week, only to have it all count for nothing as some totally incompetent official dictates the outcome of a game.
>
> Grievance because of the fact that not only can they ruin a whole week's work, but that they can send in official complaints about me, making it sound as if I am some sort of foul-mouthed, brainless yobo, rather than the hard working, perfectly civilised, respected football man that I am. Also that they take so much time and effort, that they obviously have, to make sure that their version of events is absolutely word perfect and identical. Has anybody got that sort of perfect ability of recall? (I don't think so). Then they march onto the next game, leaving the rest of us in despair.
>
> What Mr. Burns has so obviously decided not to mention, and is the whole crux of this incident, is that he made probably the biggest error of his career, at a crucial time during a local derby game, when my team were getting back into a very tough match. He blew his whistle after the ball was thrown into play, in the most dangerous area of the field, the Box, causing every player on the field, bar two, to stop playing, then allowed play to continue and award a goal after Darlington waltzed unchallenged to tap home. I stood and watched him blow. He has not been big enough to admit this and in my opinion that makes the unfairness of the result and the harshness of his subsequent report all the more difficult to accept.

The response came by return of post. 'We are in receipt' was the preferred acknowledgement to 'Thank you'. Houchen was told that it was up to him to decide whether he wished to have a Personal Hearing, at which all three Match Officials would be called, or to accept the contents of the Match Officials Report and merely make a 'plea in mitigation'.

Houchen drafted a reply:

> In answer to your letter of 24th October regards my being reported by the officials from our home game *v.* Darlington, the dice seem to be very much loaded against me.
>
> With the option of attending a hearing whereby three officials will continue to back themselves and each other, with me attempting to prove otherwise, this seems to me to be a case I simply cannot win.
>
> And to incur the costs that a hearing like this could entail on the kind of income I earn at Hartlepool makes it for me unrealistic.
>
> I reiterate I swore once at the linesman in frustration at the ref gifting the game to the opposition. I deny any other offence 'but merely wish to come along to make a plea in mitigation'.

He decided, on reflection, to settle for saying, 'My only option seems to be to make a plea in mitigation.'

The *Mail* ran a two-page spread on 'THE BURN-ING ISSUE'. Former County Durham head teacher and World Cup official George Courtney was quoted:

> Referees have always been the Aunt Sally of the game, the natural scapegoat. I did a game at Blackburn twenty years ago and I think I booked eight players and sent one off, and I was pulverised. Some things don't change. I sympathise with the referees and I support them, and I think it's high time that they got support from the clubs and their players. They will always be wrong as far as fifty per cent of the population is concerned – that's the nature of their role.

Houchen's lieutenant, Mick Tait, said:

> The referees are being filled with so much information from the FA and FIFA that they're not allowed to referee games the way they should anymore… It's as if they've been told not to use their common sense. I read in a national

newspaper that players want common sense and consistency. You can't have it all ways, but surely common sense is more important?

A goal from Stephen Halliday ensured 'Pool a point at home to Swansea, but four days later the team were sunk by a sixty-ninth-minute Sean Devine winner at Barnet. There was further trouble: In the eighty-fourth minute of the game, the manager of Hartlepool United ran some ten yards onto the field of play to remonstrate about a foul challenge by a Barnet player, for which he was cautioned. After the ref had issued the caution to the Barnet player, he approached the Hartlepool dug-out and informed Mr Houchen that he would be reported for his actions.

In his latest missive, Mr Houchen wrote:

> …yet again I am in the position of defending myself against untrue and unjust allegations from a match official.
>
> I have been called to committees twice before, once for a personal hearing and once for our club. On both occasions I felt very fairly treated and was respectfully listened to by yourselves, and hope you will do so again.
>
> I totally deny the suggestion that I ran 10 yards onto the pitch during this match. I did react along with the other members of my staff to a particularly bad challenge which took place close to the dug-out, which at Barnet is no more than 2 yards back from the pitch. I may well have strayed a couple of foot over the line, as both sets of coaching staff had done during the course of the game, and no doubt had occurred in previous home games.
>
> For me to be singled out like this I can only conclude that there must be some kind of witch-hunt against me at the moment, and the sooner officials get back to refereeing, instead of seeing us all as the enemy to score points off by reporting us at every turn, the better.
>
> I deny doing anything in this match to warrant charges of misconduct and I think my job is difficult enough without dealing with malicious officials and answering Football League charges as often as I seem to be doing.
>
> I am very passionate about my job and football, but most importantly, honest and hard-working.

By the time Mr W.R. Hammond, a professional, tossed up at Lord's in 1946 before the first Test Match after the War, *Wisden* was no longer according amateurs among his teammates the title of 'Mr'. But other semantic refinements still endure in the sporting world. As you inhale the glossy aroma of your freshly purchased football programme, you notice the name of the referee – Mr N.S. Barry (Scunthorpe), perhaps, or simply N.S. Barry. However, with the allotment of blame in the paper the following morning, he becomes Neale Barry.

Keith Houchen had become preoccupied with N.S. Barry. He was the ref who had sent him off against Gillingham.

Things had started off badly that afternoon. As normal, the ref checked the players' kits before they went out, but then sent the Hartlepool 'keeper back to change his shirt. Having acquainted Mr Barry with his feelings on the subject, the Hartlepool player-manager sensed that the referee was on the look-out for him. Sure enough, when Houchen disputed a throw-in, he got sent off for 'foul and abusive language' – the common flag of convenience for frustrated refs.

When I started out, if you said effing this to a ref he would come back with effing that, and you just got on with it. But I was fed-up when refs lied and I wasn't even saying effing anything.

Barry was the ref who booked Houchen at Barnet. Houchen, and Barnet's manager Ray Clemence – a friend – were standing cheek by jowl behind the line. 'For God's sake, the ref will do you if you run on again,' 'Pool's physio said to Houchen.

I didn't want to get another fine, so, much as it went against the grain, I thought I would apologise to him at half-time.

I had a lot of run-ins with him in my last two years. He was the most vindictive man, and he was determined to ref at a higher level.

I was at a hearing at Lancaster Gate and, as I turned to go out, one of the committee said to me:

'Oh, by the way, you've got Neale Barry again for your match on Saturday.'

'Bloody hell!' I said.

'Don't worry, we're just pulling your leg,' he laughed.

A week after the Barnet game, the trudge down to Exeter cost a 2-0 defeat. The butt of the guests' bile on this occasion was Steve Flack. In the *Mail*, Damian Spellman reported:

Ex-boxer Flack, not for the first time, hit the floor like he had been picked off by a sniper in the crowd.

He cheated all afternoon. I asked the referee nicely at half-time to watch him jumping and diving about, and then he goes and does it in the box and the ref gives a penalty. Not content with that, the ref sends my player off.

Denny Ingram followed Glen Davies into the bath for another second yellow card.

I apologised to my players after the game for bringing them in from around the country to see what happens when you come to Hartlepool…They're playing their hearts out and getting cheated every time they play. I just want to know what's going on. All I want is a level playing-field where everyone gets the same decisions. We can't play against these officials every week.

The score at Exeter was duplicated at home during the week by Northampton. Spellman observed:

> In a desperate first half, 'Pool gifted Northampton two goals – the first with only 45 seconds on the clock – and looked the very model of incompetence.

Four Hartlepool players got booked. For the second half the manager threw on Alain Horace, a French trialist born in Madagascar. Such an exotic cocktail was not without precedent in the Hartlepool side. Tewfik Abdallah, born in Cairo, who numbered Derby County, Cowdenbeath, Bridgend Town and Providence Clamdiggers among his other employ-ers, made 11 appearances for Hartlepool at the end of the 1923/24 season.

'It'll be alright,' physio Gary Hinchley reassured Houchen. But Houchy knew that the one thing that could have been of help was beyond the physio's salvation – his own legs. As he had anticipated because of the lack of fire-power, 'Pool had nose dived. But despite the need for a half-time bollocking in the Northampton game, Hartlepool's performances had not always warranted the bad results.

'Do you think I was paranoid?' he asks today, explaining that major decisions which occasionally go against you were going against the team in every game.

The team was not being allowed to win matches. I had been on radio and TV and in the papers, and I think that the way refs worked, being the type of people they are, they took offence at it, and I think a lot of them were looking for us. Certainly, I don't think we were getting a fair shot at it towards the end.

Was this really the effect of Hartlepool's dreadful disciplinary record on the refereeing grapevine, or just the depressive coincidence of a terrible run of results?

Whatever the case, they'd be able to beat Brighton, and without another tussle with the ref. The Seagulls were propping up the League and had lost 15 away games on the trot.

There must be a happier way to fulfil your life than this, Houchen mused as he stared into the shaving mirror. He thought about the letter Harold Hornsey had shown him, in which an established manager was dropping a hint that if Harold sacked Keith he would be happy to take over.

I was tortured by the idea of being the manager who took Hartlepool into the Vauxhall Conference.

The punters ho-hoed as the ball rippled one of the HOUCHEN OUT banners festooning the ground. With visiting supporters screaming ARCHER OUT at Brighton's chairman, the hatred became antiphonal. You could identify almost every one of the 1,683 voices in the crowd.

The players set about their game, puffing and snorting, and occasionally dropping their guard to see where they were punching. At ten-past-three, Adrian Roosevelt Mike, to give him his full name, put the home side ahead.

This time it was going to be OK, and – for a change – a Saturday evening to look forward to in the Houchen household. However, a quarter-of-an-hour later, the visitors were awarded a penalty. In the no-man's land of such a moment, with hope hanging by the thread of the goalkeeper's glove, debutant Paul O'Connor dived the wrong way. Denny Mundee scored. And, before the break, a goal from Hobson added even further to the woe.

> Me brother's in Borstal,
> Me sister's got pox,
> Me mother's a whore down Hartlepool docks,

> Me uncle's a pervert,
> Me aunty's gone mad
> And Jack the Ripper's me dad,
> La, la, la…

On the resumption, the fans turned their drollery onto one of the players, 'What are you doing out this half, Beechy?' they chanted.

The *Hartlepool Mail* was one of the few papers still to publish a Saturday evening sports edition and, on the 'phone from the press box, Spellman spluttered:

> Chris Beech was suffering a nightmare afternoon as everything he tried fell
> to pieces before his eyes.

There was one more cock-up to come as 'Pool went 3-1 down. The cheers had lost their echo.

Mark Cooper's late goal was of little consolation. The mob gathered around the dug-out. Afterwards, they banged on the shutters of the main office.

I had to walk away from all that nonsense. I didn't deserve it. I'd put too much into the club to be treated like that. I'd put in so many hours. I'd tried and tried to get it going. I thought, 'I just can't stand it.'

My players had got into the habit of losing. They were doing some daft things that day when we should have been winning comfortably. The whole ground was singing 'Houchen Out'. I was standing behind the dug-out and thinking, 'I don't need this'.

Houchen disappeared down the tunnel before the end and soaked himself in brandy, but his legs had toppled over weeks before. And without those legs, Hartlepool United were almost on the floor.

On Monday morning, 4 November 1996, the club released a short statement announcing that Houchen's contract had been terminated by mutual consent. Houchen was sanguine:

> The way it was going, it was hurting me and the chairman too much. We both
> care too much. I was looking for heart and bottle from the players and I didn't
> get it – that was the worst of it. We have put everything into this job. I could

have made myself ill if things had gone on the way they have…The facts are that bad refereeing started this run off – some very, very bad decisions have contributed massively to me losing my job.

I felt very, very let down by the supporters of Hartlepool United Football Club.

We have a chairman who is Hartlepool through and through. He loves the club. I regard him as a friend. Like him, when I started here, I desperately wanted the club to do well. But people are asking the impossible. I was backed for a month, and barracked by a large majority for the rest of my time in charge.

I would like to go on record and say that the supporters of this club have got to back the chairman a lot more. By attacking his manager and his decisions, they're attacking him. If he's not here, there's no Hartlepool United. It's as simple as that.

I just could not believe how they turned against me when I took the manager's job on; I'll never forget it. And I don't know where it came from, or why. The year before when I was player-coach, I was Player-of-the-Year by a million miles. The nearest challenger was one man and his dog in the local park. And then they turned nasty. These were local supporters' club people, and it was so vicious.

There are a lot of shit people following every club. They are everywhere, that type, with brains the size of a pea. I wouldn't keep the players they wanted, players who were patently not good enough and were really, really bad professionals. If I was going to make it into something, and I wanted to make it into something, then it was no good with crap pros.

Houchen would attend fans' forums, arranged by the club. Billy Horner had survived unusually long as Hartlepool manager partly on account of the amount of time he devoted to meeting the public, supporters and people in business. The good will and rapport it fostered was incalculable. Supporters, baffled by Houchen's experiments with three and four-man defensive line-ups or his willingness to radically alter team selection from game to game, could pose their questions. At one of these forums, Houchen got stitched up when the commercial manager made the mistake of sitting him beside goalkeeper Brian Horne.

Horne had done the rounds since making his name at Millwall, where he had won five England Under-21 caps, but he was barely twenty-seven when he signed for Hartlepool at the beginning of the 1994/95 season. The fans were quick to applaud his 'dead flash saves' but slow to acknowledge his errors. A sociable youth, who liked a beer, he was fine away from the job, but training was little to his liking:

He'd be stood with his hands in his pockets; he'd just got up; there was stubble on his face; his hair was all over the place – he'd been out on the piss the night before.

Quick reflexes were not enough to compensate for the appearance of a 'Fatty' Foulke.

What is he doing in my dressing room?… When he took his kit off, it was revolting. He was an absolute slob.

Training, of course, has been an encumbrance to many over the years. In the late 1920s, manager Bill Norman ordered his players to get ready for a training session one freezing day at the Victoria Ground. When they demurred, Norman took all his clothes off and rolled in the snow in front of them. They got the message.

One of the messages that Houchen instilled, as had Curtis and Sillett at Coventry, was that players should jog everywhere once training started. Players were fined for having their hands in their pockets:

Put football kit on and put your hands in your pockets – what's that all about?… George and John used to sit in the office with the window open watching for this. You had to be switched on, and I totally agree with that in sport.

Houchen never trusted Brian Horne at crosses and used to get back to cover in case of problems. Once, at Gillingham, Horne attempted to punch the ball clear, only to palm it off Houchen's head and into his own net. 'Fucking hell, you and crosses!' screamed Houchen. Standing on the penalty spot, and much to the amusement of the locals, Horne then proceeded to land three rather more accurate punches on his manager. At Torquay in 1982, two Hartlepool players had set a precedent for the Lee Bowyers and Kieron Dyers of today when they were sent off for abusing one another, but verbally rather than physically.

'Get your kit off and get in the bath. You'll be first on the bus,' Houchen shouted at Horne at half-time as he sent on Steve Jones, the reserve 'keeper. Not surprisingly, Horne never played for Houchen again.

'Are you a bad player?', 'Why did they leave you out last week?' the fans ironically enquired of their bar-room friend in an attempt to discomfort the manager beside him.

What really hurt the chairman and me is that some of the people who purport to support this club would rather back fat unprofessional players than people who really care about Hartlepool United.

Houchen retains a conflict of feeling:

There are a lot of nasty people who support Hartlepool. There are several hundred nice, proper, people but the majority of them are nasty people. There are more of them at Hartlepool than elsewhere – without a shadow of a doubt.

Despite all this, Houchen cared deeply about his job. He remembers:

All the stand was missing down one side, with just two little cabins. It was pretty bleak. But then they built the new stand and the ground looked all neat and nice, and I wanted the team to go with it. I just think that all that time it had been a horrible run-down little football club, with players who couldn't play and the people on the terrace having a go at them, it couldn't change. Nobody ever made Hartlepool into anything. Wherever I went in my career, everybody was dead derogatory about Hartlepool, and I always stuck up for them.

Houchen was a little too ambitious maybe, a little too idealistic, too keen to impose himself and his discipline.

What I really needed was fifty grand, for a new goalie, a new centre half and a centre forward. I couldn't even replace me.

Harold Hornsey had nonetheless made some extra cash available in the summer and the squad was substantially reshaped. In came the experienced former Middlesbrough goalkeeper Stephen Pears, young defenders Glen Davies and Chris McDonald, and a teenaged winger, David Clegg from Liverpool. Mark Cooper from Exeter and Chris Beech of Blackpool brought new direction to the midfield. Beech would not be the only one of Houchen's recruits to reap the approval of the bank manager, making Hartlepool a handsome profit on his transfer to Huddersfield.

That's the other thing. You would bring in players and they would see what it was all about and not fancy it. You're at a big club and suddenly you're at Hartlepool. When they're shouting at you, you can hear them. It's not like a roar and players don't like it.

Defeats started to mount up and the confidence born of such a promising start soon evaporated. Houchen, in his attempt to find the string to open the parachute, had been trying to change things around but sometimes his efforts seemed to leave the players bewildered.

'I'll be hurting just as much as I am now if they don't start winning,' said Houchen, as he closed the book on nearly twenty continuous years as a professional player and manager.

I want them to do something. I've put a lot of hard work into this club and I want them to do well.

Settle his contract, put his assistant Mick Tait in charge, he suggested, and fulfil the proposals for his own benefit match.

It was not a testimonial, it was a benefit match, as the chairman knew I could never play again having wrecked my knee in the Hartlepool cause.

Middlesbrough subsequently accepted an invitation to turn out for Houch on 19 July 1997.

Mick Tait suggested that Houchy should lead out the Hartlepool team. Houchen shuddered at the idea – he didn't wish to be subjected to abuse from the few Hartlepool fans present. He was grateful that there were enough Middlesbrough supporters to make up a crowd of 2,500. At the end of the game he walked out of the ground with £23,000 slung in a sack over his shoulder. He has never been back.

11

Thirsk

K eith Houchen is not quite at ease with Hartlepool, even now, either as a football club or as a town. This was where Billy Horner, a decent and diligent man, had fostered Houchen's talent, where the youngster had made his name and gone on to spend a major part of the career that was so precious to him. And it was where the prodigal son returned, giving his all as his knees ground on through growing pain. So, for all the refereeing run-ins and the ups and downs of a life dependant on the kick of a ball, Houchen's mildness and sense of perspective lend surprise to the bitterness of an occasional aside:

The environment has to be just right for me, and Hartlepool never had the right feel.

The surprise is in the knowledge that Keith Houchen would have gone to the end of the earth for the club that employed him, and even for the town itself which was home to his wife and her family. It was what made him react to Sandy Clark haranguing the players about the lowliness of playing for Hartlepool United. The club mattered to him and he wanted the very best for it. Houchen had inherited Billy Horner's conscientiousness. It was the only thing – short of a bookful of blank cheques – that could sustain a club like Hartlepool. Therefore, it hurt that there were many who clearly didn't understand how much he cared. It hurt to hear a caller to the local radio station saying that he would rather throw a tenner out of the window than pay for a ticket to Houchen's benefit game. And it hurts now to hear someone say that he was only in it for the money.

But there were those who did understand. Some time later, Keith and Yvonne were shopping in York. When they returned to their car, they found an anonymous note waving in the wind. It had been left under the windscreen wiper:

> Thank you for everything you did at Hartlepool. I'm sorry it ended in the way it did.

Houchen received a letter from a gentleman in Newcastle:

> I wanted to write to you to express my disappointment at your departure from HUFC.
>
> I think you should know that not all HUFC fans were represented by the noisy elements, who have such short memories. I remember, only too well, what the club was like before you took over, also that you have significantly improved the side. We know that they can play football and it is difficult to understand what's happened in the last few weeks. Above all I remember, not too long ago, that the commonest phrase used by the announcer was '…and the scorer Keith Houchen!'
>
> I have spoken to you once or twice recently at the open day at Victoria Park – and was impressed by your obvious feeling for the club (we talked about the appalling referees we have suffered).
>
> I'm sorry and ashamed that your association with the club has ended in such a fashion. I can only hope that some of your memories will not be soured and that you will look out for our results.
>
> Last of all, let me wish you success in the rest of your career in football. I am sure I'm not the only one.

The secretary of the Milton Keynes branch of the Hartlepool United Supporters Club wrote to say how sorry he was to read about Houchen's departure.

Houchen is surprised that so many fans find difficulty in seeing their idols as human.

I've always looked at football as just a job. It looks glamorous but it's nothing like that behind the scenes. Footballers swear, spit and lose their tempers. My terminology is that ninety percent of them are 'dirty-arsed working blokes,' so they don't come across well in certain situations. They're just working class men making a lot of money.

Supporters spew out of bars and through turnstiles to watch these dancing cigarette cards – footballers arranged in a game of *Battleships* already played out in the mind. And heroes don't get headaches or suffer bad bio-rhythms; they don't have a child in trouble or letters from the bank. They catch their breath beyond the ends of the newspaper, cogs in a fantasy that ticks and tocks to fans' favours. If the machinery doesn't deliver, there must be somebody to blame – a particular player, the manager, the chairman, certainly the ref. It's always someone's fault. Thus, in an inarticulate pang of bouquets and *You'll Never Walk Alone*, football wobbles when grief swaps shirts at the final score of all. We dribble life up its own tail, only to discover that there is more to pity than just a game.

Houchen's career seems like a romantic parabola, beginning and ending at the same unfashionable club and reaching a peak in such an exceptional way. But, it was a career that begs questions about the more impoverished end of professional football in England and its place in the community. The people of Hartlepool owe Houchen more than he owes them and overindulge sympathy for the lot of the little club.

It was a career with more than the usual ups and downs. Houchen has no desire again for the office desk although Billy Horner regards him as by far the best management material he ever saw at Hartlepool. He was a natural communicator both as a coach and with those around him, and strong enough to delegate as well as take responsibility. Horner tried to persuade him to stay in the game. He thinks that Houchen was badly let down by some players not pulling their weight, and that the apparent failure to be able to get the best out of them was what turned the fans against him.

Did the Hartlepool fans feel let down by the player-manager getting himself suspended three times in one season? There were certainly never any letters begging him to keep his mouth shut.

Houchen recalls that at one of his disciplinary hearings, despite all the points accumulated for dissent and otherwise, an FA representative confided that the general quality of refereeing was pretty duff. It may or may not be significant that some of the referees have now graduated to the Premier League.

Horner feels that the tensions of management, disloyalty among some of the players, and frustration with the increasing unwillingness of his own legs, crystallised in an overwhelming way in Houchen's relationship with officials. Horner refers nostalgically to his own playing days when refs were part of a common experience and would chat with players during the match, when they were allowed to be more than just traffic policemen.

Today, there is less room for the Neil Midgleys of this world. Not one for the constant whistle, extravagant gesture, or the flamboyant delve for the notebook – he stopped doing that when the contents of his pocket fell onto the grass as he was vainly searching for the red card – he sought to get through a match with a quiet word here and a few warnings there.

Uniquely in sport, the continuing prosperity of professional football depends in part on perpetuating the abuse of referees. How could you possibly fill all those national newspapers every day of the year with such a disproportionate amount of copy on football on the premise that refs do a difficult job honestly and competently, and that their inconsistencies are not just understandable but even desirable – even if it were true?

Football has become the media's most significant conduit with the mass market. The common denominator is contentiousness and sensationalism. Balance and sound reasoning get easily compromised, with Television better at offering opinion than true enlightenment. How often does Television analyse an incident through the eyes of the referee, let alone offer us the opinion of an ex-referee rather than a player or a manager? When it suits the studio slant, of course, as with the Liverpool *v.* Milan European Champions' League Final in 2005, the punditry can become almost *Pravda*-like in its oversights.

The 'I know the ref has a difficult job BUT…' caveats were out in force when international referee Anders Frisk felt compelled to give up his whistle. The chief football correspondent of *The Daily Telegraph* implied that the issue was secondary to UEFA's continuing equivocation over racism. However, some refs may wonder when they look at the paper or switch on the telly whether the two things are not a branches of the same tree.

The abolition of the maximum wage in 1961 provided an unforeseen catalyst, with ever fitter players playing ever faster football. The game became more demanding to officiate, and players took the law into their own boots. If an opponent stepped out of line, he quietly had the hell kicked out of him.

Television began to poke its nose in, with every footstep open to debate. The product looked increasingly nasty. Instructions went out to clear it up: red and yellow cards were issued, the tackle from behind outlawed, and the screws told to take a grip.

The kids in the playground started to whine about inconsistency. It was then that the powers-that-be made their big mistake. Consistency was to be imposed by relieving refs of their discretion. The ref was to become a robot. And, from then on, communication began to break down.

Has Houchen laid to rest the gremlins of all those scraps with referees? He was not the first, and will by no means be the last, to believe there was a conspiracy against his team. For Alex Ferguson, the conviction helped hone the fine art of intimidating officials:

> It seems to me we are not going to get another one [penalty], no matter what the circumstances. One of our players will need to get shot for us to get one.

We just couldn't win a game. Some of the matches we should and could have won. We played far superior to the opposition but we weren't allowed to win; honestly, we weren't allowed to win. I remember Cambridge in particular. We had perfectly good goals disallowed, and penalties not given and them suddenly given a penalty for nothing.

At the end of the day, I think the referee grapevine was at work. I had been on radio, TV, newspapers, saying, 'Look, this has got to stop.' I think that the way they worked, being the type of people they are, they took offence at it and I think a lot of them were looking for us. I certainly don't think we were getting a fair shot at it towards the end.

Billy Horner continues to live in Hartlepool but is no longer involved with the football club. On his hearth is a gallon bottle of Bell's, the memento of a Manager-of-the-Month award. It remains unopened: neither he nor his wife drinks whisky. He is scouting in the North-East still for Rangers. Horner intends no criticism of Houchen when he says that his own coaching duties deflected him from exploiting the unique knowledge he had of prospective local talent which could have been so beneficial to the club. He regards his own most significant decision when manager of Hartlepool to have been in taking the youth team into the Northern Intermediate League, which could provide Hartlepool's youngsters with the opportunity to compete with the best from the big clubs in the area. So cash-strapped were the club at the time that they could only muster the fifty quid required for application an hour before the deadline. The league was eventually disbanded in favour of the new FA Academy Leagues – a dubious benefit, according to Horner.

Both Hartlepool and Hartlepool United have changed out of all recognition. The town is still an outpost on the GNER. The Hartlepool Dock & Railway Co., a stone's throw from Stockton and Darlington, laid its tracks in 1835. You alight from the curve of the platform under broached girders and high defences of red brick. The Victorians made their way from there to The Grand to negotiate the community's part in the Industrial Revolution. The shrunken fishing port where the monkey had been tried as a spy became a source for coal and timber, with ironworks and shipyards. By 1900, the ports of the Hartlepools were amongst the four busiest in the country.

Gulls cry, and you emerge now from under the glass awning of the station as if from a potting shed. The surrounding streets feel deserted, bled of the businesses that established them, but reflective in the afternoon sun. What became of the horses and the holsters?

The football ground is perched in the middle of the town, its old-fashioned floodlight pylons a portent for the small-town pride that has all but peeled from the game. Black and white or red and white are the favours of children's dreams, where docks have given way to satellite screens.

However, despite occasional moments, the 'Pool rarely bulge the locals' chests. Two up against Peterborough, a fan confides on his mobile, 'It'll be 5-0, they're shite,' at which a Peterborough player swings a boot at the ball and scores. Laughter all round, and disappointment again. Times, though, are changing. The money that Horner and Houchen and all those other managers craved, the opportunity to create more than just a footnote to Brian Clough or the Busby Babes, reinvigorated the club. For a time, Norwegian oil money turned a very occasional aspiration of Division Three into realistic hopes of today's Championship.

The town no longer reeks of the desperation of unemployment. For a long time, the local MP was Peter Mandelson who became president of Hartlepool United. Once asked what he would save if his house were on fire, Mandelson replied, 'My Hartlepool United scarf.'

Few footballers were ever possessed of such discerning feet – and autobiographies – as that magician of the North-East, Len Shackleton. Chapter 9 of his *Clown Prince of Soccer* is a blank page, at the top of which are the words: *The average director's knowledge of football.* The title page of the new edition adds the following: *From a game with a business in it, to a business with a game in it!'* Shackleton, who joked after scoring six of the thirteen goals on his Newcastle debut that Newport 'were lucky to get nought', was not afraid to rattle the shackles of servility in soccer.

What would Shackleton have made of the new money over at Darlington, where the Quakers were bought by George Reynolds, who cleared the club's £5.5 million debt with a single cheque?

Reynolds was born into dire poverty in Sunderland and spent much of his youth in a workhouse orphanage. School reports were littered with phrases such as 'mentally deficient, educationally sub-normal, retarded and backward'. According to the fly-leaf of his autobiography:

> He quickly moved into a world of violence and crime, and was soon smuggling gelignite in the fridge of a Mr Whippy van, and blowing safes. But after a four year spell in prison he moved into business, amassing an estimated £300 million fortune through chipboard and kitchen worktops.

This was not perhaps the most predictable association for a club which in the early 1950s had a right-winger by the name of Baden Powell. Clearly, Reynolds's teachers overlooked certain qualities. Come the millennium, the man was ranked 112th in *The Sunday Times* Rich List.

Reynolds received a police warning after threatening Peter Barron, the editor of *The Northern Echo.*

> Nobody has a go at me. I find out where they live and knock on their door.

Arthur Pickering's occasionally barbed observations from the sports desk never prompted such unpleasantness from the boardroom at Hartlepool.

Reynolds invested £27 million in Darlington Football Club, and £30 million in the Reynolds Arena with its marble toilets and gold plated taps. However, a reluctance to invest in his tax commitments has since led to George Reynolds being returned to prison.

The town of Darlington, and its old football ground, Feethams, was as different in character from Reynolds' folly or from the rival town and its football ground as could be imagined. Simon Inglis describes it:

> The neighbouring superstore apart, its environs are unashamedly charming; almshouses by the main gate, the tree-lined River Skerne along the east side, faced by a line of trim Victorian villas, and the narrow, cobbled Polam Lane which runs along the west side to a footbridge over the river to a lodge and public park… The cricket pitch appears first, often in winter with a game of hockey thoughtfully provided for some pre-match entertainment. To the right is the cricket pavilion, to the left, the groundsman's house. From there a drive leads past the cricket scoreboard to another set of gates into the football ground. Nothing could seem more natural than this happy juxtaposition.

Keith Houchen, understandably, observes the modern Hartlepool United with some envy:

You look at Hartlepool and you expect them to get a result, it is a well-run professional club now. Chris Turner was probably the first manager in Hartlepool history to have had the facilities to do the job properly and what he did, and where he got to, is what I envisaged, and was what I wanted to do with them.

I think that the supporters had got so used to moaning and swearing and having a go at the people running the club that that they just did it automatically. So when I went from player-coach to player-manager I was the one who got it all.

Victoria Park is trim, the pitch unmatched in the North-East. Before the War, the Regal Cinema advertised 'Dainty Afternoon Teas' on the front cover of the programme. As the ground fell apart, the visitors' dressing room came to be known in the business as the 'Black Hole of Calcutta', Torquay - after an all-day journey - complaining about 'a slum'. As you sit in the Mill House Stand, the masts of HMS Trincomalee tower over the Clarence Road side of the pitch. Built in Bombay in 1817 of malabar teak, the frigate is central to the £20 million Hartlepool Historic Quay and dock area, which has been regenerated with a 500-berth marina. Meanwhile, the greyhound track at the Town End, where 17,000 people once poured in to watch local heavy-weight Brian London, has given way to Morrisons.

Towards the southern end of the bay, along the beach from the power station, is Seaton Carew with its higgledy-piggledy of seaside shapes and colours. To the north is the Headland and the imposing Abbey Church of St Hilda. The Abbess, of whom the Venerable Bede recorded: 'all who knew her called her Mother, such were her wonderful godliness and grace', lingered in Hartlepool before moving down the coast to Whitby and its kippers. The fourteenth-century Town Wall of Hartlepool was built to repel Scots as well as tempests, but the Scots were back in occupation during the Civil War.

Towards the end of the eighteenth century, John Wesley became a regular but frustrated preacher among 'this dull, heavy, sleepy people,' as he described them.

> Surely the seed will spring up at last, even here, where we seemed so long to be ploughing on the sand.

The poet Thomas Gray had taken a different view. Averting his attention from elegising in the country church yard at Stoke Poges, Gray eulogised the Hartlepools and their people, 'I have nowhere seen a taller, more robust or healthy race,' he said, and expressed himself 'delighted with the place'. Sadly, as one who despised the sporting fraternity, Gray would probably have felt ill at ease in a Hartlepool United scarf.

After leaving Hartlepool, Houchen recalls receiving an extraordinary letter from the Football Association. It was about his relationship with officials and said that before he accepted employment from another club he would have to sign an enclosed letter undertaking to be a good boy. It would have been interesting to see how this would have stood up in court, but Houchen has got off the carousel and has no intention of remounting.

He no longer feels especially interested in the professional game. He is happy and intensely grateful for his career, but there is more to life than professional football. Beguilingly modest, he recalls that at the height of his publicity Yvonne once had cause to tell him off for not acting himself. He remembers with humour how his daughter once came home from school and asked him, 'Dad, are you KEITH HOUCHEN?'

When Houchen was on a golfing trip to Spain with friends a few years ago, Roy Evans, then manager of Liverpool, and a couple of other football personalities, made their way over to greet him. It felt flattering but nonetheless strange that they should want to include him in their group.

It was a sad, and wonderful, career. Sport is defined by moment, not logic or emotion. Technique, or skill as we used to call it (Paganini, in a different field, referred to *The Philosophy*), is victim to chance. Keith Houchen's career splintered regularly and painfully, but on several celebrated occasions it stretched the boundaries of experience and elation.

It was a career that in competitive first-team matches was played out on the grounds of eighty-eight different Football League clubs, as well as many in Scotland and, of course, some elsewhere. Show him a photograph now of any game in which he has played, and he can identify the venue from the merest plank or floodlight pylon.

I was a nice bloke with a nice manner. I always tried to look like that, but as a person I developed and became a little bit wiser and a little bit harder. I think football makes you hard. You have to be hard to survive, but I think I always tried to do it right.

I wouldn't change anything when I look back, but I would love to have played for my home town team. I only ever played one senior competitive game at Ayresome Park, and that was in the Full Members' Cup the season I left Coventry. When my contract came up for renewal after my first year back at Hartlepool, John Pickering, Bryan Robson's assistant at Middlesbrough, got in touch with me. They wanted someone to help the youngsters along, someone they could also call on if needed. But I stayed at Hartlepool because I wanted to carry on playing regular first team football. Middlesbrough were prepared to match the wages I was getting at Hartlepool, where I agreed to take a pay cut after John MacPhail took over.

All I wanted in my career was somebody to have real faith in me and give me three or four seasons and treat me how I felt that I should be treated.

It's all maybes, but I certainly underachieved. I should have played at the top level a lot longer, and should have done a lot better than be famous. It's nice to be well-known – not famous is it, daft word, but well known for a famous Cup Final goal. I wouldn't change it. It's fantastic, but I think I should have been well known for a lot more than that. I should have played a lot better than that. When I think of Chapman and others getting England caps – John Fashanu got an England cap, for God's sake – I was a far better footballer than that.

It sounds like I was constantly falling out with people at every club I played, but that wasn't the way it was. I think I wasn't achieving what I wanted to achieve and I was restless more than anything else. I think it turned into confrontation because of that. That's what a lot of it was, looking back. Then, when I was my own boss it became confrontational with the local press, with the local supporters, with everything else, because I was wanting to achieve something I wasn't able to achieve. Maybe that brought out the confrontational side of me, looking at it philosophically.

I couldn't understand from being a kid, from being the best player in Middlesbrough, playing for the town team, playing for the county team, not quite making the England Schoolboys but going up to Crystal Palace where there were several England Schoolboys on trial with them, that from there I couldn't break into football, and that when I did it was with Hartlepool who were bottom of the pile, and when I was really playing well at Hartlepool I was stuck at Hartlepool. 'What have I got to do?' I thought.

The Houchens live near the market town of Thirsk, home to the vet James Herriot and birthplace of the eponymous Thomas Lord of Marylebone. Keith has a fulfilling life with Yvonne, his wife for nearly twenty-five years, and their two children, Cara and Ross. Cara has graduated from university back in her father's home town where he now rents out accommodation to students. Ross is already independent, and keen to develop his musical interests. Yvonne works in a bookshop, from where she feeds Keith's voracious appetite for reading – at least two books a week, usually fiction or biography.

Keith works for the Press Association logging those esoteric but apparently vital statistics about shots and fouls and assists, also passing comment on the officials. As he walks through the stands to the press box, his stride the unmistakable souvenir of years of professional battering, he is struck by the indifference of today's players. Houchen's contemporaries notice the same thing. It is not that they expect today's players to doff their caps at them, but Keith remembers being in awe of older players he used to meet. The culture, to use an overworked word, and the heritage of the game are of little concern to today's professional, cocooned as he is like a matchstick ship in its bottle.

Keith also spends a lot of time coaching youngsters for Middlesbrough, as well as in local schools. Coaching is important to him, and he plans his sessions very carefully. He recognises the need for a structure, but despairs of dogma and lack of flexibility. He values the intuitive and responds to the flow of the moment. But when he is dealing with aspiring professionals there can be nothing casual in the kick of the ball, and he insists on the correct technical approach all the time.

There is something of this in his reflections on refereeing. He is offended by the intimidation and abuse of referees that besmirches the television screen, but frustrated at the incompetence of so much refereeing and the failure of refs to grasp the tenor of certain situations. It is not as if the rules are as difficult as in some other sports. Few referees have been through the loop of the professional game as players themselves, and consequently do not read it with the informed eye of professional experience. Professional players should be fast-tracked into becoming refs.

Until a few years ago, you could always tell when a manager had run out of excuses for his team. Suddenly, his newspaper column was full of red herrings about the need for summer soccer or professional referees. The Doncaster referee Roger Furnandiz was waxing wistful in Keith Houchen's office one day before taking charge of a game. Professional referees, of course, have come to stay, even if climate change has seen to summer soccer. However, for Furnandiz, refereeing was not the career it has become for some of his colleagues, and he certainly wasn't interested in issuing cards as an investment in his own ambition.

It seems incomprehensible to Houchen that there should be so much diving and cheating. In his day, it was a badge of honour to stay on your feet, to demonstrate your resilience. It's what was meant by 'A man's game'.

But I can remember telling Stephen Halliday when I was his manager, that when you weave your way through the penalty area, you shouldn't go out of your way to stay on your feet if someone fouls you. There's a difference.

For those who have never broken their connection with the game, the memories may come tinkling out to order, the raconteur a puppet within his own mind. It is refreshing to meet someone whose memory is more than just a filing cabinet of stories, whose feelings spontaneously come alive in the gesture of his hand.

He appears the same as ever, tall and dark, handsome with a quizzical expression and an easy smile. He looks as if he has just emerged from the dressing room, but the kit is in the locker, the performance left behind. He is still there in the mind's eye – lean, determined, insistent, his back as straight as a mountain face, his foot wrapped obstinately round the ball. At fourteen-and-a-half stone, he weighs in two stone heavier than in his playing days. But for someone who is no longer involved in day-to-day coaching, he remains very fit.

On 19 April 2005, the Cup Final team reassembled at Highfield Road for a belated testimonial match for Michael Gynn. Houchen's long legs are recognisably a bit bandy, and he was disappointed that as a result of a recent operation on his left knee, where a cartilage had again been giving him gyp, he had to watch proceedings from the dug-out.

There were one or two players displaying their 'kites' but Tommy Hutchison, who was one of several interlopers, had no sign of a paunch. He shamed many around him with his fitness at the age of fifty-seven. 'Yes, but he wasn't very good at covering back for Greggie Downs,' joked Cyrille Regis after the game.

The man at the centre of that moment that May afternoon in 1987 did not go on to become a David Beckham, neither did life shrivel up for him in anticlimax. So many things coincided in that exceptional second that you wonder what effect the experience had on the human being.

Enter the station house in which the Houchens live on a long since closed branch line near Thirsk, take off your shoes, and imagine what Lloyd Grossman and David Frost might make of it as they go *Through the Keyhole*. There are two photographs next to the fireplace, one of the famous goal, another of the winning team, but nothing else of football. Look at Keith in the group. He is part of the celebrations, of the joy, but not utterly consumed by it. He remains his own man.

Look out from the conservatory across fields to the sunset beyond and you are high enough to be engulfed by winter snow. The warmth of the home has a perspective of orderliness and good taste. A delicate lead figurine dances from the gravel, and pets quietly intrude. A chicken, as solitary as the last of the ten green bottles, defies marauding foxes to provide an egg or two.

Open the door of the Range Rover and you discover a net bursting with footballs freshly flecked with the earth of a nearby school playing field. Traumatic trips between Thirsk and Hartlepool, those moments at York and Wembley, and so much more, have earned Keith the serenity he now finds in coaching children.

There is more to this story, much more, than the riveting intensity of a very rare moment. But in one north London suburb, marshalled by that mysterious white horse, such moments place you in an extraordinary panoply: of Lew Hoad and Pancho Gonzales, Stanley Matthews,

Billy Graham and Bill Haley, of Fanny Blankers-Koen and 'They think it's all over', Mick the Miller and Mick Jagger, 'Hurricane' Higgins, Mister Softee, Busby, Trautmann, Live Aid, Karol Wojtyla – and Keith Houchen.

Keith Houchen
Career Summary

	LEAGUE APPS LEAGUE GOALS		FA CUP APPS FA CUP GOALS		LEAGUE CUP APPS LEAGUE CUP GOALS		OTHER APPS OTHER GOALS	
HARTLEPOOL UNITED								
1977/78	13	4	0	0	0	0	0	0
1978/79	38+1	13	1	0	2	0	0	0
1979/80	35+6	14	1	0	2	0	0	0
1980/81	42+3	17	1	0	2	0	0	0
1981/82	32	17	1+1	0	2	1	(3)	0
ORIENT								
1981/82	14	1	0	0	0	0	0	0
1982/83	32	10	2	0	1	0	(3)	0
1983/84	28+2	9	1	0	2	1	0+1	0
YORK CITY								
1983/84	1+6	1	0	0	0	0	0	0
1984/85	35	12	5	3	3	2	2	1
1985/86	20+5	6	4+2	0	3	1	2	1
SCUNTHORPE UNITED								
1985/86	9	2	0	0	0	0	0	0
COVENTRY CITY								
1986/87	20	2	5	5	0	0	0+1	0
1987/88	13+8	3	0	0	2	0	(1)	0
1988/89	10+3	2	0+1	0	0+1	0	1	0
HIBERNIAN								
1988/89	7	2	1	0	0	0	0	0
1989/90	27+2	8	3	3	3	0	4	1
1990/91	17+4	1	2	1	2	1	0	0
PORT VALE								
1991/92	18+3	4	1	0	2	1	0	0
1992/93	26+2	6	1	0	0+1	0	1+1	0
HARTLEPOOL UNITED								
1993/94	34	8	1	0	1	0	1	0
1994/95	32	13	1	0	4	1	2	0
1995/96	36+2	6	0	0	3	0	0	0
1996/97	2+3	0	0	0	1+1	0	0	0

Figures in brackets are for appearnces in the Football League Group Cup, Football League Trophy and FA Charity Shield

Bibliography

The Annual Register, or a view of the history, politics and literature for the year 1788, London, 1790.

John Ayto and Ian Crofton *Brewer's Britain & Ireland: the history, culture, folklore and etymology of 7500 places in these islands,* Weidenfeld & Nicolson, London, 2005.

Cliff Bastin, *Cliff Bastin Remembers: an autobiography in collaboration with Brian Glanville and others,* Ettrick, London, Edinburgh, 1950.

Dave Batters, *York City: A Complete Record 1922-1990,* Breedon, Derby, 1990.

Arnold Bennett, *The Old Wives' Tale,* London, 1908.

Arnold Bennett, *The Card,* London, 1911.

Ian Bevan, Stuart Hibberd & Michael Gilbert, *'To the Palace for the Cup': An Affectionate History of Football at the Crystal Palace,* Replay, Beckenham, 1999.

Jim Brown, *Coventry City: The Elite Era: A Complete Record,* Desert Island, Westcliff-on-sea, 2001.

Tony Brown, *The F.A. Cup Complete Results,* T. Brown, Beeston, 1999.

Brian Clough, *Cloughie: Walking on Water: My Life,* Headline, London, 2002.

Richard Cox, Dave Russell and Wray Vamplew (editors), *Encyclopaedia of British Football,* Frank Cass, London, 2002.

Rod Dean with David Brassington, Jim Brown and Don Chalk, *Coventry City: A Complete Record 1883-1991,* Breedon, Derby, 1991.

Charles Dickens, *The Letters of Charles Dickens,* Oxford University Press, Oxford, 2002.

Peter Dunk, Glenda Rollin, Jack Rollin, Leslie Vernon, Tony Williams (Separate Editors), *Rothmans Football Yearbook,* 1977-1997, Separate publishers.

Dorothy Eagle and Hilary Carnell, *The Oxford Literary Guide to the British Isles,* Oxford University Press, Oxford, 1977.

Alan Earnshaw, *An Illustrated History of Trains in Trouble: a Century of British Railway Disasters 1868-1968,* Atlantic, London, 1996.

Mervyn Edwards, *Potters at Play: a Look at Popular Entertainment in the Six Towns,* Churnet Valley, Leek, 1996.

Mervyn Edwards, *Molly Leigh: A Burslem Legend,* 2005.

Colin Foster, *Hartlepool United: In the Beginning 1908-1921,* Katcha, Hartlepool, 2005.

David Frith, *By his Own Hand: A Study of Cricket's Suicides,* Stanley Paul, London, 1990.

Bamber Gascoigne, *Encyclopaedia of Britain: The A-Z of Britain's Past and Present*, Macmillan, Basingstoke, 1993.

Walter Gill, *The Hartlepool Story: A History of the Area of the Present Borough (8000 B.C. to A.D. 1988)*, Printability, Wolviston, 1990.

Geoffrey Green, *The History of the Football Association 1863-1953*, Naldrett, London, 1953.

Oliver Green (introduction), *Metro-Land: 1924 edition*, Southbank, London, 2004.

M.W. Greenslade, *A History of Burslem*, Staffordshire County Council, Stoke-on-Trent, 2000.

I. Hassey, *Meeting my Match*, Toame Publications, London, 1977.

Barry J. Hugman, *The PFA Premier and Football League Players' Records 1946-2005*, Queen Anne Press, Harpenden, 2005.

Gary Imlach, *My Father and Other Working-class Football Heroes*, Yellow Jersey, London, 2005.

Simon Inglis, *League Football and the Men Who Made It: The Official Centenary History of the Football League 1888-1988*, Willow, London, 1988.

Simon Inglis, *Soccer in the Dock: A History of British Football Scandals 1900-1965*, Willow, London, 1990,

Simon Inglis, *Football Grounds of Britain*, Collins Willow, London, 1996.

Simon Inglis, *Engineering Archie: Archibald Leitch – Football Ground Designer*, English Heritage, London, 2005.

Simon Jenkins, *England's Thousand Best Churches*, Penguin, London, 1999.

Brian Johnston, *Chatterboxes: my Friends the Commentators*, Methuen, London, 1983.

Michael Joyce (editor), *Football League Players' Records 1888-1939*, T. Brown, Beeston, 2002.

Neil Kaufman and Alan Ravenhill *Leyton Orient: A Complete Record 1881-1990*, Breedon: Derby, 1990.

John Keith, *Dixie Dean: the Inside Story of a Football Icon*, Robson, London, 2001.

Stephen F. Kelly, *The Kingswood Book of Football*, Kingswood, London, 1992.

Jeff Kent, *The Valiants' Years: The Story of Port Vale*, Witan, Alsager, 1990.

Jeff Kent, *The Port Vale Record 1879-1993*, Witan, Stoke-on-Trent, 1993.

Ed Law, *Hartlepool United: A History of One of the North-East's Oldest Clubs*, Breedon, Derby, 1989.

John R. Mackay, *Hibernian: the Complete Story*, Sportsprint, Edinburgh, 1990.

Magnus Magnusson (editor), *Chambers Biographical Dictionary*, Chambers, London, 1990.

Stanley Matthews, *The Way it Was: My Autobiography*, Headline, London, 2000.

Brian Moore, *The Final Score: The Autobiography of the Voice of Football*, Hodder & Stoughton, London, 1999.

Tom Morgan, *Wembley Presents 25 Years of Sport, 1923-1948*, Wembley Empire Stadium – Pool and Sports Arena, Wembley, 1945.

Sydney H. Pardon, Hubert Preston, Graeme Wright (Separate editors), *Wisden Cricketers Almanack*, 1891, 1897, 1947, 1987, Separate publishers.

David Pickering, *The Cassell Soccer Companion: History, Facts, Anecdotes*, Cassell, London, 1994.

George Reynolds, *Cracked It: The amazing true story of a safe blower and bare-knuckle fighter who became a multi-millionaire soccer boss*, John Blake, London, 2003.

Stanley Sadie (editor), *The New Grove Dictionary of Music and Musicians*, Macmillan, London, 1980.

Paul Screeton, *Who Hung the Monkey? (A Hartlepool Legend)*, Printability, Wolviston, 1991

Peter Seddon (compiler), *A Football Compendium: an expert guide to the books, films & music of association football*, The British Library, Wetherby, 1999.

Bibliography

David Sekers, *The Potteries,* Shire Publications, Princes Risborough, 2000.

Michael Schmidt, *Lives of the Poets,* Weidenfeld & Nicolson, London, 1998.

Len Shackleton, *Return of the Clown Prince,* GHKN Publishing, Durham, 2000,

Jack Simmons & Gordon Biddle (editors), *The Oxford Companion to British Railway History,* Oxford University Press, Oxford, 1997.

Gordon Small, *The Definitive Hartlepool United FC: A Statistical History to 1998,* T. Brown, Beeston,1998.

Siné (Maurice Sinet), *Massacre,* Penguin, London, 1966.

John Staff, *Scunthorpe United Football Club: The Official Centenary History 1899-1999,* Yore Publications, Harefield, 1999.

Alfred Tennyson, *English Idyls, and other poems,* London, 1842.

Dennis Turner & Alex White, *The Breedon Book of Football Managers,* Breedon, Derby, 1993.

Stephen Wade, *Foul deeds and suspicious deaths in and around Scunthorpe,* Wharncliffe, Barnsley, 2005.

Frank Wappat, *The Chick Henderson Story: the story of the million selling singer from Hartlepool,* Printability, Wolviston, 1990.

J.M. Ward, *Dawn Raid: The Bombardment of the Hartlepools: Wednesday, December 16th, 1914,* Printability, Wolviston, 1989.

Keith Warsop, *The Early FA Cup Finals and the Southern Amateurs: A Who's Who and Match Facts 1872-1883,* T. Brown, Beeston, 2004.

John Weir (editor), *Drink, Religion and Scottish Football 1873-1900,* Stuart Davidson, Renfrew, 1992.

Wembley 1923-1973: The Official Wembley Story, Kelly and Kelly, London, 1973.

Other titles published by Stadia

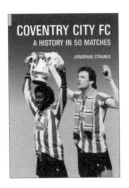

Coventry City A History in 50 Matches

JONATHAN STRANGE

Focusing on 50 significant matches, this history of Coventry City traces the emergence of the Singer's club, through the heyday of the Bantams and 'The Old Five', to Jimmy Hill, the Sky Blues, 1987 and beyond. As well as the triumphs and great escapes it also relives bad defeats, personal tragedies and scandals – four of the matches were actually 'fixed'. Jonathan Strange offers an affectionate but distinctive view of events in this illustrated history.

0 7524 2718 0

One Hit Wonder The Jimmy Glass Story

JIMMY GLASS WITH ROGER LYTOLLIS

It was goalkeeper Jimmy Glass's 95th-minute goal in the last game of the 1998/99 season that kept Carlisle in the Football League. Jimmy's journey through every level of the game, from Premier League to Sunday league, takes him to twenty-two clubs in seventeen years and sees him battling to stay afloat in a sport awash with money but drowning in debt. This amazingly honest account gives the inside story of the most dramatic period of change football has ever seen.

0 7524 3181 1

The Tony Ford Story

KEITH HAYNES AND PHIL SUMBLER

Tony Ford holds the record for the most appearances of any outfield player in the history of British football. In a career spanning four decades, his name has become known and revered in towns and cities across England by fans seduced by his skill, professionalism and above all the sheer joy he has always taken from the game. He represented his country prior to the 1990 World Cup and at the turn of the century was awarded an MBE and the PFA Merit award for services to football.

0 7524 2418 1

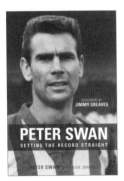

Peter Swan Setting the Record Straight

PETER SWAN WITH NICK JOHNSON

Still remembered as one of the biggest scandals in English football, the match-fixing case of the early 1960s robbed Sheffield Wednesday and England centre half Peter Swan of the best years of his career. A four-month prison sentence was just the start of it; upon his release Peter found he had been banned *sine die* by the FA. He eventually returned to football eight years later. With a foreword by Jimmy Greaves, this is the inside story of one of football's most controversial episodes.

0 7524 4022 5

If you are interested in purchasing other books published by Stadia, or in case you have difficulty finding any Stadia books in your local bookshop, you can also place orders directly through the Tempus Publishing website

www.tempus-publishing.com